Leading from Within

Leading from Within

Conscious Social Change and Mindfulness for Social Innovation

Gretchen Ki Steidle

The MIT Press
Cambridge, Massachusetts
London, England

This book was set in Stone Sans and Stone Serif by Toppan Best-set Premedia Limited. Printed and bound in the United States of America.

Library of Congress Cataloging-in-Publication Data

Names: Steidle, Gretchen Ki, author.
Title: Leading from within : conscious social change and mindfulness for social innovation / Gretchen Ki Steidle.
Description: Cambridge, MA : MIT Press, [2017] | Includes bibliographical references and index.
Identifiers: LCCN 2017011530 | ISBN 9780262037198 (hardcover : alk. paper)
Subjects: LCSH: Social change. | Social entrepreneurship. | Mindfulness (Psychology)
Classification: LCC HM831 .S734 2017 | DDC 303.4--dc23 LC record available at https://lccn.loc.gov/2017011530

10   9   8   7   6   5   4   3   2   1

To every emerging change agent who dreams of creating transformation for a better world.

Contents

Preface

When I was ten years old, my father, a US Navy test pilot, was assigned to a flight squadron attached to an aircraft carrier stationed in the Philippines. My mother, two younger brothers, and I relocated our lives to Subic Bay Naval Base for the two years my dad was deployed at sea. For the most part, our existence was defined by the relative freedom we enjoyed as kids in the security of a US naval base. But it was my exposure to poverty and disparity through our off-base excursions, including one particular two-week exchange program, which would be the catalyst for a process of inner and outer transformation that has led me to the writing of this book thirty-three years later.

I don't remember whether I had the cultural curiosity at that age or if my parents simply signed me up "because it would be good for me," but I soon found myself the guest of a little Filipino girl named Girlie and her family in a rural Philippine fishing village. We slept in their two-room bamboo nipa hut, perched perilously on bamboo stilts, with more than a half dozen other family members, and chickens scratching the sand below us. I went to school with my host each day and marveled at how the children squeezed together to squint at the blackened piece of plywood that served as a chalkboard while sharing a few donated books. I was terribly shy in those days, and even more terribly polite. I did what I thought I was supposed to do, and tried my best to smile through what was initially a terrifying experience of being in an entirely unfamiliar place with no one to retreat to for safety. I ate the peculiar little red sausages my host family offered, took a cold shower from a bucket, and tried to ignore the stench of the public latrine. We drank coconut milk from the husk, chopped open by machete. We splashed through the ocean waves on banca boats with wooden outriggers, and sipped Coca-Cola from plastic baggies, having returned the valuable bottle to the store clerk. We ended each day sitting together and giggling on bamboo steps as young and old gathered under the fluorescent light from an outdoor market stall and danced to Michael Jackson on an old radio. It was 1984 after all.

When it was time for me to leave, I realized how easily my life had quickly melded with what was one of the most loving and united communities I had ever experienced. Growing up in suburbia, we rarely shared time with the rest of the neighborhood in the same way. While we kids were always shooed outdoors to play wherever we lived, here there was a different feeling of safety to the adventures that unfolded within a village that seemed always to have a gentle, watchful eye surrounding us.

Nevertheless, now was my turn to share my life with Girlie as she came to live with me for a week. I was excited to show her my room and toys, and imagined she would delight in the conveniences and relative luxury she would experience. But she did not. She was horribly homesick, and fearful of things like flushing toilets and stereo speakers. Reentering US culture on our military base was almost as strange for me too. Suddenly the cool, clean floors of our modest navy duplex felt sterile. The television and games that sprinkled our playroom as well as the abundance at the dinner table were lacking something.

What I remember as an almost-vague impression at that time has sharpened as I have grown older and left me with two distinct revelations. First, I had experienced economic poverty up close. The disparity between our two lives felt unfair, and I recognized within myself a sense of obligation to respond in some way.

But I also realized that Girlie did not want to trade lives with me. She enjoyed the embrace of community—something that for me, a nomadic "navy brat," had always been in short supply. It was not my place to decide what people valued or wanted for their lives. That was up to Girlie and her family. Yet I was in a privileged position to help.

In the thirty-plus years since that formative experience, I have been guided by an inner curiosity, sense of justice, and compassionate drive to serve in similar communities of disadvantage. My career, passions, and blind luck have seemingly conspired to deliver a consistent learning curve of global injustice, struggle, courage, and change. From India to Darfur, South Africa to Thailand, and Haiti to Rwanda, I have had the great fortune to work and learn on the front lines of social change where it is needed most.

Through these travels, I have seen so many well-intentioned social change efforts miss their mark because they have been driven by single parties with too narrow an agenda and too little understanding of what individuals and communities really need to alleviate an issue at its roots. I have worked alongside impassioned yet angry activists, burned-out aid workers, and traumatized first responders. Their heroic work takes enormous self-sacrifice fed by a pure conscience, which I absolutely honor. But it can also become distorted from the unconscious material that often underlies our good intentions and exhausted from a lack of self-care.

It was in talking with women in refugee camps and local communities across Africa that I finally found my own approach to affecting social change. Circling back to my experience in the Philippines, it was essential to me that I only serve in a way that respected the local women's dignity and would support them in pursuing their own visions for change. In 2004, I founded Global Grassroots, a nonprofit organization that blends mindfulness-based leadership training with a social entrepreneurship incubator to help undereducated women and girls turn their own ideas for social change into sustainable community organizations benefiting other women and girls. In our first decade of work, we trained over 650 emerging change agents among the world's most disadvantaged women in post-conflict East Africa—women who have initiated organizations that now serve tens of thousands of others each year. These "micro-NGOs" are working to eliminate domestic violence and sexual exploitation, provide clean water and sanitation, ensure girls attend school, protect women's rights, and attend to a whole host of other priorities women and girls need to thrive.

It is through this work that I have seen consistently that a personal investment in self-awareness shapes humble and inspiring leaders who have expanded capacities for sparking change in others, building relationships, and designing solutions that will have lasting impact. I have come to believe wholeheartedly that there are two domains—personal and societal transformation—that are integral and essential for a whole, just, and compassionate society.

I know that this basic concept of inner-driven change is not new. Throughout time there have been inspirational leaders guided by their sense of spirit, faith, or self-awareness who have endeavored to alter society for the betterment of others. I recognize that my passion for what I have been calling "Conscious Social Change" is standing on the shoulders of the accomplishments, insights, and courageous sacrifices of these change agents, some well known, others now long forgotten, and some forever anonymous.

I am also recognizing a growing movement where inner wisdom meets social justice. This work has been described by different names at different times, including deep change and transformational change. Some efforts have been rooted in the realm of activism and organizing, while others have been focused more within a particular field of social change work. While I am offering one set of organizing principles that I am giving a name to here, the label is less important than the common values that define our approaches and exciting array of their applications. Actors across a diverse range of fields and issues are increasingly experimenting with myriad contemplative practices to inform or deliver their social change work. Business and social entrepreneurs are increasingly recognizing that investment in self is essential for stress management as well as productivity, creativity, and good management.[1] In the wellness community, more and more practitioners are finding a sense of responsibility to go beyond the benefits for the self to advance the well-being of the entire collective.[2] Research is still lagging, but increasing dialogue and study among scientific, practitioner, and academic communities are generating increasing evidence of the efficacy of these personal practices along with the neurobiological and psychological explanations for why they work. What I feel has been missing most, and what I hope to offer here, is a road map for how individuals can integrate mindfulness into every aspect of the social change design process, and why doing so contributes to more effective, impactful, and sustainable transformation. With this book and its companion, Toolkit for Conscious Social Change, I am eager to make my contribution to this emerging field, and share the philosophy, capacities, practices, and frameworks that have facilitated my work within and outside Global Grassroots.

I must offer the caveat that I am not an academic expert on social entrepreneurship, international development, neuroscience, or mindfulness. I am instead a long-term, experiential learner. I am a seeker of intensity and meaning, and an impassioned change agent, fascinated with fixing what is unjust around me. That also makes me a hands-on specialist in the messy terrain of initiating and failing at things, putting myself in vulnerable situations, and stepping into the often-exhilarating and more frequently excruciating maelstrom of personal transformation. It took me a while to find my niche, but my practical apprenticeship, if you will, gave me gems of insight from a broad range of industries and teachers that have contributed to my conception of Conscious Social Change. I share it here with openness and curiosity as well as with a beginner's mind that welcomes feedback from seasoned and new actors in this field. I invite you to experiment with this offering to help broaden our collective understanding of its different applications, adaptations, and limitations.

I fully believe, and endeavor to show you in the following pages, that anyone can create change mindfully, whether you are acting alone and the arena is your own community, or you help steer a multinational organization with the opportunity to shape the lives of millions. This book is for social entrepreneurs, business executives, activists, international development professionals, and volunteers who want to understand the applicability of mindfulness to enhance social impact as well as ensure sustainability for self, others, and the planet. It is written for wellness practitioners who want to support others to realize their own potential. And this book is for anyone who wishes to advance real transformation within and beyond themselves and their organizations. May we consider ourselves as colleagues and fellow seekers working together toward a more conscious society.

Guide to Practices

Chapter 1: The Science of Mindfulness
- Breath-Noticing Meditation
- Mindfulness of the Senses
- Mindful Body Scan
- Mindful Walking
- Mindful Tasks
- Loving-Kindness Meditation

Chapter 3: Cultivating Presence
- Noticing the Three Centers
- Mindfulness of the Breath: A Tool for Relaxation and Insight
- Noticing Our Environment
- Noticing the Inner and Outer
- Fifty-fifty Awareness with a Group
- Noticing the Self and the Other in Conversation

Chapter 4: Becoming Whole
- Reactivity: Transforming Reaction into Wise Response
- Attachment: We Want Change
- Aversion and Finding Inner-Driven Compassion: But Change Is Hard!
- Identifying Shadows: Who Do You Think You Are?
- Mapping Dominant Culture
- Understanding Our Blind Spots and Role in the System
- Finding Power from Within
- Transforming Limiting Beliefs
- Intentions

Acknowledgments

Since 2000, I have had the honor of learning from some of the world's most extraordinary change leaders and mindfulness teachers, including Alice Wells of One Breath Circle; Ouyporn Khuankaew of the International Women's Partnership for Peace and Justice in Chiang Mai, Thailand; Jessica Dibb and Ron Orem of the Inspiration Community; Dr. Richard P. Brown of Columbia University; Dr. Patricia Gerbarg of New York Medical College; Adam Musa of Darfur, Sudan; Seraphine Hacimana of Abanyamurava in Gahanga, Rwanda; Zolecka Ntuli of Cape Town; Sharon Salzberg of the Insight Meditation Society; Claudia Horwitz founder of stone circles; the Rev. angel Kyodo williams of the Center for Transformative Change; Bill Drayton and Bill Carter of Ashoka; Isobel Shih of Georgetown; shaman Anna Kheler of Pomfret, Vermont; and the dozens of other change agents I have met throughout my travels. I am grateful for the many realizations that have come through my studies and work with these remarkable individuals. I also thank those who have served as my personal champions in different ways, helping me initiate or further my work, including David Germano of the Contemplative Sciences Center at the University of Virginia; Alan Pesky of the Lee Pesky Learning Center; Pat Palmiotto, John Vogel, Merritt Patridge and Richard McNulty at the Tuck School of Business at Dartmouth College; Jane Wells of 3Generations; Natalie Lynn Rekstad of Black Fox Philanthropy; Theresa Donovan; Lina Srivastava; Jennifer Holden; Cristina Ljungberg; Lauren Purnell; Barbara Johnson; and my brothers, Eric and Brian Steidle. I extend my special gratitude to Bob Prior at the MIT Press; he has wholeheartedly believed in me and this philosophy, and consequently made it possible for me to move beyond my perfectionistic hesitation so as to make this book a reality. I must honor my young daughter, for she is truly my greatest teacher, holding me accountable for being present in every moment, and helping me to slow down and engage in life ever with a beginner's mind. I give thanks for her father, Andrew Wallace; my parents, RADM Craig and Marcia Steidle; and my Global Grassroots colleagues, who with care and encouragement have enabled me the space and time to write. Finally, I extend gratitude with love to my partner, Daniel Ellis, who has served unfailingly as champion, sounding board, editor, and life support throughout this entire project, and through whom I have learned the true meaning of partnership and devotion.

Introduction

To become a truly transformational leader requires an investment in both inner and outer work. There is self—the capacities, knowledge, and insights you cultivate as a leader. And there is the other—the world around you that you affect. These two sides are inextricably linked, with each realm informed by and dependent on the other. Whether by accident, necessity, or with great intention, we all evolve as we go about life with our unique circumstances and relationships. Every day we are given the opportunity to engage with the external reality of the world, and then learn and grow from those experiences. With some level of inner awareness, we can recognize and transform our own limitations and capabilities, and then turn back to our environment to affect change with insight from our discoveries. If we bring consciousness to this process, there results a deepening wisdom fueled by the intersection of our inner and outer landscape. We become more effective leaders by being more attuned to our own inner selves as well as our interconnection and interaction with the world around us.

Yes, leaders exist that appear almost devoid of internal wisdom. The world indeed assesses leadership too often by the one-dimensional measure of success, or the degree of political or social sway that can be held. Leadership, unfortunately, can be won, bought, taken by force, or stolen by manipulation. But holding the title of "leader" is something quite different from practicing leadership. Cultivating your skills as a sincerely impactful leader involves making a contribution to that which is greater than yourself. As much as leadership is frequently measured by accomplishment—even accomplishment of how well you do serving others—it must also be measured in terms of personal growth, self-awareness, and consciousness.

This is leading from within, and it is critical for leaders involved in creating change, whether within existing institutions or as creators of new solutions. Those of us who are called to advance a more just society have a responsibility to create transformation while embodying the same principles of integrity and justice we hope to see in the world. Our outer work will reflect our inner work. And inner work begins with mindfulness.

Mindfulness is defined as becoming aware of the present moment, whatever may be happening, without judgment, yet with curiosity. Inside and out, it is simply paying attention to reality, whether that is our own internal emotions or the political climate around us. Whatever is. But something that seems so simple can also have far-reaching impact beyond the individual. It allows us to understand ourselves and change from the inside out, build stronger relationships, respond more wisely instead of reacting, be guided by our own unique wisdom and insights, learn from and find meaning in our work, and step into our leadership capacity to serve the needs around us responsively, creatively, and compassionately.

When mindfulness is applied to social innovation, it transforms the way we understand issues and advance change. What I call Conscious Social Change is a design philosophy and methodology of creative, compassionate problem solving and solutions building grounded in mindfulness and self-awareness. It is a process led by change agents who invest in their own self-understanding and personal transformation while striving to advance positive change for the common good. Cultivating self-awareness invites a balance of engagement with the outer world, which is always providing opportunities for learning, and an investment in inner inquiry, which allows us to integrate and utilize each lesson. When an individual interested in creating social change chooses to deepen their self-awareness, they have a greater likelihood of making wise, ethical decisions aligned with what a community most needs.

Conscious social change uses a direct experience learning methodology to understand change from the inside out. There are five key capacities of conscious social change that we will learn to develop throughout this book, and they all hinge on our awareness. These capacities and their guiding questions are as follows:

1. Cultivating presence: What is happening?
2. Becoming whole: What is true?
3. Ensuring well-being: What is needed?
4. Engaging mindfully: What is helpful?
5. Leading from within: What is possible?

As a fundamental skill, we must first cultivate our own ability to be present. We drop the narrative of our own perspective and allow awareness to move in with nonjudgment. This leads us to see how change affects us personally, and where stress, suffering, reactivity, and fear originate. From this place of self-understanding, we can see more clearly, and find compassion for what is wrong and what is needed in our society—even among our opposition, those who perpetrate violence, and all those who hold partial responsibility for the issue. Next we work to find wholeness in the areas of our lives that may need attention. We work on the unexamined parts of ourselves that cause us to act unconsciously to avoid discomfort. This builds compassion for the ways other people resist or grasp at change in their lives. We also learn how to restore balance through self-care when our work becomes too stressful or we get off track in our approach to protect ourselves from fatigue and disillusionment. Engaging mindfully helps us stay attuned to the needs of those we serve before our own agendas and look at our own role in upholding the status quo. Mindfulness helps us determine what is the wisest response in any moment so that we not only do not create harm but also transform suffering. We avoid sticks and carrots, and instead employ design tools driven by our inner understanding of change and shaped by the ideas and wisdom of the entire community. This ensures solutions are innovative as well as effective at the systemic and root levels of a social issue. Finally, this process helps us find what we are most called to do so that we can pursue our passions and embody mindfulness, leading from within while helping others. As we open to our own unique contributions, conscious social change invites us to recognize the same in all stakeholders, allowing full collaboration inspired by a common cause.

This book offers a pathway for inner and outer transformation to contribute toward a better world. Drawing from and integrating my life's work to date, I will explain the what, why, and how of conscious social change. I will examine mindfulness, present the neuroscientific evidence of its benefits to the individual, and argue its relevance to social change. And I will provide practices that you can conduct, alone or with your community, to foster mindfulness and enact conscious social change. Each subsequent chapter will introduce readers to one of the five capacities of conscious social change, which together form a new paradigm for approaching leadership and social entrepreneurship. Finally, I will share how-to practices, theoretical frameworks, and practical tools that can support an individual

1 The Science of Mindfulness

I'm twenty-six years old, and far more intense than I should be in my mid-twenties. It's my final term at Dartmouth's Tuck School of Business, and I am making my daily ten-mile commute to school from the small farmhouse I rent in the New Hampshire countryside. I am late to class. I often am, as I suffer the compulsion to tie up all loose ends before moving onto the next project or chore. I cannot leave dishes in the sink, an e-mail unsent, or a nagging task unfinished, and it is for this fault that I often step out the door a few minutes late for the next item on the schedule.

I am largely unaware of this tendency at the time, as I have not yet started any personal growth work and know nothing about mindfulness. But I do know that I am frequently late. Expecting a quiz that usually lasts only the first five minutes of my cost accounting class, I know I need to get there fast, so I am simultaneously driving like a maniac down my dirt road with one hand and sipping from a coffee cup with the other, going through a mental list of homework and other project to-dos in my head. Suddenly I feel the steering wheel pull to the right and find myself in a ditch. I don't think I've even noticed the last five miles I've driven and now here I am, adrenaline racing through my veins, but my vehicle no longer racing toward school. It seems the universe is deliberately slowing me down—literally stopping me in my tracks.

I am reminded of how frequently I get sick the moment I go on vacation. The intensity of school, like my earlier investment banking days, keeps me functioning in survival mode right up until I allow myself to relax. Then, as the stress hormones subside, I become susceptible to any bug in the vicinity. I end up spending every vacation nursing a cold rather than enjoying myself with friends and family. It often feels as if some greater force is overcompensating for my lack of rest to make a point: I desperately need to slow down. And here it is again.

As I sit in the ditch, I realize I need to do something about my stress level and balance. If I can't even pay attention to my driving, my mental distraction is actually putting my life and maybe even another's at risk. Luckily I am not yet working in the realm of service or social change, where a larger community might be subjected to my unconscious behavior; I am still a solo act. But deep down I know something needs to shift. Stuck in that ditch, I make a commitment to seek out some way to help me come back into balance.

I consider the friend I had met a few years prior, Alice Wells, founder of One Breath Circle. I had been struck by her presence, even though I did not know that was what it was called. Alice also had a full schedule with just as many obligations, yet she always seemed so calm. She moved slowly and gracefully, always taking time to speak with me as though I were the only person in the world and time was infinite. Though she suffered and celebrated life's ups and downs like all of us, she exuded a peaceful, joyous engagement that seemed somehow independent of whatever stresses or conflicts may be going on. I didn't know what this capacity might be labeled or how one might go about getting it. But I was sure she had it. And I was sure I did not.

Alice's lifestyle included mind-body work, organic foods, homeopathy, and Eastern spiritual practices, which seemed exotic and intriguing, although I was far from diving into any realm that seemed too radical. At that time, I was just starting my professional life, and wearing a skirt with a hem above my knees was about as risky as I got. My only understanding of the link between mind and body was that if I exercised intensively and used mental discipline with my diet, I could think I felt OK. But I wasn't ready for mindfulness yet.

I didn't know what I needed. I would wander through the aisles of health food stores and buy books on the art of doing nothing. I had dark days, drank wine, and felt lost. I had good days, created art, made music with friends, and danced on my cottage's flat rooftop. But there was more to it somewhere. I felt like I was trying on spiritual clothes, searching for something, but not sure what it was. It was a whole three years after driving into that ditch and more stress in my post-MBA work environment until I decided to take a chance by exploring a course in personal growth and breathwork at Alice's suggestion. Breathwork is a mind-body practice that uses a form of deep breathing to help relieve stuck emotion, access deep insight, alleviate pain, and enliven the body, heart, mind, and spirit.

I stepped into that first personal transformation course with a lot of skepticism, but just enough curiosity. I stepped out permanently changed. I realized that up to this point, the map I had been following was one I had been given rather than the one I might forge on my own. I was simply doing what was expected of me. I was raised with a strong moral code along with the expectation that I should work hard, achieve, and earn the title of "success"—a word I actually never stopped to define for myself.

I quickly realized after experiencing mindfulness for the first time, that what I was actually searching for was myself. And I just as quickly discovered that if you go in search of yourself, you may not always like what you find. Someone told me once that personal transformation always *works*. It will always deliver what you need, though it may not always be what you want or with the timing you expect. Complete with uncertainty, vulnerability, a closet of my own chaos to heal, and new possibility, my journey had begun.

Mindfulness, Presence, and Consciousness

Jon Kabat-Zinn (1994) has offered one of the most well-recognized definitions of mindfulness as "paying attention in a particular way: on purpose, in the present moment, and non-judgmentally." Mindfulness is both a form of brain training and empirical inquiry that allows us, through our own observation and experience, increasing levels of self-awareness, insight, and transformation.

In order to be mindful in our actions and relationships, we first have to cultivate the capacities for mindfulness and presence in ourselves. Mindfulness is a practice of noticing the present moment whatever it is, without judgment, preference, and aversion. It is simply paying attention to whatever is happening with openness and curiosity. Showing up with a commitment to be awake, sit with any discomfort, and stay open to what it has to teach us.

There are four categories of mindfulness practices that we will explore in this book. One category involves focused attention that is usually cultivated during a formal practice, like meditation, where we set aside explicit time from our day to concentrate on something specific like our breathing. A second category entails bringing a more open awareness to everything happening around us more informally as we go about our day. The third involves working to cultivate certain qualities like compassion and loving-kindness through intentional contemplative exercises. And the fourth category concerns seeking deeper understanding about ourselves, others, and our experiences by using mindfulness practices that invite insight. Some practices offer benefits in more than one category.

Under the first category, meditation is a formal practice of focused concentration on an object of our attention, such as our breathing, and contributes toward mindfulness of the self. It can be conducted while sitting, standing, or walking. While some may also practice meditation while lying down, it is not recommended for beginning meditators who want to remain alert and awake. In meditation, we practice building our concentration by bringing our attention back to the chosen object again and again whenever we notice the mind wandering. Meditation thus serves as a mental discipline that helps us clear the mind so that we can become observers of our experience with greater acceptance of what we discover.

Our thoughts, emotional states, and physical sensations can all be targets of our awareness through such formal, focused-attention mindfulness practices. For example, we can take a moment to close our eyes and notice how our body feels. We may notice that we have some tension between our shoulders, our chronic back pain is flaring up again, or we feel rested, energetic, and want to go for a run. We may notice that our poison ivy itches, the chair we are sitting on is not comfortable, our sweater feels soft on our skin ... The list of what we can notice goes on and on.

From this practice of focused attention, we can achieve not an intellectual understanding but rather a deeper wisdom or insight about ourselves as well as acceptance and curiosity about what we find. Meditation trains us to be with our physical and emotional discomfort or pain without reacting or pushing it away. We feel it, notice it, and can just be with it without resisting. Once we quiet the mind, and put our agenda and narratives aside, we might then be able to perceive a nagging itch, the stress that comes from too full a schedule, or the underlying jealousy of an insecure relationship. Instead of being unconsciously swayed by these sensations and emotions, or manifesting these stresses in harmful ways, we pause to observe how they are affecting us. We are granted the opportunity to be aware and the wisdom to see that everything is impermanent, including our thoughts, sensations, and emotions as we watch them come and go.

One of the most widely clinically studied formal mindfulness practices is Mindfulness-Based Stress Reduction (MBSR), a practice developed by Kabat-Zinn in the early 1980s initially for patients with chronic pain. MBSR uses a group process whereby formal instruction is offered in sitting meditation (using a breath focus), body scans (noticing sensations throughout the body), and mindful hatha yoga practices in eight weekly 2.5- to 3-hour sessions, plus an all-day intensive gathering in the sixth week, where discussion is facilitated as to how the mindfulness practices are used daily to help cope with stressful situations. Individuals practice formally on their own each day, guided by 45-minute CDs, and are also encouraged to use open-focus mindfulness to enhance their awareness throughout their day (Carmody & Baer, 2008). Another widely studied meditation technique is Transcendental Meditation, which involves focused concentration on the silent repetition of a mantra, sound or phrase.

In addition to formal practice, we can practice mindfulness informally. As we go about our day, we can also bring greater awareness to our external environment, such as the traffic, fresh (or not so fresh) air, or singing birds. We can have mindfulness in our conversations as well as our actions, from what we say to how we climb the stairs or wash our dishes. Virtually anything and everything can be a target for mindfulness; all you have to do is simply notice it fully with complete attention. When you are able to be really aware of everything that is happening around you and internally at the same time, we call that state "being fully present."

Throughout this book, we will explore various practices, methods, and disciplines to experiment with mindfulness, both noticing our inner landscape and outer experiences. It is important to understand that the simplest technique—for example, just noticing the experience of breathing—can actually be difficult and takes practice. The average individual takes seventeen to twenty-two thousand breaths a day (Calais-Germain, 2006). How many of those are we actually aware of?

Unfortunately, most of the time we are not mindful and are instead operating on automatic pilot. A 2010 study conducted by Harvard researchers revealed that our minds wander nearly 50 percent of our waking hours (Killingsworth & Gilbert, 2010). Excluding the time that we are sleeping, that is perhaps only eight hours of paying attention to our lives each day.

And we all know what our quality of attention is like during those eight hours if we are tired, stressed, or worried. Further, most of that time we are multitasking, unable to pay attention fully to any one thing. Our brains are flooded every moment with vast amounts of data, but we are only able to be conscious of a small fraction.

Mindfulness, as we will discover, like any other skill, takes disciplined effort to cultivate. But we must also be gentle with ourselves, as we would in learning anything new, and let go of our expectations as we conduct these practices. All that is needed is to show up and try to pay attention. As even experienced meditators know, if we bring a quality of "beginner's mind" or openness to each time we sit as if it were the first time we ever tried it, we will be both humble in our approach and learn something new.

> When people start to meditate or to work with any kind of spiritual discipline, they often think that somehow they're going to improve, which is a sort of subtle aggression against who they really are. … On the contrary, the idea isn't to get rid of ego but actually to begin to take an interest in ourselves, to investigate and be inquisitive about ourselves. … One of the main discoveries of meditation is seeing how we continually run away from the present moment, how we avoid being here just as we are. (Chödrön, 2001)

When we practice any form of sitting practice, we try to sit in a way that feels *noble*. You can sit in a chair or cross-legged on the floor. This means sitting with your spine straight and your chin level. You want to feel as if there is a string attached to the top of your head pulling you upward. If you are in a chair, sit up straight with your feet firmly planted on the floor. If you are on the floor, you may want to sit on a small pillow or folded blanket for more comfort as well as to help provide you with the right support for your back and legs. Your hands may rest with palms down on your thighs or may be in your lap with palms cupped upward. You should feel alert and engaged, but not so much so that you are tense. You should feel slightly relaxed, but not so much so that you will fall asleep. You are seeking a balance between effort and relaxation.

You may close your eyes if it feels comfortable to do so, or let your gaze rest softly on the floor in front of you. But if you have your eyes open, be certain that you are not looking at anything in particular. Instead, let your gaze soften (even slightly out of focus) as you choose a point on the floor in front of you. Now try this breath-noticing meditation.[1]

Take three deep breaths to help you relax, and invite any tension, mental distraction, or emotional material you may have with you from before this practice to decrease or melt away.

Next, bring your attention to your experience breathing normally:

- Feel the air coming in through your nose or mouth and filling your lungs. See how far into your body you can still feel it.
- Notice its temperature and the sensation in your mouth, nostrils, or throat.
- Now place one hand on your ribs and one hand on your belly. Feel your body moving as you breathe.
- As you breathe in and out, notice how deep and fast your breath is.
- Notice if you pause after you breathe in or out.

If you experience a thought coming into your head while breathing that distracts you or discover your mind has been wandering, just observe it and say to yourself, "That is a thought," and then try to bring your attention back to your breath. Continue for five minutes staying as focused as you can. Or as an alternative, see if you can count ten breaths without losing your attention. If you lose your attention, simply take notice and start again. See what happens to your thoughts as you pay such close attention to your breath. There is no need for judgment on how well you do at this exercise. Consider it an experiment, and anything you notice is valid.

You may conduct this breath-noticing meditation on your own or with a group. On your own, you can set a timer for your practice, or set your watch or a clock nearby. If you are with a group, the facilitator can ring a bell to signify the end of the practice.

When you finish, gradually bring your attention back to the room. Notice how you feel. Notice any changes compared with how you felt when you began the practice. What did you notice about your breathing that you had never noticed before? How did this exploration of breath affect you?

This is the training. If your mind were a muscle, this practice would equate to doing your first set of weight lifting repetitions. As with physical strength, mindfulness is a capacity for which to strive. It is not inherent. It doesn't often come easily. But it does come with commitment and practice. Like hitting the gym, a routine of meditation "exercise" will manifest, over time, in a quality of calm and awareness.

The more we develop a practice of mindfulness, and start to observe our internal and external experiences, a strange thing may begin to happen: we find we become aware of our awareness, or the fact that we are observing ourselves. This sense of the inner observer is an orientation that develops through mindfulness practice that characterizes consciousness and presence.

Let's say you sit down for fifteen minutes of meditation where the intention of your particular practice is to focus your attention on your breath, as we did previously, and let go of any thoughts or daydreams that arise. Perhaps after two minutes, you realize you have been daydreaming about what to have for breakfast. What follows is a feeling of frustration and then a thought, "I am really not doing well focusing on my breathing today. My mind keeps wandering! Maybe I should just quit."

Rather than letting your attention run away with the feeling of frustration and judgmental thoughts about how poorly you are doing, and giving in to the reaction (quitting), what if you take a step back as your inner observer and just be present with the emotion? First you notice that experience as simply an emotion arising (frustration) and thought (judgment about your performance). With curiosity, you fully feel that emotion with intensified awareness. You might notice frustration feels like tension in your belly or maybe a headache. And as you recognize your thought, you might think next, "Wow, I'm feeling really frustrated and I just judged how well I was doing today. Why am I being so hard on myself?" With greater focus, we step out of our stream of thoughts so we can recognize our judgment too is simply something else that is happening. We don't have to get involved, or react to it or push it away. We just notice it is there with curiosity. And often it shifts. Gradually we come to have the felt sense of watching ourselves, and from this place of presence, we are open to deeper insights and a judgment-free perspective of what is arising for us.

Eventually you will go back to noticing your breath again, and all its qualities going in and out of your lungs, until something else arises that you experience and observe—a fly that lands on your nose, the sound of a siren coming through the window, or remembering something you were supposed to do. These are all just experiences to notice.

The more you practice mindfulness, the longer you may find you can hold moments of awareness, and the more you may find insight in what arises. Our moments of being fully present will increase with continued practice and effort, but they will also shift with the nature of our lives and demands on our attention. The process and practice itself is always evolving, and will always be influenced by our state of mind, personal circumstances, and what is happening around us. And that is absolutely OK.

> Being fully present isn't something that happens once and then you have achieved it; it's being awake to the ebb and flow and movement and creation of life, being alive to the process of life itself. (Chödrön, 2001)

Greater consciousness comes through mindfulness practice and cultivating a state of being fully present. I define consciousness as both the awareness of your awareness and the integrated insight that comes from the awareness. In other words, we use mindfulness practice (being aware) to cultivate the capacity to be fully present (being aware of the awareness), which contributes to our ability to gain deeper understanding and clarity from our observations (insight and meaning). We integrate, make sense of, and embody these insights into how we approach the world, which in turn leads to a state of deeper knowing or consciousness. It is here in this place of noticing and curiosity where transformation happens.

So what might this kind of transformation look like? It could be anything, but it almost always comes from the wisdom that is already contained within you:

- *What's happening?* "I'm aware of how harsh I can be in judging how well I am doing with meditation today."
- *What's really true?* "I sense that there is a part of me that expects to achieve things more easily. I remember feeling this when I tried to learn a new language as an adult. I felt awkward and incompetent. I feel compassion for that part of myself that has attached its sense of worth to being good at things."
- *What's needed in this moment?* "Maybe this one time, I can just be with the process rather than being so results focused."

There is a felt sense, a leaning in for greater attunement, and a process of just being with what is. This orientation may or may not move us to action. The simple truth is that by practicing mindfulness and cultivating the capacity to be fully present, this will lead us to moments or states, if not a long-term trait, of greater consciousness so that we know how best to respond moment by moment. This is why we can see mindfulness as an empirical inquiry process that derives wisdom from our own experience. As mentioned above, mindfulness is also a form of brain training, as we will explore next.

Benefits and Science of Mindfulness

Science is beginning to find evidence for the many benefits of mindfulness that ancient spiritual traditions have understood for centuries. There is a growing body of research on the neuroscience of mindfulness, interpersonal neurobiology, and the outcomes of mindfulness practice on the brain, the mind, our behavior, and our mental, emotional, and physical health. One important finding that science has brought us relatively recently is that even as adults, we can still change and develop our brain. Defined as neuroplasticity, our brains continue to evolve in response to various stimuli. Mindfulness practice, which we can look at as a form of brain conditioning that involves intentional, focused attention and awareness, stimulates the brain, changing and strengthening certain neural networks. These changes lead to the development of certain capacities, states of being, more coordinated and regulated responses, emotional balance, and greater resonance with others.

So what is happening in the mind and brain to enable these outcomes? Beyond the personal benefits, how might it impact your work as change leaders? Let us first explore the scientific research that explains the physiological processes, and documents the facets and outcomes of mindfulness practice, and then we will apply these to social change throughout the remainder of the book.

The brain is the topmost portion of the nervous system that extends through the body, made up of an estimated one hundred billion neurons, each connected through up to ten thousand synapses. These linkages are formed and strengthened through our experiences, each of which stimulates neural firing—an electric charge—that then determines the release of either activating or inhibiting neurotransmitters, which in turn decide whether the connecting neuron will fire or not. Neuroplasticity describes the process of the change or growth of new neurons and synaptic connections in the brain. This results in both structural changes in the brain and changes in brain function.

The human brain includes the following primary areas. First is the brain stem, which is responsible for regulating our respiratory, cardiovascular, and central nervous systems. Second is the limbic system, which includes the amygdala, hippocampus, hypothalamus, and anterior cingulate, and is responsible for our hormone regulation, emotional experiences, memory, and attachment or bonding. Finally, there is the cerebral cortex, the upper and outer layers of the brain. It includes the middle prefrontal cortex, which is responsible for our higher thinking and relating functions. Behind the prefrontal region are the motor and premotor areas responsible for our motor functions, and that contain the mirror neurons responsible for our ability to relate to and resonate with the emotions and actions of others. The back of the cortex is responsible for our perceptions of our external environment.

Neural integration involves the linkages that allow the coordination and balance of interconnected parts of the brain, thereby optimizing brain functioning. Horizontal integration, for example, enables the left-brained functions of logical and organized thinking to coordinate with the right-brained emotional, creative, and nonverbal functions. Vertical integration enables the lower-brain instinctual reactivity to be understood through the higher reasoning that drives connection and moral decision making. Integration involves a process of rewiring and forming neural connections between various parts of the brain to allow those parts to work more harmoniously together over time.

Research has shown that mindfulness in particular stimulates the middle prefrontal cortex, a part of the brain associated with many integrative functions including self-observation and awareness of one's own thought processes, regulating emotions and fear, attunement to others, optimizing body systems, empathy and morality, and intuition and insight (D. J. Siegel, 2007; Davis and Hayes, 2001). Also relevant to our discussion is the autonomic nervous system, which regulates all the automatic functions of the body including breathing, heart rate, blood pressure, digestion, and the internal glands and organs. Our autonomic nervous system is made up of two parts. One is the sympathetic branch or stress response system that activates to protect us from danger (fight or flight), and releases adrenaline, cortisol, and other chemicals into our system to ensure we can move quickly with strength, be hyperalert, and respond with energy. The other, the parasympathetic branch, is what slows us down, and helps us relax, feel safe, and stay grounded. Normally our body regulates between the two as necessary, such as when a loud noise startles us, thus activating the stress response system, and then we realize we are not in danger and relax again. Relaxation occurs when the stress response turns off and the parasympathetic system turns on.

As a result of the stimulation of these parts of the brain and nervous system, the repeated practice of mindfulness helps us develop a range of capacities. Ruth Baer and colleagues determined the following five facets of mindfulness that can be reasonably assessed (Baer, Smith, Hopkins, Krietemeyer, & Toney, 2006):

- Nonreactivity to inner experience
- Observing/noticing sensations/perceptions/thoughts/feelings
- Acting with awareness and concentration, reduction in automatic pilot, and nondistractedness
- Articulating experience with words
- Nonjudgment of experience

Each of these facets of mindfulness practice results over time in particular benefits to the individual. In the beginning these benefits may be experienced as a particular state, such as empathy, that you feel during a particular occasion or for a period of time. The more we stimulate the brain through mindfulness practice and build such capacities to achieve such *states*, the more that these activated neural networks within the brain begin to strengthen. This means that they increasingly become an actual *trait*, our new default for how we respond to the world. Through mindfulness training, we can actually change the structure and functionality of our brain along with the capacities of our mind.

A quick note should be added here about the difference between the brain and mind. What we refer to as the mind are the psychological states and processes of a person that allow them to be conscious, think, feel, perceive, judge, imagine, remember, relate, and reason (Velmans, 2009). Among neuroscientists and mental health professionals, there is disagreement about how to define exactly what constitutes the mind. There is most certainly a relationship between the mind's capacities and the brain's functioning. Some argue, however, that the mind is limited to this neural activity, while others contend that the mind extends beyond and exists independently of the brain and body.

Daniel Siegel (2007) defines the mind as "a process that regulates the flow of energy and information" that is both embodied (defined by specific neurobiological processes in the brain and body) and relational (determined by the dynamic between people and things in our external environment in relationship). This definition captures both the inner mind-body relationship and outer interpersonal dynamic that influences the mind. I especially like this definition because we know that the mind can affect the brain and body, such as with formal mindfulness meditation, as I will explore shortly. And we know that changes to the brain can also impact the nature of our mind, such as with a traumatic brain injury. We know that our mind is shaped by our relationships, such as how we were raised, and our mind can also have an impact on those same relationships: as mindfulness increases, our awareness, consciousness, and the way in which we relate to others change too. These are not just unidirectional links. They are integral and interdependent.

Mindfulness practice, in particular, has a direct impact on both the embodied and relational dimensions of the mind. In fact, the positive impact of mindfulness on the mind is where its greatest relevance to social innovation and social change exists. From science, we have some understanding of what is happening in the body, including the brain and broader central nervous system, during conscious engagement of the mind. We can actually change the structure and functioning of our brain through mindfulness practice. This in turn affects the way we relate to and understand others in the external environment where social change unfolds.

> Mindful awareness, as we will see, actually involves more than just simply being aware: It involves being aware of aspects of the mind itself. Instead of being on automatic and mindless, mindfulness helps us awaken, and by reflecting on the mind we are enabled to make choices and thus change becomes possible. (D. J. Siegel, 2007)

Psychotherapeutic and neuroscientific research has found evidence to support a wide range of outcomes or benefits of practicing mindfulness that can be examined as either embodied (internal) or relational (interpersonal) processes of the mind (Davis & Hayes, 2001; see figure 1.1). These outcomes or benefits have also been shown to be able to predict certain psychological conditions. For example, Baer and colleagues found that the development of the three facets of nonreacting, acting with awareness, and nonjudgment positively correlate with various psychological conditions, including self-compassion, emotional intelligence, and openness to experience, while they also negatively correlate with other conditions, including neuroticism,

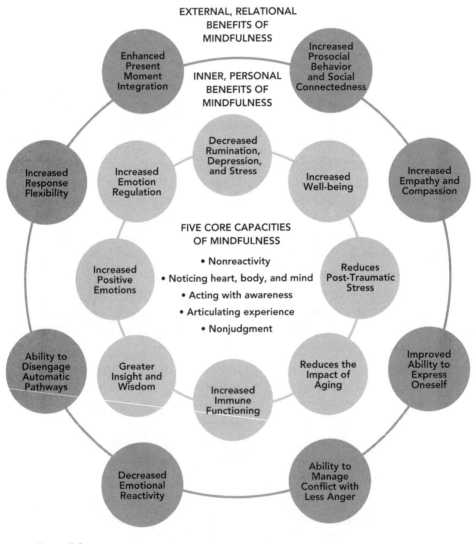

Figure 1.1

absentmindedness, and dissociation (Baer, Smith, Hopkins, Krietemeyer, & Toney, 2006). Let us explore the primary outcomes of mindfulness practice on both the brain and the inner, relational domains of the mind.

Internal Experience and Embodied Processes of the Mind

When you think about those in your life who exhibit a greater capacity for present-moment awareness, it is most often accompanied with a detectable level of inner calm, peace, and happiness, as I found in my friend Alice. Indeed, research has shown evidence that practicing mindfulness leads to increased positive affect, which means we actually feel more positive emotions, such as happiness, and less distress. Several studies have indicated that practicing meditation and mindfulness can result in more positive emotions and self-compassion, while decreasing stress, rumination, and anxiety (Davidson et al., 2003; Erisman & Roemer, 2010; Shapiro, Brown, & Biegel, 2007).

Rumination is the act of thinking about something, along with its causes and consequences, over and over again, which is an underlying cause of stress and anxiety. Remember the last time you were replaying an argument or composing a conversation in your head? Despite growing only more frustrated by the imaginary exchange, we can't seem to help but play and replay the irritating words that were spoken, or the vindicating zingers we wished we had said (or regret that we did). Mindfulness helps alter these patterns of rumination, which in turn reduce the resulting stress and anxiety (Corcoran, Farb, Anderson, & Segal, 2010). A 2013 meta-analysis of 209 studies across more than twelve thousand patients shows that mindfulness-based therapies resulted in clinically significant benefits in treating anxiety as well as depression (Khoury et al., 2013). With the mindfulness facets of observing, nonreacting, and nonjudging, we can become the observer of our own runaway train and recognize our propensity to get caught up in those thoughts. We also come to understand that our reactivity, defensiveness, and resistance to those thoughts are what cause us anxiety. We can see how our thoughts are often conditioned by our particular circumstances, and that they are not the same as our personal identity. By disrupting the power of our constant stream of thoughts, we increasingly recognize that thoughts, like emotions, shift and change, and thus we are more able to consider multiple perspectives since we do not so easily get attached to our own.

In addition to reducing rumination, mindfulness decreases stress and depression. Depression often involves a shutting down or repression of emotion. Mindfulness serves as an antidote. The facets of observing, describing, nonreacting, and nonjudging allow us to be with our feelings and thoughts, and by doing so, recognize that our experiences are just transient phenomena, not who we really are. One study found that mindfulness helps to reduce resting amygdala activity, an area of the brain associated with stress and depressive states (Way, Creswell, Eisenberger, & Lieberman, 2010). Another clinical study showed that with mindfulness, the ability to identify and describe one's inner states was associated with a reduction in depressive symptoms, negative emotional reactivity, and neuroticism (Barnhofer, Duggan, & Griffith, 2011).

Mindfulness practice also increases our capacity for emotional regulation. Emotional regulation can be described as "the processes by which individuals influence which emotions they have, when they have them and how they experience and express these emotions" (Gross, 1998). Essentially, it ensures we are not simply prisoners of our own emotional reactivity, flying off the handle with anger one moment and then overwhelmed with guilt the next. Many psychological disorders, such as borderline personality disorder and post-traumatic stress disorder (PTSD) involve the inability to regulate intense emotions effectively (Corcoran, Farb, Anderson, & Segal, 2010). The middle prefrontal cortex is the part of the brain that helps to monitor and regulate the activation of the limbic system, which is responsible for our emotional response. Mindfulness practices help promote stronger integration between these two areas, giving us balance between our emotional richness and our capacity to regulate without overwhelm and chaos (D. J. Siegel, 2007). Emotional regulation assists us in coming back to a neutral state of balance and peace more quickly after experiencing intense or distressing emotions, and our ability to continue to pursue desired goals in spite of such emotions (Erisman & Roemer, 2010). Emotional regulation also benefits from the decrease in rumination and increase in our attention, which support better awareness and management of our emotional experiences.

Mindfulness training is essentially a practice in greater attention concentration. The more that we pay attention to what is happening around and inside us, the more these moments of enhanced awareness experienced in our practice become longer-term traits of greater presence. Studies of mindfulness practice reveal increased awareness and attention, including increased processing speed of information, our ability to overcome distraction and have fewer thoughts that are unrelated to the task at hand, and enhanced metacognition—our ability to recognize thoughts and emotions from a decentered perspective, as mental or biological experiences rather than reality (Corcoran, Farb, Anderson, & Segal, 2010). This in turn contributes to our ability to reduce maladaptive tendencies in response to our emotional experiences, such as rumination, anxiety, and emotional reactivity.

Mindfulness leads us to greater insight and wisdom too. The middle prefrontal cortex, which is strengthened by mindfulness practice, draws from our own autobiographical memory and limbic system, which gives emotional context to our experiences, to allow us a sense of self-awareness and insight from our present as well as past experiences that also influences our view of the future (D. J. Siegel, 2007). Intuition and morality are also controlled by the functions of the middle prefrontal cortex, which involve using inputs from the larger body for reasoning and considering what is best for the larger whole. The more we strengthen the prefrontal cortex through mindfulness practice, the more we gain states of insight, knowing, intuition, and stronger moral reasoning.

While one might consider mindfulness to be only the purview of the cognitive mind and emotions, in fact mindfulness impacts the physical body. A study conducted and published by Richard Davidson and colleagues at the University of Wisconsin at Madison in 2003 demonstrated that mindfulness practice can positively affect the immune system. After an eight-week period of a structured mindfulness practice, meditators demonstrated increased levels of activity on the left side of certain anterior regions of the prefrontal cortex of the brain, shown to be associated with more positive emotions and less anxiety. This correlated with an associated greater immune response to an influenza vaccine, compared to a control group (Davidson et al., 2003).

With greater health, we might also expect a positive impact on aging. Aging is hastened by stress from the long-term activation and dominance of our stress response system, the sympathetic branch of the autonomic nervous system. It effectively wears out our organs from overactivation and excessive pressure on our cardiovascular system, affecting our heart, kidneys, and blood vessels (Elliott & Edmonson, 2006). Telomeres are the protective ends of chromosomes that wear down with exposure to chronic stress and depression, contributing to cell death, which is a sign of aging. Mindfulness is again an antidote. Not only does practicing mindfulness moderate stress, but research shows that it may actually help to lengthen telomeres, reducing the affects of stress on aging (Epel, Daubenmier, Moskowitz, Folkman, & Blackburn, 2009). Further, meditation practice has been found to result in a thickening of the cortical regions responsible for somatosensory, auditory, visual, and interoceptive processing, which also thin with age (Lazar et al., 2005). One study involving experienced meditators showed that the cortical thickness of forty- to fifty-year-old participants matched that of twenty to thirty year olds (ibid.).

Several mindfulness and mind-body interventions have been shown to mitigate the symptoms of PTSD. An eight-week pilot program in mindfulness among mental health workers in New Orleans, beginning ten weeks after Hurricane Katrina, demonstrated measurable impact on overall posttraumatic stress, including reexperiencing, hyperarousal, and anxiety (Waelde et al., 2008). The study's authors hypothesize that breath awareness reduces hyperarousal, and the capacity to focus on the present reduces stress associated with traumatic memory. Research has also found that particular practices in voluntary, slower yogic breathing, especially at a pace of five breaths per minute, called coherent breathing, help to optimize the stress response system and contribute to a significant reduction in PTSD symptoms (Gerbarg, Wallace, & Brown, 2011; Gerbarg & Brown, 2015; Gerbarg & Brown, 2016). I will revisit such conscious breathing practices in a later chapter. Breath and mindfulness-based programs are now being used across a variety of professions to address stress and PTSD, including among first responders, survivors of violence and mass disaster, combat veterans, and humanitarian aid workers.

All these positive impacts of mindfulness practice on our physical and emotional health lead to a greater sense of well-being. Here I define wellbeing not in the hedonic sense of happiness achieved through external stimuli or achievement. Instead, I consider the inner-derived sense of wellbeing that would exist in the absence of such external forces. B. Alan Wallace and Shauna Shapiro (2006) and Carol Ryff (1995) propose eudaimonic models of well-being that include: intention, aspirations, and volition toward one's and other's happiness; the ability to sustain one's attention voluntarily; self-acceptance; mastery; autonomy; purpose; clarity of mind; positive relations; personal growth; and emotional balance.

There is a growing body of research that demonstrates the effectiveness of mindfulness practice on well-being. Mindfulness practice, especially the practice of bringing your attention back again and again to an object of focus with intention, contributes to intentional and attentional balance as well as cognition, such as the metacognitive ability to detach from our thoughts for greater clarity. Additionally, neural integration in the brain is fundamental to well-being, enabling us to make sense of or create meaning out of our experiences. The prefrontal cortex's primary functions is integrative, and as we have seen through several studies, mindfulness promotes greater activity and thickening of the prefrontal cortex.

A 2008 study of the formal practice of MBSR demonstrated that it does significantly increase mindfulness capacities, and that mindfulness results in measurable improvements in psychological well-being (Carmody & Baer, 2008). In particular, the act of conducting a daily body scan practice is significantly related to developing the mindfulness facets of observing and nonreactivity to inner experience, and correlates to a reduction in interpersonal sensitivity and anxiety. Second, mindful yoga was found to be significantly associated with an increase in the capacity for observing, nonjudgment, nonreactivity, and acting with awareness, which results in improved well-being along with a reduction in stress, interpersonal sensitivity, anxiety, phobia, and psychoticism. Finally, formal sitting meditation is associated with acting with awareness and nonreactivity, leading to outcomes of psychological well-being and a reduction in psychoticism.

As we improve our physical, emotional, and mental functioning through mindfulness practice, we can then identify the positive benefits that influence our interpersonal engagement with others—the relational dimensions of the mind.

External or Interpersonal Engagement and Relational Processes of the Mind

There are many benefits of mindfulness that affect our interactions with our external environment and relationships that extend from those that accrue to us personally. First, mindfulness enhances our present moment integration. This is our ability to make sense of what is currently happening around us. Research shows that mindfulness increases not only our attentional capacity but also our cognitive flexibility, which means our ability to adapt different cognitive processes in response to new, unexpected experiences (Moore & Malinowski, 2009). With enhanced present moment integration, we have the opportunity to gain deeper insight from our observed experiences. For example, through our ability to observe our mind, body, and emotions, and that which is taking place around us moment by moment, we can more easily recognize the ways we create our own suffering or anxiety. We tend to suffer most by judging or comparing ourselves to others, resisting unpleasant experiences and change, reacting or blaming, clinging to desirable experiences, and trying to be right. The more we notice our emotions and subsequent reactivity, the more we are able to disengage from our habitual ways we have always reacted to similar stimuli, whether our reactions are instinctual or have been conditioned as a result of our life experiences. With the impact of mindfulness on our attention, awareness, and cognitive flexibility, we can better choose to respond in ways that are not automatic. This is also supported by the balancing and coordination of the sympathetic and parasympathetic branches of the autonomic nervous system, influenced by mindfulness practice that enhances integration between the subcortical regions responsible for igniting our fight-or-flight response, and the middle prefrontal cortex, which helps make sense of and respond consciously to our experiences.

A related capacity supported by mindfulness is increased response flexibility. This is our ability to pause and control our responses to choose how we respond as opposed to react. Instead of letting the experience of a sensation, thought, or emotion result in an impulsive reaction, mindfulness allows us to notice the experience, pause, and draw insight as to whether a reaction and what kind of action would be optimal in response. This process involves integration between the middle prefrontal cortex and sides of the cortex in assessing experiences, exhibiting restraint, and then utilizing choice in our response.

The combination of enhanced present moment integration, the ability to disengage automatic pathways, increased response flexibility, increased positive emotions, and decreased stress—all fostered through mindfulness—leads us to experience decreased emotional reactivity. This is a reduction in how reactive we get in response to our emotional states and external stimuli. For instance, mindfulness decreases the occasions where we feel anger and then react with anger instead of simply noticing that we are mad. Nonreactivity involves the regulation of the complex layers of emotional activity, which is stimulated in the subcortical limbic amygdala—the affective arousal areas of the brain, and coordinated and balanced by the prefrontal cortex—the integrating and modulating area of the brain, which controls the functions of the activating and rest/restorative branches of the autonomic nervous system. Mindfulness strengthens the relationship and integration between the limbic areas and prefrontal cortex, influencing our brain's capacity to find balance between the felt experience of emotional abundance, on the one hand, and our sense of meaning, emotional stability, and clarity, on the other hand (D. J. Siegel, 2007). Mindfulness also helps modulate the extent to which we view something as a threat, and then respond with greater anger or reactivity (Epel, Daubenmier, Moskowitz, Folkman, & Blackburn, 2009).

As we continue to practice mindfulness, we will find we cultivate the ability to manage conflict with less anger. As we develop the capacities for noticing, nonjudging, restraint, and response flexibly with deeper awareness, we find that we can experience conflict, opposition, or frustration without feeling emotionally triggered. This is in part because we get better at separating from and noticing what is arising for us with curiosity instead of reacting. We also start to understand that our emotions are transient phenomena that do not reflect our true identity. From this perspective, we are less likely to take other people's behavior personally, as we recognize they too are experiencing emotional material that comes from within. This is a fundamental capacity for building stronger relationships and transforming conflict into deeper human understanding.

Mindfulness further deepens our sense of empathy and compassion, the root capacities that enable us to feel and understand others. Empathy is the ability to put oneself in another's shoes and feel what they may be feeling. Compassion, in contrast, is a sense of empathy for the other's suffering *and* a fundamental desire to see the cessation of that suffering. Empathy is enabled by the limbic system, which responds to what we perceive in other's intentions, emotions, and behavior, then the insula communicates with the middle prefrontal regions where we interpret what might be happening in the other.

The capacity for empathy begins to develop at the earliest ages through our development of strong attachment. As babies, we develop relational bonds for the first time through eye contact, a response to our cries, smiling, and the sense of touch we receive from our caretakers. Mirror neurons in the presence of relationship enable these bonds to form in the brain. Mirror neurons are specific kinds of neurons that have been observed in the premotor cortex to fire both in response to an observed action and when the observer is executing that same action (Gallese, 2001). This can include simply watching someone move an object. We are also capable of mirroring sensations like pain and emotion, essentially contributing to our recognition that we are similar beings and resonating with the process of experiencing the same thing simultaneously.

Andrew Meltzoff and M. Keith Moore (1977) suggest that this mirroring behavior is innate to human beings, and can be recorded as early as twelve to twenty-one days old in infants, given their capacity to imitate facial changes such as opening the mouth or sticking out the tongue. Smiling is one action triggered by mirror neurons that is also reinforcing to bond development between infants and their caregiver. Smiling provides positive feedback to the caregiver and in turn supports the caregiver's role in attending to that infant's need. In one study, Lane Strathearn and colleagues at Baylor College of Medicine determined that mothers who were shown images of the smiling face of their own infant (as opposed to the smiling face of a strange baby or other emotional faces of their own child, including sadness), responded most strongly, stimulating dopamine release and activating all the brain's reward centers, including the areas involved in processing emotion, cognition, and motor/behavioral outputs. They explain that "the ability to link these sensory cues with the underlying needs of an infant, and differentially respond to such needs, is thought to be the basis for establishing secure mother-infant attachment" (Strathearn, Li, Fonagy, & Montague, 2008). Early childhood mirroring provides this sense of secure attachment and resonance with another. Secure attachment helps us develop the felt sense of being heard, seen, and understood, and capacity for empathy in understanding others.

Vittorio Gallese defines empathy as being driven by the embodied experience of the "lived-body," which enables us to recognizes others as like us. Through the mirror neurons that simulate action/emotion/sensation observed as well as discharge on that same action taken, emotion felt, or sensation experienced, we have the capacity to see ourselves through the eyes of another and see others through our own imagined experience of their reality. Gallese (2001) states, "My thesis is that many aspects of our felt capacity to entertain social relationships with other individuals, the ease with which we 'mirror' ourselves in the behavior of others and recognize them as similar to us, they all have a common root: empathy. ... Self and other relate to each other, because they both represent opposite extensions of the same correlative and reversible system self/other." It is this "neural matching system" or "resonance mechanism" that is critical in forming bonds or intersubjective links, and thus the capacity for empathy between people. Evidence of mirror neurons is the most extraordinary example of our brain's ability to adapt in response to relationship.

It has been demonstrated time and time again in research studies over the last twenty years that practicing mindfulness helps to increase empathy and compassion for others as well as self-compassion, which reduces stress and negative emotion, and increases positive emotion and altruistic responses (Shapiro, 2013). Several studies have demonstrated the ability of mindfulness practice to improve self-reported empathy, including after participating in an eight-week MBSR program or four-week Zen program, and among psychotherapists, who found mindfulness helped their ability to have a felt sense of their client's inner experiences, be more present, communicate, and support their clients in articulating their experiences (Davis & Hayes, 2001). One study demonstrated that nonjudgmental acceptance results in more helping behavior, but those who practiced present moment awareness also felt more positive emotion connected to that helping behavior (Cameron & Fredrickson, 2015). Another study showed that with only thirty minutes of compassion meditation training per day for two weeks, altruistic behavior increased, and neural changes were detected in the circuitry associated with more empathic concern, compassion, and response to suffering (Weng et al., 2012). A practice for compassion is contained at the end of chapter 6.

Self-compassion is a slight variation of compassion, also fostered by mindfulness. According to expert Kristin Neff (2016), self-compassion involves extending compassion to yourself, as you would another—recognizing your own suffering, feeling moved by it, and then inviting kindness toward yourself as you consider how to offer care and comfort in alleviating that suffering. A study by Elizabeth Kingsbury demonstrated the link between mindfulness, self-compassion, and three elements of empathy, including being able to take on another's perspective, the level of distress one feels when considering another's experience, and the ability to feel concern in response to another's experience. The nonjudging and nonreacting capacities of mindfulness as well as self-compassion had a direct relation-ship on high levels of perspective taking and low levels of personal distress. High levels of reported self-compassion significantly influenced empathetic concern as well as perspective taking (Kingsbury, 2009).

A related concept is loving-kindness. Loving-kindness is an open state of feeling kindness, warmth, and goodwill toward others, and like compas-sion, can be cultivated through specific meditations to evoke these feeling states. Emma Seppala, the science director of Stanford University's Cen-ter for Compassion and Altruism Research and Education, has identified several benefits of loving-kindness practices. Loving-kindness has been shown to increase positive emotions such as love, joy, contentment, grati-tude, and hope; reduce negative emotions; improve a sense of purpose; reduce stress, illness, and depressive symptoms; and increase life satisfac-tion (Seppala, 2014; Kang, Gray, & Dovidio, 2013). In particular, practic-ing loving-kindness meditation activates and strengthens the areas of the brain responsible for empathy and emotional intelligence, and increases gray matter volume. As a result, loving-kindness meditation increases pro-social and helping behavior, decreases bias toward others, and increases the perception of social connection. One study demonstrated that a six-week program in loving-kindness was able to significantly reduce implicit bias against stigmatized groups, including blacks and the homeless (Kang, Gray, & Dovidio, 2013). Loving-kindness meditation has also been shown to reduce self-criticism and improve self-compassion. Clinical research has fur-ther demonstrated that loving-kindness meditation can reduce migraines, decrease chronic pain, decrease PTSD, and decrease schizophrenia spectrum disorders. To try a loving-kindness meditation, see the practices at the end of this chapter.

In addition to all the beneficial outcomes of mindfulness practice from the facets explored above, studies have suggested further potential benefits of mindfulness, including an improved ability to express oneself; greater patience, gratitude, and social connectedness; a reduction in fatigue and burnout; and more effective psychotherapeutic relationships (Davis & Hayes, 2001).

Some of the limitations of the current studies include the lack of ran-domized control trials and challenges of the accuracy of self-reported mindfulness. It is possible that the more mindful you become, the more you are aware of the ways you are mindless, skewing results that depend on self-assessment. Research that incorporates biological as well as performance measures to verify self-reported data can strengthen results and provide greater insight into the physiological changes taking place with mindfulness practice (ibid.). Furthermore, most research has not involved controlled, longitudinal studies, sample sizes are small, and many findings have not yet been replicated (Tang, Hölzel, & Posner, 2015). Additional controlled studies that can evaluate longitudinal changes over larger samples of novice meditators, taking into account the difference in effort at the early stages of learning versus long-term practice, as well as studies that can explore the correlation between functional brain changes and self-reported behavior and well-being are needed (ibid.). Finally, bias can be seen in self-selection interventions, where participants who believe in the benefits of mindfulness may be more likely to choose to be a part of such a study and consequently self-report such benefits (Goyal et al., 2014).

Relevance to Social Change

A vital tenet of this book is that mindfulness is not only relevant but also critical to transformative social change. Examining the list of benefits, it is perhaps easy to recognize how. Indeed, there are likely few areas of human endeavor that would not be positively served by increased mindful "fitness." But as I look specifically at the role of change agent, I will delve more deeply into the methodology of conscious social change. Key questions I will need to answer are:

- Why does empathy and compassion matter?
- How does mindfulness influence our understanding of social issues and problem solving?
- How does mindfulness affect our reactivity and awareness, and how does that influence the ways we understand change in ourselves as well as others?
- How does mindfulness influence our ability to stay well while doing this work?
- How does mindfulness influence how we respond to as well as work, manage conflict, and build relationships with others?
- How does mindfulness and investing in self-awareness help us maintain a sense of purpose and meaning, and inspire others?
- What does mindfulness look like in action and leadership?

In 2004, as mentioned in the preface, I founded Global Grassroots, an international nonprofit organization that blends mindfulness-based leadership with social entrepreneurship to help women and girls in post-conflict East Africa develop their own ideas for social change into sustainable non-profit organizations. As part of our leadership development curriculum, we use a variety of contemplative practices as a means to foster inner wisdom, heal the wounds of violence, inspire compassion, and fuel creativity. I have reliably seen that this investment in mindfulness and inner work reaps unimaginable rewards among some seemingly unlikely leaders. Consider Brenda, a promising university student who participated in our 2014 Young Women's Academy for Conscious Change, a seven-month program that helps female high school graduates design and implement their own community service projects in their home villages as their first experience in conscious leadership.

Brenda's project revolved around the elevated school dropout rates of girls in her village. Due to teen pregnancy, early marriage, or the stresses rooted in a poor farming season, half of school-age girls habitually dropped out before graduating. As part of her program, Brenda personally mentored fifteen orphans and helped to keep them in school while teaching her community the benefits of educating girls versus encouraging them to end their education. She then developed a loan saving scheme among twenty-seven girls and ten parents to help them set aside school fees, and found financial sponsorship for another orphan. Next she developed a community piggery project where new piglets are sold to raise further school fees, and convinced two other dropouts to return to school. I sat down with Brenda at her graduation from our program in Uganda in August 2014. With a shy but confident smile, she told me how grateful she was for assistance in turning her own story into a passion to help others, for Brenda herself had been orphaned at the age of eleven, and had suffered all the depression, stigma, and withdrawal that such a hardship brings. Given the opportunity for reflection, understanding, and integration, Brenda was able to alleviate her own personal trauma as well as address a social need with compassion and collaboration. She laughed and told me her "heart had been healed." She said she no longer felt unhappiness. Brenda explained that at age fourteen, she wrote in a journal a plan to help other orphans one day and had dreamed about it for years—the same idea she had implemented. "Now it has come true!" she exclaimed, her voice bubbling with pride.

Empathy and Compassion for Social Change

All effective social change is built on our understanding of those we aim to serve, our insight into the root causes of a particular issue, and the relationships we build in carrying out our work. We call this attunement, which involves bringing our capacity to be present and aware to our engagement with another. And it is defined by our capacity for empathy and compassion.

As I just explored, mindfulness practice improves our self-awareness and presence as well as our awareness of the experience of others. This is the root of empathy and compassion, both of which are critical to effective leadership. Building our capacity to be fully present, we approach relationships differently. Looking inward, we discover our personal challenges with change, recognizing our own resistance and forgiving ourselves for slow progress. From this place, we can share the experience of those we are seeking to help or asking to change.

The more we develop empathy and listen more completely, the more we can understand the motivators, fears, and suffering of others. With compassion, we attend to various needs with greater insight and less judgment. This enables us to build bonds of resonance, connect more effectively, build trust, and find common ground around issues of priority. Our deeper level of attunement contributes to a desire to understand others while fostering a greater sense of connection and trust. From this place of connection, we are more likely to surface the information needed for more effective cross-cultural or intersectional understanding as well as collective problem solving. There are also techniques for using mirroring and empathy in listening that help to support stronger relationships, as we will learn in chapter 6.

Mindful Relationships for Social Change

As we develop our mindfulness capacities for observing, nonreactivity, and nonjudgment, we become more capable of recognizing and understanding our own inner landscape. In addition to fueling compassion and empathy, mindfulness supports us in finding self-compassion for our own process of transformation. We feel greater social connection and may even find a greater sense of interconnectivity with others. With self-awareness, we become more familiar with and begin to mitigate the ways we are triggered in relationship with others. We are less likely to perceive the acts of others as threats and more capable of disengaging our automatic pathways to choose consciously how to respond. This means we are more likely to act in ways that reduce the reactivity and anger that can escalate conflict.

Now we can build relationships based on stronger connection and human understanding. We are more present in relationship and can listen more proactively, permitting us to see more clearly the needs of those we aim to serve as well as those with whom we will collaborate. We remain curious, nonreactive, and nonjudgmental in our engagements, building trust and receptivity. As we become more accepting of ourselves through mindfulness practice, we are more likely to find acceptance and compassion for others. We are also less likely to perceive other's actions as a personal threat or act against us than a reflection of their own suffering. As such, we are more likely to be able to forge relationships across perceived boundaries.

Mindfulness and Mental Well-being for Social Change

Mindfulness influences our ability to stay well while doing this work. As mentioned previously, mindfulness practice results in a reduction in stress and anxiety coupled with higher immune functioning. Present moment awareness provides us with the opportunity to notice what is happening to us before we become too disillusioned or burned out. Through the facets of observing, nonreactivity, and nonjudgment, mindfulness training gives us a greater ability to be patient and endure discomfort, accepting our current circumstances. Simultaneously, as we disconnect ourselves from our automatic pathways of behavior, we can make a more conscious, proactive response to what we need instead of reacting to our discomfort. And it has been shown that acceptance (versus reactivity or aversion) reduces suffering and the stress response (D. J. Siegel, 2007). This supports a sense of possibility, choice, and agency, reducing our sense of suffering, which comes largely from wanting things to be different than they are. Here we can consciously choose to invest in our own restoration when we need it, and avoid the negative coping mechanisms that lead to avoidance, depression, burn-out, and disillusionment. I will explore mindfulness and its impact on our well-being in more detail in chapter 5.

Mindfulness and Meaning for Social Change

Finding meaning is the integration or "making sense" of one's experience. Integration is an indicator of emotional intelligence. If we see our life's path as a meaningful progression, each little (or big) event becomes an important opportunity for learning (higher brain functioning) rather than simply a random event that requires a reaction (lower brain functioning). This is critical to a social change leader in their ability to advance long-term transformation. When we make sense of things and find meaning through integration, we uncover a sense of greater understanding and connection, both with our life's events and others, leading us in turn toward a more universal and collaborative approach to solutions building. Everyone and everything becomes a part of our journey; thus we pay more attention and everyone matters. We also know finding meaning through integration is critical to well-being, resilience, and happiness, which is supported and enabled by mindfulness practice. In chapter 7, we will learn more about how to blend our passions, gifts, and capabilities through collaboration in service to the greater good.

Mindfulness is simply a function of practice. Like exercise, the more you practice, the more you benefit. Below are a few initial mindfulness practices to try. You need no special equipment, capability or previous experience as a prerequisite. Whether you are perfectly able-bodied or have any form of physical disability, these simple and safe practices can be attempted by all, as they invite you to notice your unique experience, primarily residing in your internal landscape. Experiment with each of them for at least a week in order to explore which one resonates most and which ones you find most challenging. Then choose one as a daily practice to invest in over time.

It is remarkable that the simple series of practices that fall under the umbrella of mindfulness can result in so many capacities and outcomes benefiting the individual and our interpersonal relationships. Mindfulness teaches us how to be, and within Western cultures that are oriented around doing and achievement, mindfulness can sometimes feel passive and unproductive. Science has proven otherwise. Mindfulness training is brain training and an empirical inquiry process that enables us to transform our brain structure, brain function, the processes of the mind, how we understand ourselves as well as others, our physical, mental, and emotional health and well-being, and how we relate and respond to our inner landscape and the world around us. Why wouldn't we try it? From a more mindful outlook, we can learn to act consciously in ways that inspire meaning and positive change in our own lives along with the lives of others who suffer. Mindfulness is an essential and integral part of conscious social change.

Practices

Mindfulness of the Senses
Recommended duration: seven to fifteen minutes
Recommended frequency: daily for at least a week

Allow yourself to notice—hear, smell, see, touch, and experience—all that is outside of and around you:

- Notice what you hear in and outside the room.
- Notice the temperature and humidity.
- Notice any smells.
- Notice your clothes or any breeze on your skin.
- Notice how the chair or floor feels while it holds you up.
- Notice the light passing across your eyelids and so on.

Allow yourself to notice everything you can for seven minutes. When your timer goes off, slowly open your eyes when you feel ready.

Discuss or write in a journal about your experience: How do you feel? What did you notice? What was that experience like being your own observer? How often do you get to stop and just look inside? What wisdom came out of that experience for you? Has there been anything that you have experienced that has changed your perspective?

Mindful Body Scan
Recommended duration: ten to fifteen minutes
Recommended frequency: daily for at least a week

Conduct a body scan (if you have any disability that makes it difficult to feel certain parts of your body, simply notice with curiosity and compassion everything you can about your experience, including the edges of sensation and anything that arises for you from this exploration):

- As you breathe in, see if you can feel whether you have any tension in your neck. As you breathe out, imagine that tension leaving your body.
- Next when you breathe in, allow your attention to move down your spine. See if you have any tension in your spine and release this with your next out breath. With each breath, allow yourself to become more deeply relaxed. Let a few breaths go by before you try each of the next instructions.
- Now as you breathe in, feel your heart area and then your stomach, and notice how you feel in those two places. Notice how your body moves in your chest, ribs, and abdomen as you breathe. If you have any tension in those areas, invite it to melt away as you breathe out.
- Now notice your shoulders, arms, and hands as you breathe. Do they feel strong? Tired? Tense? As you breathe in, imagine you are breathing energy into those muscles. As you breathe out, imagine any tension disappearing. Do this as many times as you need to until you start to release the tension.
- Next breathe into your hips and pelvis. Notice how you feel as you sit on your chair or the ground. Feel the strength of the surface below you holding you up. Breathe out any tension and let yourself relax into the surface (but without slumping).
- Now bring your attention to your legs. Notice how they feel. As you breathe out, allow any tension to melt through your feet into the floor.
- With a deep breath in, allow (imagine) your breath and attention to go all the way to your feet. Feel your feet, heels, toes, and ankles. Consider with gratitude these feet that, for many, carry you each day. What do your feet need? As you breathe in, send your feet a sense of calm, strength, energy, and healing—whatever they need, and then breathe out any pain or tension into the floor.

When you have completed the practice, notice any overarching changes in the body. What did you notice that you may not have noticed before?

Mindful Walking
Recommended duration: ten minutes
Recommended frequency: daily for at least a week

Mindful walking allows you to bring exquisite awareness by moving in slow motion. Practice this in your own home or outside in a private setting, ideally in a beautiful natural environment, or if you are lucky to have access, walk in an intentional space like a labyrinth or on a garden path that forms a circle. If walking is not possible or easy for you, use any form of motion to invite awareness, including slow stretching or transportation by wheelchair or vehicle.

Begin by taking three deep breaths and stretch your body. How does it feel today?

Next, begin walking slowly—almost slow enough to start feeling off-balance. Feel each foot lifting and placing on the ground or floor. You may want to say in your head "lifting" and "placing" as you move each foot. Try to synchronize your breathing with your steps so that you breathe in as you lift a foot and breathe out as you place your foot back on the ground.

As you walk, pay attention to how your feet feel. Notice your muscles moving, the strength of your skeletal system holding you up, and your breath. If you are outside, you may also notice the sounds, temperature, scents, and sights around you.

Walk for at least ten minutes. If you find your mind wandering during this exercise, simply notice yourself thinking and label it "thinking." Invite your thoughts to drift or fade away like a cloud in the sky or leaf floating down a creek. Then bring your attention back to your body moving.

You may practice this alone or in a group. Alone, you can walk in a circle or allow yourself to move in whatever direction you feel pulled with each step.

When in a group, it is beneficial to practice walking together at the same slow pace in a circle so that you experience the process of moving as a collective. Notice any feelings that arise in response to your lack of control over the pace of the circle. Notice if you have any impulse to want to "fix" it or blame others. Or notice whether you shift into a state of collective flow. Notice that you are one part in a larger system and what that feels like. Notice how much your attention rests on your own experience versus that of the other participants.

If you are facilitating, you can ring a bell at the end of the time frame you have set aside for this practice. As the bell rings, be mindful of how you transition back into a normal pace, or sit back down to reflect together or in solitude. After completing the practice, take a moment to sit or stand and reflect on how your mind, heart, and body now feel in stillness. You may want to journal about your insights, or discuss them with the group or a partner.

Mindful Tasks

Recommended duration: ten minutes

Recommended frequency: daily for a chosen task for one to two weeks

Whatever task you may be doing, bring 100 percent of your attention to everything you are experiencing. Be your own observer. For example, if you are washing a dish, slow down your process and

- Notice the container or dish.
- Feel the temperature of the water, texture of the sponge, and soap and bubbles on your skin.
- Acknowledge the time of day and any distinctions of the light at that time of day.
- Notice the sounds of the experience of washing and the sounds around you.
- Consider the colors of the bubbles and items in the sink.
- Take in the scent of the soap and food, whether or not they are pleasant, and notice which you prefer or not.
- Experience the movements of your hand in the water.

If you are working at a computer,

- Notice the feeling of your fingers on the keyboard.
- Notice how your body feels sitting in the chair: Are your feet rooted on the floor, do you have any tension in your shoulders, are you alert or tired, and so on?
- Notice where your eyes move, how often you look up or look around, and the quality of the light around you.
- Try to notice yourself breathing as you type.
- Notice the sounds around you—the sounds of your keyboard and computer, and the sounds around you in your workspace, or any music or other entertainment you listen to while working.

- Notice when and why you pause in what you are doing.
- Notice how you use your hands: Are you only typing or do you stop to touch your face and hair, or scratch or cough or bite a fingernail, and what other unconscious habits do you employ?
- Notice what thoughts accompany what you are doing.

If you are eating,

- Notice the color of the food on your plate and smell of each item, and how it changes as you eat.
- Contemplate how many hours of people's time and natural energy went into its creation from the sun, rain, and soil that nurtured the seed, to the cultivation and harvest of the plants, to the packaging and delivery of the raw ingredients, to any manufacturing that took place to the preparation and presentation of the meal.
- Notice the texture, temperature, and consistency of the food when you taste it.
- Which items do you touch with your hand and which with a utensil, and how does that change your eating experience?
- Consider the nutrients that are present, and notice what you crave as well as what your body needs and wants.
- Eat slowly until you notice yourself becoming full.

Other tasks that could be a source of mindfulness include:

- Getting dressed in the morning.
- Walking up or downstairs.
- Standing in line.
- Playing or listening to music.
- Riding on public transportation or driving.
- Creating art.
- Time with a pet.
- Cleaning the house or fixing something.
- Weeding, planting or watering a garden.

Loving-Kindness Meditation
Recommended duration: as long as it takes to complete the practice
Recommended frequency: daily for at least a week

Sit in your meditation posture, as described in the initial breath-noticing practice. With this meditation or reflection, we will bring kindness and compassion to others, even our enemies. Pick something that you wish for yourself. Such as "May I (or another) be happy. May I live with ease. May I be healthy. May I be safe. May I be joyful. May I be peaceful ... " Now close your eyes and begin taking deep breaths.

- Offer your blessing to yourself.
- Offer your blessing to each of your family members.
- Offer your blessing to those around you who support you.
- Offer your blessing to those you know who are in need.
- Offer your blessing to those who challenge you most.

Conventional Change

Change is happening every moment whether we are actively engaged in creating it or not. It is valuable to explore the predominate model by which change takes place in our lives and then look at what distinguishes conscious social change, especially in its mindfulness.

As illustrated in table 2.1 below, when we are involved in seeking change, the conventional way in which this manifests usually involves change that benefits the self (e.g., we choose to educate ourselves or work out at the gym) or the self-interests of a defined group (e.g., low-income workers advocate for a raise in the minimum wage, or large financial corporations seek a relaxation of regulatory policy) (Quinn, 2000). Certainly there are broad-reaching, positive outcomes that can be achieved. Yet in most conventional change cases, the primary goal is typically the benefits accrued to the self or group.

Furthermore, in the conventional model what drives our underlying actions and visions of what change should look like is most often what external forces, such as cultural norms, deem important (e.g., status, power, education, material wealth, appearance, or what we have come to think of as fair or right) or depends on the direction of an authority (e.g., upper management has dictated what shift has to happen, policy must be implemented and enforced, or the leader of an activist movement has set the vision for change).

Frequently, such conventional change tries to compel people to change with incentives or punitive measures. Such "sticks and carrots" most often result in incremental change within norms of behavior that are temporary only so long as the reward or punishment is in effect. Consider taxes on

Table 2.1
Conventional change vs. conscious social change

Conventional model of change	Conscious social change model
Outer driven: we try to achieve what society says we should have—wealth, status, or beauty—or seek approval and direction externally.	Inner driven: we are driven by what we feel most passionate about and called to do in the world.
Self-focused: we look at what's in it for us.	Other focused: we look at how we can benefit the common good.
To create change, we tell or force people, and are motivated by our needs. This creates a sense of division: us versus them. We use threats of punishment or rewards to get people to comply with what we want.	To create change, we begin with self-examination to understand how much of the problem is our own, develop compassion for others, seek the insight and participation of others in designing a solution, stay attuned to the changing reality, and look to collaborate to optimize social value creation.
The results are usually incremental change within the norms of behavior, often without people changing at a deep level; instead, they are just complying to avoid punishment or get the reward.	The results are systemic change at the root levels and individual transformation that lasts longer term.

cigarettes to reduce smoking. Studies have shown that for every 10 percent increase in cigarette prices, smoking demand is decreased by 4 percent (Bader, Boisclari, & Ferrence, 2011). While this has been an effective deterrent against smoking among certain populations such as youth, however, it has had limited impact on the behavior of heavy or long-term smokers. More is needed to transform such behavior permanently. Remove the tax and it is possible that demand will rise again.

Such change also tends to orient itself with an "us versus them" paradigm that can go so far as to demonize the opposition. For example, US political rhetoric, especially surrounding the 2016 presidential election, increasingly focused on fear of the broader immigrant community, stemming from a desire to limit outsiders deemed dangerous, connected to terrorists or a drain on the economy. As a result, hardworking families of legitimate refugee status, or citizens of certain ethnic, religious, and racial backgrounds, have faced a rise in widespread discrimination.

Even well-intentioned activists can target opposition to such an extent that they too come to adopt harmful tactics that obstruct or sabotage progress, or even utilize violence, as seen in cases such as ecoterrorism and abortion clinic bombings. This not only perpetuates division but also may even unintentionally uphold the inequity and disconnect between those of privilege and power, and those without.

Conscious Social Change

While these conventional approaches to change may play significant roles in achieving benefits for individuals and groups, or enabling policy change, there are other methods that can lead to deep transformation with inclusivity, compassion, and connection among a broader stakeholder ecosystem. With conscious social change as an alternative paradigm, we can use mindfulness to help us understand and engage others on an equal level, shifting away from models that blame, try to force compliance, or perpetuate division. As we explore transformational practices that support self-awareness, we gather the tools to understand change in ourselves, and that leads us to understand more clearly how others react as they grasp at or resist change. From this deeper, inner-driven understanding, conscious social change looks not just at a onetime fix but also how change can happen in a way that transforms individuals, groups, systems, institutions, and whole societies for the better and long term.

Conscious social change is a process led by responsible and ethical change agents, who engage in their own efforts toward deeper self-awareness, while striving to create positive change for others. These two components of inner and outer change, or personal and social change, are integral to and essential for a better society. Unlike conventional change, as depicted in table 2.1, conscious social change is an inner-driven paradigm—meaning that much of what guides its actions comes from self-understanding and an internal sense of purpose (Quinn, 2000). This model begins with self-examination, and seeks to understand others through one's own direct experience with change, fear, anxiety, and reactivity. From here we can identify the drivers of or obstacles to change among all participants so as to choose strategies that will support long-term transformation.

Conscious social change is other focused, looking to benefit the greater common good, not just the self-interests of a smaller group. Conscious social change does not operate with an orientation of us versus them. Instead, it recognizes our shared experience, finds ways to heal and connect, actively listens, and facilitates solutions in ways that speak to the underlying essential nature of people as human beings. Conscious social change is a more collaborative approach, and as a result works at the roots of the issue to create lasting transformation at a systemic level, determining how we can alleviate the underlying reasons for inequality, suffering, and other social ills, not just treat symptoms. And it does so while embracing the wisdom, participation, and leadership of as many stakeholders as possible, especially the most marginalized.

Five Capacities and Five Questions

There are five key capacities of conscious social change and five questions that guide its implementation. It always begins with a process of inner awareness and then turns outward to inform our work with others. I will discuss each of these in turn throughout the book:

1. Cultivating Presence: What is happening?
2. Becoming Whole: What is true?
3. Ensuring Well-being: What is needed?
4. Engaging Mindfully: What is helpful?
5. Leading from Within: What is possible?

Conscious change leaders have a responsibility to advance social justice with awareness, integrity, and compassion—even for our "enemies." This begins with a deep understanding of ourselves and our own needs. The first capacity is cultivating presence. This is the fundamental step of quieting, calming, and becoming aware. It is the movement away from immediate reaction and toward a profound attention to what is going on. Without recognizing what is happening with our thoughts (e.g., daydreams or worrying), emotions (e.g., anger or embarrassment), or physical experiences (e.g., fatigue or pain), these things can distract us from what is happening right now in front of us. This mental "busyness" can also unconsciously affect how we interact with others. If we are hurt, we may be cold or short with people. If we are stressed, we may listen poorly. Instead, with increased self-awareness, we can begin to separate ourselves from these occurrences and observe them with greater insight. Cultivating presence starts with practicing mindfulness. To guide us, we use the key question, *What is happening?*

The second capacity is becoming whole, where we are proactive in addressing our own wounding, fears, limiting beliefs, impulses, and shadows that can distort our perspective as well as cause us to act unconsciously in ways that can cause harm. Conscious social change invites us to examine our role in the systems, including dynamics of power and privilege that uphold the status quo. It asks us to work on ourselves to make sure we are not contributing to the problem or creating division before we try to change others. The more we look deeply into ourselves, the better we come to understand our compulsions to fix things and the underlying reasons for our anxiety. This is our proverbial "stuff," and this is our chance to recognize it for what it is and attend to it when it gets triggered. The more we are mindful of our own fears, the better we can respond during conflict with wisdom and respect for others. Once we recognize the challenges that adapting to change pose for each of us, the more likely we are to approach the change we wish to see in another, in institutions, and within broader society with deeper compassion (Rothberg, 2006). The deeper we go in our personal exploration, the more surprised we may be to discover that in many ways, we are actually just like everyone else. In developing this capacity for wholeness, to guide us through a process of getting at the roots of our own inner experience, we ask the question, *What is true?*

The third capacity is using self-awareness for ensuring well-being. Here we ask the question, *What is needed?* By committing to ongoing personal transformation practices, we can more readily attend to our own balance so that we avoid burnout and disillusionment. As we learn more about our own unhealthy coping mechanisms for stress, we can employ intentional self-care mechanisms to ensure our own restoration in ways that honor the needs of our hearts, bodies, and minds. With balance, we stay grounded and completely available to do our work in the world.

The fourth capacity is engaging mindfully for social justice. Here we apply the same process to broader society that we utilize in our inner work, asking, *What is happening, what is true*, and *what is needed?* As we diagnose our issue and design a solution mindfully, we also ask a fourth question: *What is helpful?* This is a fundamentally inner-driven approach that benefits the common good. In approaching social change more consciously, we recognize through deep listening the inherent wisdom in those we aim to serve. We honor that each stakeholder has insight from their particular experience with the issue that is valuable to our understanding of the whole system and a potential contribution toward the larger solution. We can also work to identify any collective unconscious material, such as fears and assumptions, which may distort truth and cause harm. Instead, we engage collaboratively to design a more informed and innovative intervention that gets at the roots of the problem. This allows us to work toward systemic transformation with deeper human understanding as opposed to a reliance on punitive measures to force change. With mindfulness, we learn to approach our work without as much ego. In this way, we can avoid imposing our own agenda when it may not align with what is most needed. We can then more clearly discern the wisest response and our particular contribution (which may include no action) in any moment, such that we not only avoid harm but also facilitate agency, connection, and optimal learning among all parties. The resulting solution will be issue driven, not activity driven. In other words, our mission is to alleviate the underlying issue as opposed to just advance our programs or agenda. We do not measure our success based simply on the scale of our work. Rather, we evaluate our effectiveness in remaining responsive to shifts in the issue and needs of those we aim to serve. Moreover, we can foster organizational cultures that support deep listening, individual renewal, and continual learning for everyone involved.

Finally, we develop the capacity for leading from within, embodying mindfulness as a leadership ethos. Conscious social change is a mind-set as much as a methodology. We continue to commit to both an inner and outer transformation process with a beginner's mind. We invest in regular individual or organizational practices that enable well-being and reflection. We care for our relationships and social change work, letting them deepen our human understanding. The more we cultivate self-awareness, the more likely we will find our unique purpose or passion, and thus inspire others to do the same, energizing and unifying collective efforts behind a common cause. We are unafraid to take informed risks and stretch ourselves. With conflict, we look first at what change may be needed within ourselves. We act with intention and integrity, holding a vision for the highest benevolent outcome, but letting go of what we cannot control. We know how to use our power and potency to speak truth for justice, but we lead with humility, embracing compromise as a step toward progress. Here the final question we are left to ask is, *What is possible?*

Because conscious social change draws from a broader set of ideas and perspectives over the imposition of a narrow agenda, solutions are more likely to be dynamic and innovative. The more comprehensive your understanding and resources to draw from, the more creative your outputs. Because conscious social change fosters a community's engagement and ownership rather than division, solutions are more likely to have longevity and be self-sufficient with diverse support. Because endeavors are informed by mindful awareness and the need for balance, solutions are more likely to be sustainable for the self, others, and the planet.

Phases of Social Change Solution Development

The conscious social change methodology can be applied at any point in the problem-solving process, many of the tools for which are introduced in this book and developed further in the accompanying Toolkit for Conscious Social Change (www.conscioussocialchange.org):

- *Problem diagnosis:* This includes learning how to work deeply at the roots rather than at the symptomatic level, mapping the entire system and engaging all stakeholders, including the most marginalized, opposition, and perpetrators, utilizing deep listening and participatory skills.
- *Solutions design:* This involves deep and inclusive collaboration, seeking common ground as a basis for change, employing compassion from an inside-out understanding of the common experience of change, and choosing interventions that will contribute toward systemic transformation.
- *Organizational design:* This includes organizational structures, decision making, communications processes, practices used in conducting business operations, policies that support well-being, and collaborative methods that inspire meaning and creativity.
- *Implementation and evaluation:* This can include dealing with opposition and conflict mindfully, building community understanding through mindful communications, designing metrics and evaluation methods that are participatory and aligned for deep transformation, and employing ethics in decision making.

Conscious social change can also be applied to a range of processes and functional areas within each of these four phases of problem solving above, including research, pilot testing, hiring, fund-raising, communications, fiscal policy, and reporting, among others. Rather than provide a formula for what a conscious social change organization or any of the functions above might look like, I honor that each strategy will be informed by the people among whom it will be implemented. Regardless, I would propose that if each step is driven by mindfulness, there is a higher likelihood that the outcomes will also be mindful and have sustained impact.

Over the course of the following five chapters, I will go deeper into each of the five capacities, present how mindfulness is relevant in achieving these capabilities, show how to develop skills through practices or tools you can use, and weave throughout research, profiles, and anecdotes to illustrate the capacity in action. The companion Toolkit for Conscious Social Change contains even more in-depth practices to explore and cultivate these capacities, and apply them in your social innovation work.

3   Cultivating Presence

It is so easy for all of us, especially those of us who identify as change agents, to want to fix things when we come face-to-face with another's suffering. Yet sometimes our simple presence is all that is required.

I'm sitting on a bench next to the South American woman, as her friend disappears into the search headquarters looking for information. I can hardly speak Spanish, and Melinda does not seem inclined to speak English with me. I know her as the woman at the Jerome building who has been desperately awaiting word from the rescue teams on the status of her husband and son, trapped or crushed beneath the apartment building when it collapsed in Haiti's worst earthquake. I had flown to Haiti to volunteer after the massive 7.0 magnitude quake hit just sixteen miles west of the capital, Port-au-Prince, on January 12, 2010. I thought that my skills as a breathwork practitioner would be of service to those traumatized by the disaster.[1]

I had sought out additional training on the eve of my departure to Haiti from two professors of clinical psychiatry who were also mind-body trauma-healing experts. Richard P. Brown, professor of psychiatry at Columbia University, and Patricia Gerbarg, professor of psychiatry at New York Medical College, had developed and had been using a breathing method called Breath~Body~Mind (BBM) to address PTSD among survivors of the 2006 tsunami in Southeast Asia, Hurricane Katrina survivors in Biloxi, Mississippi, and first responders to the 9/11 terrorist attacks in New York City with great success. They provided me with additional coaching in their methodology, which would be more adaptable to working with larger groups, across language and cultural barriers, without a long-term therapeutic relationship like my own practice required.

I understood the physiology of trauma, knew how to use breath to help reset the nervous system and address PTSD symptoms, and was familiar with working in disaster and war zones from my years of work in Africa, including Rwanda and the Darfur refugee camps of eastern Chad. But when I arrived in Haiti, I was surprised to discover people were not at all interested in trauma healing. It was too soon. Their focus was on survival, and like Melinda, they were desperate to find their loved ones. Emotional well-being was not topping their list.

As I sit on the bench now with Melinda, my mind is filtering through every solution, skill, and fragment of knowledge that could help me respond to the woman sitting solemnly next to me. Suddenly, I notice my reactive compulsion to fix, the unbearable discomfort with not knowing what to do, the urgent driving force of the need to be of help in some way. Slow down. Breathe. I focus on my own breathing again, slowing its pace intentionally. Funny how what I thought I'd be bringing to the people here is actually what I need most. I pull back into the inner observer. Catching myself in a wave of what had been—even well intentioned—reactivity, I let myself just be with the experience of silence. I am reminded of a lesson from my breathwork teacher: sometimes all you need to do is be with someone. In so doing, you are showing them that just *being*, showing up exactly as you are, is simply enough. I stay for a moment. I am there. She looks at me. I see her. She sees me. That is all that is needed.

> When one realizes one is asleep, at that moment one is already half-awake.
> —P. D. Ouspensky, *In Search of the Miraculous*, 1949

Presence is the ability to bring complete awareness to what is happening around you and what is happening inside you right now, in the present moment. To be here now. Under this overarching capacity, we are guided by a key question as we examine with curiosity our inner and outer landscape: *What is happening?* This includes awareness of our mind's activity, our emotional experiences, our physical state and sensations, the space around us, and our interactions with others. Our ability to be our own witness can also lead to greater insight into those experiences. This capacity is cultivated through mindfulness. This can include a focused attention on one particular aspect of our experience, such as trying to sense what we are feeling in any moment. Or we can practice bringing a more open awareness to all occurrences happening simultaneously. It is useful to start with a simple mindfulness practice of noticing our normal pattern of breathing.

Breathing is an experience that is always with us, and serves as an easy anchor for our attention whether we are formally sitting in meditation or going about our daily business. Let me offer a quick aside to discuss breathing, and why it has such significant potential to support mental, physical, and emotional well-being.

Breathing

Every major spiritual tradition has some reference to breath practices in its literature, and most have some practices using breath awareness for personal transformation. The earliest written documentation reveals conscious breathing being used in spiritual training approximately three thousand years ago, but some scholars suggest it was in use much earlier as part of ancient Vedic-Yogic traditions that emerged between eight and ten thousand years ago (Mijares, 2009). Before there was a written record, spiritual teachers had been orally handing down secret, mystical breathing practices between teacher or guru and students for hundreds of generations. Eastern traditions tend to use breath as a tool for self-awareness and/or moving energy toward the realization of the true nature of all things, leading to enlightenment. More recent Western traditions, such as Holotropic Breathwork or Integrative Breathwork, use breath as a therapeutic tool for psychological healing via a mind-body philosophy whereby the individual is guided by their own inherent body wisdom in exploring and integrating unconscious material to reach wholeness.

It may be helpful to understand what is happening in your body when you take a breath, and thus why it has been used for centuries as such a powerful, whole-body tool for self-awareness. When the carbon dioxide in our blood rises to a certain level, the brain stem initiates a breath. The diaphragm, a dome-shaped musculotendinous sheet between the lungs, sternum, ribs, and lumbar vertebrae, flattens and pushes down. This allows the lungs to expand, causing a change in pressure or vacuum, which draws in air. Air is pulled through the nose or mouth into the lungs, which are made up of three hundred million little soft sacs. These pulmonary alveoli, lined with a dense network of capillaries, make up the surface area on which the exchange of oxygen and carbon dioxide takes place, affecting seventy-five trillion cells. Luckily, the body is made to never stop breathing. If you held your breath until you began to lose consciousness, the body's internal regulation would take over, and you would immediately start breathing again. The average person reaches peak respiratory function and lung capacity in their mid-twenties. Then they begin to lose respiratory capacity of between 10 and 27 percent for every decade of life.

There are many physiological benefits of breathing deeply. Seventy percent of the body's detoxification takes place through the exchange between air and blood. It makes sense that we use Breathalyzer tests to measure our blood alcohol content, as our body works to cleanse itself of alcohol with each breath. Breathing also allows for the massage of the organs in the abdominal cavity, which supports their circulatory release and functioning, including the liver, spleen, stomach, kidneys, pancreas, and large intestines.

A significant number of physical ailments are linked to poor respiratory functioning, including chronic fatigue, headache, high blood pressure, depression, and low back pain. The Nobel Prize was awarded Otto Heinrich Warburg in 1931 for research that "the prime cause of cancer is the replacement of the respiration of oxygen in normal body cells by a fermentation of sugar" (Brand, 2010).

The autonomic nervous system controls our automatic breathing function in addition to a range of other automatic functions needed for our survival, including heart rate, digestion, and reflexes like coughing and swallowing. As I discussed previously, the autonomic nervous system has two branches. The sympathetic branch is the stress response system, which is also responsible for our fight-or-flight response in the presence of a threat. The parasympathetic branch is responsible for our rest and relaxation, and is particularly influenced by sensory perceptions from the body delivered through the vagus nerve networks that connect most of our internal organs and tissues to the brain. Our respiratory function is one of the most critical of these interoceptive pathways because life depends on our ability to breathe. So while the autonomic nervous system controls unconscious breathing, changes in our breath patterns can also affect our sympathetic and parasympathetic balance. For example, if our breathing were to be obstructed by choking, it would signal to the brain the presence of a threat, and activate our stress response system and other reflexes to immediately respond to the emergency. When normal breathing is restored, the stress response system quiets down as the relaxation branch engages. Higher-frequency breathing has been shown to correlate with sympathetic dominance, while slower-paced breathing stimulates the parasympathetic branch (Elliott & Edmonson, 2006).

We tend to breathe twelve to fifteen breaths per minute on average, taking seventeen to twenty-two thousand breaths in a day. Breathing at a normal resting frequency of fifteen breaths per minute actually results in slight sympathetic preference (ibid.). In other words, our stress response system remains in a state of partial activation or readiness even at rest. In addition, heart rate variability, a marker of cardiovascular health, age, and stress, is influenced by breath. A low heart rate variability, associated with a higher risk of cardiac arrest and coronary heart disease, correlates with sympathetic emphasis and a shallow, more frequent pace of breathing (ibid.). The constant activation of the stress response system is linked to a whole host of physical ailments, psychiatric disorders, and aging (ibid.; Gerbarg & Brown, 2016).

On the other hand, it has been shown that slow, gentle breathing activates the parasympathetic branch of the autonomic nervous system, effectively stimulating our rest-relaxation system (Bhimani et al., 2011; Jerath et al., 2006; Gerbarg and Brown, 2015). Furthermore, using Ujjayi breath—whereby the practitioner focuses attention on the sound and feel of breathing by creating resistance in the throat—also helps to bring online the parasympathetic branch (Zope & Zope, 2013). This is possibly partly due to stimulation of the vagus nerve, which run through the throat. Finally, yogic breath practices that involve the khechari mudra, where the tip of the tongue is curled upward and backward touching the roof of the mouth at the edge of the front teeth, has been shown to limit the capacity of the nasal airway, effectively reducing the frequency while increasing the depth of breath, both of which contribute to autonomic balance and our ability to relax (Elliott & Edmonson, 2006). There is a reason we have phrases in our language such as "Take a deep breath!" that we use to support individuals in slowing down and achieving a state of calm.

In addition to the physiological benefits, conscious breathing supports greater emotional and mental wholeness too. When we breathe consciously, it activates different neural pathways than when controlled automatically. Conscious breathing is controlled by the cerebral cortex, enabling breathing to serve a bridging function that not only exerts influence over the autonomic nervous system but also connects our physical experiences, emotional states, and higher thinking capabilities.

Breathing is a constantly changing force that serves as a mirror of our inner state and shifts in reaction to our external environment. For instance, when we are afraid or startled, or are experiencing pain, what do we do with our breath? Usually we suck in and hold our breath, or quicken it. In contrast, when we see something beautiful or experience joy, what do we do with our breath? Imagine yourself walking out onto a balcony or mountain summit overlooking the most beautiful view you have ever seen. Usually we expand our breathing to take in more energy and feel more of those good feelings.

For most of us, however, we tend to live in somatic "amnesia" disconnected from the sensations of our bodies, until they are significant enough that we can no longer ignore them, such as a headache or back pain. This is closely connected to our challenge recognizing the emotions that trigger our reactions. But given that breathing serves as a mirror of our internal state, we can use conscious breathing as a way to strengthen our awareness of what we are experiencing. Moreover, it is possible to reverse that relationship, using intentional breathing patterns to shift our mental, emotional, and physical states as well.

When we notice ourselves breathing shallowly or holding our breath, for example, we can recognize our stress, and deliberately slow down our breathing to calm ourselves and feel less anxiety. The changes we may make to the way we automatically breathe may have significant power over our emotional and mental states, because signals from our respiratory system are inextricably linked to our survival and thus receive higher priority in the brain (Gerbarg & Brown, 2015). Using the breath as a tool and anchor for mindfulness practice, we have the capacity to integrate the unseen and seen, which connects these three "centers" of mind, heart, and body.

University of Maryland psychiatrist Stanislov Grof developed a technique called Holotropic Breathwork in the 1970s and is one of the pioneers of the use of breathing for therapeutic purposes in the West. Grof observed restrictions in breathing that correlated with traumatic memory and difficult emotional experiences. In fact, such emotional material was often linked in systems of "condensed experience" where several biographical experiences with a common theme, similar physical sensation, or similar emotional thread stimulated the same physical or emotional response, again reflected in breathing patterns. As a therapeutic breathwork practitioner, I too have witnessed that breathing is influenced not only by what is happening to us right now but also by unhealed wounding, fears, and trauma that resulted in corresponding unhealthy breathing patterns from our survival reactions at the time. Because of the mind-body bridge that breathing allows, Grof found that by using conscious, deep breathing, one can retrieve all core sensations, thoughts, and feelings of the original experience, and then complete, heal, and integrate the memories into consciousness. This is even believed to be true of implicit memory from prenatal and birth experiences.

There are countless ancient and modern, evidence-based practices that engage breath for physical, mental, and emotional wellness. With each inhale and exhale, breath represents the cycle of impermanence along with the balance between free will and letting go. Breath contains the potential of life, impetus for healing, and intelligence of our bodies. Each breath we take in has cycled through all manner of living creatures over millions of years. Breathing is a collective experience we share as well as something that is always with us as a reminder of this life and right now. How incredible to have this mechanism running constantly in the background, automatically maintaining our health and linking us to all of life, while at the same time inviting us to engage intentionally and center ourselves in mindfulness!

A Note on Practice

Presence is a state of being. And meditation and mindfulness are processes of practicing presence. We call the time we dedicate to meditation, mindfulness, or any other awareness technique our "practice." Practice can take many forms, and each individual must choose what feels right for them. Most often an individual makes a commitment to daily practice, frequently in the morning to set intentions before they get busy with their other obligations or at the end of the day as a form of reflection. Others take breaks throughout their day for practice—perhaps for sitting meditation, walking meditation, or other more dynamic practices. For some, exercise is a practice—that is, if it is conscious. (Exercise can also be an addictive coping mechanism.) For others, artistic expression is the form in which they find they can become fully present. Still others may use a reminder throughout the day to come back to presence regularly and frequently, such as the chime of an app or every time they walk through a door.

Simply noticing what is happening might seem to be the simplest instruction that anyone ever gave us and yet it can often be the most frustrating act we ever tried. We suddenly find ourselves unable to turn off the spigot of continuing, flowing thoughts. We may be overwhelmed with emotion or unable to bear the physical discomfort of sitting still. Yet it is precisely all that we experience in our practice that is fodder for transformation. We notice our angst. We notice our pain. We notice our fluctuating emotional state and aversion to being there. We notice our inability to stop thinking and our judgment. And through noticing, we are already waking up to our inner observer and the wisdom that lies within.

Different practices may serve you for different reasons at different times. There is value to committing to a single practice that you find most insightful or useful over a long period to invest in the ritual of practice and see how it shifts you. There is also value to trying new practices that you find challenging to allow yourself to stretch and learn from those difficulties. See what you enjoy, what helps you to set an intention for the day ahead, or what allows you to reflect at the end of your day and process what you have experienced. Explore what helps you feel more aware of yourself and others. When you find a practice that serves you best, try to set aside time each day to practice it. With time, these practices will become an important part of your day along with your ability to stay present with yourself and others.

Why Is Presence Cultivated through Mindfulness Important for Social Change?

There are three key reasons why the capacity to be fully present is valuable for the change leader. First, mindfulness supports greater self-awareness, which impacts how we react to the circumstances and people around us. Mindfulness practice enables us to be with our own pain, anxiety, and discomfort. The more we practice, the more we can sit with the moments of uncertainty or discomfort, like I felt in Haiti, and be aware of our own impulses that are more about immediate fixes than what may really be needed. This gives us the space to notice what is arising for us so that we can understand ourselves and respond consciously, rather than reacting to avoid or protect ourselves from vulnerability, fear, discomfort, or pain.

For example, many people are taught that it is important to not appear vulnerable. When we feel our strength threatened, whether it is because we are uncertain, made a mistake, or feel embarrassed about something, we can react in ways to reinforce our sense of strength. This can include anger, posturing, flight, blaming, and a whole host of other reactions, many of which can be unconstructive.

With mindfulness practice, we experience decreased emotional reactivity and increased response flexibility. This means we are not acting out conditioned ways of behaving on automatic pilot. We are able to disengage automatic pathways in the brain, enjoy an improved ability to express ourselves, and manage conflict with less anger. As a leader, these are key capacities for engaging with people, especially our perceived opposition, so that we may resolve conflict and see more clearly.

Second, mindfulness allows us to understand change from the inside out, which in turn leads to greater compassion and understanding of others who are required to change. We see how joy or irritation affects our interactions with others. We notice how much we want certain aspects of our life to change. When we go through the humbling personal growth process that takes place with the increased mindfulness practice of watching our vulnerabilities arise, sitting with them in curiosity, and identifying what needs our attention, we understand change takes work.

Science demonstrates that practicing mindfulness leads to enhanced present moment integration. We can see what is actually happening and not get caught up with it. Over time, we are less likely blame or lash out at others. As we practice being the observer of our emotions and thoughts, we notice that they shift over time. They are not permanent. We are not identified by our emotions. We may feel weak and clumsy one day, but we are not inherently weak and awkward people. This allows us to endure our discomfort more easily.

We recognize our good intentions and unconscious patterns of behavior, and may begin to take greater responsibility for our stuff that gets triggered. We may begin to observe that we are different than others due to our own unique life experience, and can no longer expect others to see the world and respond to it the way that we normally do. There is an entire universe accessible under our awareness.

And then, when we go to work on change with others, we are prepared that it may take them time to adapt to change and recognize the ways we are the same in how we react to protect ourselves. In fact, the more we get to know our deepest, truest selves, the more we may discover we are just like everyone else and in many ways connected to others. We are thus more able to come to the table with the understanding and compassion that can help people move out of reactive spaces, and instead, through our capacity to listen, find greater security and trust. This inevitably leads to greater conflict resolution and more effective solutions, as I will explore more under the fourth capacity of engaging mindfully in chapter 6.

Finally, mindfulness enables stronger relationships. Scientific research demonstrates that mindfulness practice leads to increased well-being and an enhanced ability to manage our interactions with others. We listen better and are able to alter our historical patterns of thinking. We end up building relationships driven by deeper human understanding and common ground, allowing us to run better-functioning teams and organizations. And we design more aligned solutions.

Inevitably, our external network of relationships with others will come to impact our personal transformation process too. Unless we are living in a cave or at sea in total isolation, we will interact with others. It is in this realm—the relational field—where we are invited to learn the most about ourselves. Here we respond and react to protect ourselves, seek what we need, and compensate where we feel lacking. It is also the territory where we find ourselves closing down or playing out our own insecurities through our various roles and interactions with others. We will continue to grow if we are open to the opportunities to learn, and we will have the opportunity to support the same in others.

Let us explore an example of how presence and empathy can directly impact engagement on a social issue. While activists, lobbyists, and policy makers may find themselves performing acts of increasing volume and visibility, or resorting to obstructionist tactics to force their opposition to yield, sometimes all that is needed is an avenue for compassion and understanding to catalyze effective transformation. It is through mindfulness and awareness of ourselves as well as our connection to others that we drive compassion and action toward the highest potential for change. This is the intersection of personal and societal transformation, the manifestation of conscious social change—where a simple act of presence can become a revolution.

Darfur Fast for Life

Beginning in early 2003, in the Sudanese province of Darfur, government soldiers and their unofficially backed "Janjaweed" Arab nomad militias carried out a campaign of terror against Darfur's non-Arab, black African tribes. Experts estimate that upward of 400,000 people were killed during the crisis and approximately 2.7 million were displaced within Darfur, while hundreds of thousands of others crossed the treacherous desert to arrive as refugees in Chad. Though attacks have declined since the height of the conflict when it was estimated that 15,000 people were being killed each month, and despite a cease-fire agreement signed in 2010, the crisis has never been completely resolved, and hundreds of thousands are still living in refugee camps on the Chadian-Sudanese border (Reeves, 2016).

On March 4, 2009, the International Criminal Court issued an arrest warrant for Government of Sudan President Omar Hassan al-Bashir for war crimes and crimes against humanity (Fast for Darfur, 2009). Within hours of the announcement, al-Bashir revoked the licenses of sixteen aid agencies tasked with providing 40 percent of the food and other aid for nearly 5 million displaced Darfuris within Sudan (UNICEF, 2009). It was estimated that within two months, over 1 million people would have no access to food. This was reminiscent of the government's previous campaigns to use starvation as a tool for mass extermination. The international aid agencies were forced to ration food to refugees at the equivalent of twelve hundred calories per day.

As reports of this forced starvation spread, activists mobilized in shows of compassion and support. Actress and UNICEF goodwill ambassador Mia Farrow had visited the Darfur refugee camps several times. She was deeply disturbed by the crisis, and vowed to go on a hunger strike for at least three weeks or until the issue was resolved. In inspiration, Darfur Fast for Life was born, led by an organization called iACT, inviting individuals to stand in solidarity with the refugees and internally displaced Darfuri to fast completely for as long as feasible, or eat only refugee rations—the equivalent of a quarter cup of yellow split peas, tablespoon of oil, and half cup of grains per day.

The movement gained traction, and many took part, sharing the physical depletion, hunger, and stress of the disempowered with a caring, global community. Across oceans, borders, and all cultural lines of identity, there grew a bonding awareness of a specific suffering and injustice. Instead of one more atrocity happening *to them,* there arose an understanding that this was us. And before too long, shared experience gave birth to shared solutions building.

Over the course of several weeks, hundreds more began to join the fast, blogging about their personal experiences, sense of despair, or committed solidarity with those in need. One of these was the late Donald Payne, US Representative from New Jersey, who committed to a water-only fast for four days. I was told that the nature of Payne's personal experience thinking about the people of Darfur and what he would have done if he had to raise his children under such circumstances was so profound that he was able to get the commitment of all the other forty or so members of the Congressional Black Caucus to agree to join him in a chain of fasting for at least one day each. He wrote in his first blog post on May 19, 2009, after completing his fast the week prior,

> On Monday, I joined the Darfur Fast for Life because I wanted to stand in solidarity with the people of Darfur and to express my outrage at the ongoing crisis in the Sudan. In addition to my personal fasting, I am launching a Darfur Fast for Life Campaign on Capitol Hill to urge my colleagues to join me in voicing opposition to the mass atrocities al-Bashir and his regime have orchestrated against the Darfuri people. It is my hope that our fasting will compel decision makers to act more decisively to put an end to the suffering of millions of innocent men, women and children in Darfur. We must do all we can until the violence, suffering, and displacement have ended. (iACT, 2009b)

In the press release from the announcement of the Congressional Black Caucus' choice to fast together for forty days, Payne said,

> After fasting last week, I invited Congressional Black Caucus Chairwoman Barbara Lee and Members of the CBC to join me in the Darfur Fast for Life. With all of the issues that this country and the world are facing, Darfur is not always at the forefront of everyone's minds. However, I, along with my colleagues, remain committed to working towards an end to the suffering of the people of Darfur. CBC Members' participation in the Darfur Fast for Life is a small gesture, saying to our Darfuri brothers and sisters "You are not alone. You are not forgotten. We stand with you." (iACT, 2009a)

Celebrities, other politicians, and whole organizations joined the fast as media attention on the issue grew. Hearings were held and rallies took place at the White House. The US special envoy to Sudan began an international tour to build momentum for peace, and President Barack Obama condemned the actions in Sudan even while traveling in the Middle East. Within three months of their expulsion, three of the aid agencies were allowed to restore operations. There was no posturing, threatening, or us versus them stance. In this profound case, what helped drive the pressure for global policy change was community and collective participation in a personal act of mindful awareness that fostered a deep, empathic connection with those suffering half a world away.[2]

This is staying present with ourselves as well as our environment, however broadly we define our environment. Investing in the first capacity of cultivating presence enables us to look deeply and listen so that we may be better poised to see clearly and understand. This is the process of asking ourselves, *What is happening?* and connecting with others from an inner realm of empathy and compassion, as we start down the pathway of conscious social change. The more we practice, the better we will be at staying grounded in ourselves even when we are in the presence of someone who is suffering, are in chaos or an emergency, and think there is little we can do in response to the sheer magnitude of the issue we face. Presence, as we will discover, is the root of our potency to move toward social justice.

Practices

How Do We Cultivate Presence?
Below are a few additional mindfulness practices for cultivating presence that you can try at home or with your team. I have always felt that there is no right practice, but that each person must explore and discover the practice that serves them most deeply. And it is also useful to change your practice when you find that it becomes comfortable, so that you continue to challenge yourself with opportunities for personal transformation. See which of these practices fit you best. Video instruction for a selection of practices can be found at www.conscioussocialchange.org.

Noticing the Three Centers
Recommended duration: fifteen to twenty minutes
Recommended frequency: daily at least one to four weeks

Read through the instructions first or have someone read them to you while you practice.

Sit in a chair or cross-legged on the floor. If you are in a chair, sit up straight with your feet firmly planted on the floor. If you are on the floor, you may want to sit on a small pillow or folded blanket for more comfort, and to help provide you with the right support for your back and legs. Your hands may rest with palms down on your thighs or in your lap with palms cupped upward. Sit with your spine straight and chin level. It is recommended that you close your eyes if that is comfortable. As an alternative, gaze softly or in an almost-unfocused stare at the floor in front of you, but at nothing in particular.

We call the body, mind, and your emotional state, or "heart," your three centers. In this mindfulness practice, we attempt to bring our attention to each one in turn. First, take three cleansing breaths to release any tension or distraction with which you may be coming into your practice.

Body: See if you can notice how your body feels. First, notice how you feel sitting in the chair or surface you are on, and how it firmly supports you. What is the temperature around you? Are there any other sensations you are feeling, such as a breeze or the clothes on your skin? Notice whether you have any tension or pain in your body. Do you feel awake, energized, tired, restless, and so on? Do you feel the need to stretch? Go ahead and move if you feel like it. Where do you find the different sensations? How strong are they? As you bring your attention to those places, does the feeling shift in any way? Stay with your body for at least five minutes.

Heart: Next, see if you can notice your emotional state or mood. Do you feel content, angry, ashamed, bored, excited, and so forth? See if you can locate that feeling and if it resides anywhere in your body—a place where you feel it strongest. You may find anxiety is associated with a headache or tension in your shoulders, for example. Or fear may feel like a knot in your stomach. You may also find you have several emotional states and that they may shift as you pay attention to them. Stay with your feelings for at least five minutes.

Mind: Now notice your thoughts. When a thought appears to you, notice if you are worrying about something in the future or planning. Or are you rehearsing a conversation or replaying a past experience in your head? Do you have any images passing through your mind? Do you have any messages you keep telling yourself? Try to notice and be with whatever is, without judgment. You may notice that your thoughts cause you to drift away from being present or aware. Once you realize you were daydreaming or thinking, go back to being your own observer, noticing what thoughts arise next, and whether they bring you into the past or future. Try to stay focused on observing your mind for at least five minutes.

When you have completed each of these three centers, see if you can feel your body, notice your emotional state, and observe your mind at the same time. See if one of your three centers tends to dominate. Which is least strong? What was challenging? How often do you take the time to just listen and feel intently—100 percent—what is happening inside and around you?

When you complete your practice, you may want to write down your insights so that you can reflect on how they change over the course of the days you are practicing. If you are practicing in a group, discuss your experiences as a whole or in pairs. Before going to sleep, contemplate how this practice may have affected your awareness throughout the day.

Mindfulness of the Breath: A Tool for Relaxation and Insight
Recommended duration: five to fifteen minutes with each activity
Recommended frequency: daily for at least a week

I encourage the use of conscious breathing to help you tune in to the best answer when you are faced with a question or decision to make. Often when we do an exercise, before we try to tune into what we know consciously, we start by taking a moment to breathe some deep breaths first to dispel stress and distraction, calm us, and help us listen to ourselves. This also helps us bring forth inner wisdom. Here we return to a more in-depth exploration of your breath.

Lead your team in the following activities:
a. Noticing your breath (pause after each instruction to notice)

Close your eyes if it feels comfortable to do so, or let your gaze rest softly on the floor in front of you. Sit up straight with your feet firmly planted on the floor, and hands resting on your thighs or lap. Let's concentrate even more closely on the breath as it naturally occurs, without changing it.

- Feel it coming in through your nose or mouth, and filling your lungs.

- Notice its temperature as well as the sensation in your mouth, nostrils, or throat.

- Now place one hand on your ribs and one hand on your belly. Feel your body moving as you breathe.

- As you breathe in and out, notice how deep and fast your breath is.

- Notice if you pause after you breathe in or out.

- If you experience a thought coming into your head, just say to yourself, "That is a thought." Then go back to paying attention to your breath.

- Let's do this for a few more breaths. See what happens to your thoughts if you are paying total attention to your breath. Start with five minutes.

Now gradually bring your attention back to the room. How do you feel? How did this exploration of the breath affect you? Discuss or journal. It is often helpful to journal daily over a period of time so that you can look back and see patterns changing over time.

b.   Deep slow breath and breath release

Take one deep breath and let it go really slowly. Notice how you feel.

Now take one deep breath and make a noise as you let it out: "Ahhhhh." Notice how you feel.

Finally, breathe in slowly through the nose and then even more slowly out through the mouth.

Continue as long as it feels helpful. A deep, slow exhale supports relaxation.

c.   Moment between inhale and exhale

Now breathe through your nose without any pauses, and see if you can find the exact moment where the in breath becomes the out breath, and the out breath becomes the in breath. Breathe continuously without pause for at least five minutes.

Discuss what you noticed.

Noticing Our Environment

Recommended duration: five to ten minutes

Recommended frequency: daily for at least a week

A friend and shaman shared this practice with me. Each morning, go outside as soon as is feasibly possible. Stand for a few moments in whatever environment awaits you outside your door. Let yourself fully feel everything about your location—the temperature, smell, sounds, light, and weather. Let your eyes rest wherever they are drawn or your ears focus on whatever sound captures your attention. Ask nature to teach you whatever it is you need to know. See what insight comes to you when you are fully present with your environment.

Noticing the Inner and Outer
Recommended duration: ten to fifteen minutes each part
Recommended frequency: daily for at least a week

By practicing mindful breathing and inner awareness, you will bring your attention simultaneously to your external environment.[3]

Part 1: First, try to conduct mindfulness of the breath or noticing the three centers as a starting practice for at least five minutes. After successfully noticing your breath and checking in with your three centers, try to hold 50 percent of your attention on your internal experience (breath or body/heart/mind), while allowing the other 50 percent of your attention to notice what is happening around you in your space. This could be sounds, temperature, light, smells, humidity, and so on. Next, open your eyes and look around, taking in the sights of your space while you also hold your attention on your breath. When you have been able to feel both your inner and outer experiences simultaneously, we call this being fully present.

Part 2: Next, try to balance your attention fifty-fifty with your inner and outer experience as you leave your space and move out into the world around you. You do not yet need to engage with another, but practice for five to ten minutes holding an awareness of your inner landscape and external environment as you move among other people. You could experience this with your family in the morning, or as you go to work or carry out errands outside your home.

Reflect daily in a journal about what you have noticed about the quality and focus of your attention along with how it shifts in relationship to the world and people around you as well as over time. What insights do you discover?

Fifty-fifty Awareness with a Group

Recommended duration: fifteen minutes

Recommended frequency: at least once with your group, and periodically
  when you need to slow down and reconnect

Sitting in a circle with your group, take five minutes to go within and notice
your breath first.

Now try to focus your awareness on both what is outside and inside
you at the same time. See if you can still feel the temperature of the room
and hear the sounds around you while you notice what thoughts you are
having as well as what your body feels like sitting in the chair. Try noticing
any feelings you have, while you also listen to the sounds of the person sitting next to you or notice what you smell. Continue this practice for five
minutes.

Now gently open your eyes and see if you can stay in touch with
what is happening inside (thoughts, feelings, and body sensations), and
notice what you see outside. Notice which part of your body you feel the
strongest—thoughts, emotions, or sensations—while you look around you.

Now turn to the person next to you, and in silence, just look them in
the eye while you maintain this sense of 50 percent attention inside and
50 percent attention on them. If you have any sight limitations, you can
consider holding the hand of the person you are connecting with to help
focus your attention on their presence. After thirty seconds of engaging one
person in this way, turn and look at or connect with someone else while
staying in contact with your feelings along with sensations inside. Be aware
of any awkwardness and your natural defenses against it. Notice if you feel
anything different with different people. Continue to switch your gaze or
contact to different people as you notice what is happening around and
inside you.

Notes for this exercise: You may have your team sit in a circle and naturally
change their gaze to different people in the circle as they feel so inclined,
noticing as they catch someone's eye how well they can keep their focus on
their inner and external worlds equally as well as simultaneously.

You may also have a facilitator keeping time and have people pair up
to eye gaze intentionally with each other. After thirty seconds, the facilitator rings a bell to signify it is time to switch partners, and people go to
find a new partner to stand or sit with. Continue switching until you have

partnered with most, if not all, the people in the room. It is important to do this experience in complete silence, but use the power of mindfulness to notice whatever is arising, from an impulse to speak or laugh to any discomfort.

Discuss your experience: What was difficult? What felt uncomfortable or easy? Why?

Noticing the Self and the Other in Conversation
Recommended duration: the length of one conversation
Recommended frequency: daily for one to four weeks

Once you have had an experience of holding your attention equally between your inner and outer experience, then try to conduct one conversation from this space. Try to hold half your attention on your three centers or breath while extending half your awareness to everything about the person you are with—what they are saying, feeling, and doing. See if you can maintain this attention throughout a conversation. Notice what causes you to lose balance or focus, and where your attention goes—Do you find yourself forgetting yourself for the other person, or noticing your own thoughts at the expense of the other? Consider conducting this experiment with a different person each day or a single person daily for a week. Do you notice how your experience changes with different people or different kinds of conversations (personal, emotional, conflict, professional, and so on)? Did any aspect of your relationship or dialogue shift as you brought more presence to your conversations?

Keep in mind that these are not mere experiments, though they may feel that way the first time you try. This is exercise. This is practice. And your mindfulness, awareness, and presence will improve over time. Embrace and endure the novice mind-set as you settle into whatever practice calls to you. But stick with it. You are stretching. Your brain is forging new neural pathways. And you will see a change.

4 Becoming Whole

I look out across the circle of twenty or so women and three men. With eyes closed, they sit diligently meditating, at least it seems. I wonder about the visions crossing their minds. Are they of hardship living in post-genocide Rwanda, or are they of hope for the change they are committing to bring to vulnerable women and girls? I notice one woman wipe a tear from her cheek. Another head bobs, fighting off sleep. I am a bit uncertain about whether the mindfulness practices I share are helpful, or if they are tolerated by a skeptical audience more likely to view meditation as a form of communing with the devil. I ring my Tibetan bells and invite the participants to bring their awareness back to the circle.

"Let's talk about how the consciousness practices we've been learning have affected your lives outside this classroom," I say, hoping for some nugget that I can turn into a lesson on why mindfulness is relevant to social change agents. Our "classroom" is really a veranda off the home my organization, Global Grassroots, rents as an office and residence for our Kigali staff, with rickety benches assembled for participants in our Academy for Conscious Change. For each new cohort, we seek out emerging change agents among Rwanda's most marginalized. We target women, including widows, mothers with HIV, violence survivors, undereducated women, and those living on two dollars a day, but we also invite men dedicated to a more equitable society for women. They come as teams to learn the social entrepreneurship skills necessary to establish a civil society organization benefiting vulnerable women and girls, but they also learn personal transformation practices and undergo the inner work that will sustain them as mindful change leaders. Over the course of eighteen months, through training, seed grants, and high-engagement support, they transform their ideas into high-impact social ventures or "micro-NGOs." Their organizations are not small businesses or income-generating projects but rather social-purpose, sustainable nonprofit organizations.

> *So, we've been practicing a technique whereby we take three breaths before responding to a situation where we feel emotionally charged. This allows us the time for self-inquiry to see what parts of ourselves are being triggered, which may drive us to react in a way that may potentially harm another or distort our perspective. With three breaths, we practice taking time for compassion and wisdom to arise, so that we can respond mindfully. Does anyone have a story to share?*

A middle-age woman named Drocella Mukantwari raises her hand. I nod, and she begins. The class breaks out in applause as I wait anxiously for the translation:

> After returning home from class one day last week, I found that my children had completely messed up my house. I was furious because I had worked hard before leaving for class to clean and straighten everything. Usually I just hit my children. But instead, I remembered what you taught me, and I closed my eyes and took three breaths. I realized I really don't want to spank my children. With my eyes still closed, I explained to my children why I wanted the house neat and asked that they return everything to its original condition before I again opened my eyes.

I glance at her and see a small smile pass over her lips as she waits for the translation to finish, "And they did what I asked. And I didn't hit my children."

Gratitude pours from my heart. I have always known this simple practice can have monumental impact, but have been uncertain whether my students would embrace it. Since 2007, I have been experimenting with different techniques, tools, and practices that I'd learned through my own personal growth work in the United States and Thailand, including yoga, meditation, mindfulness, and breathwork. Most exercises are completely foreign to my Rwandese participants. More often than not, I am greeted with sideways glances, giggles, or a steely facade unwilling to participate. Yet I have seen how critical personal awareness can be for effective social change, so I continue to offer a portfolio of experiential opportunities for those of my change agents who want to learn. Finally, here is evidence that something as simple and accessible as three conscious breaths has landed in a powerful way.

I realize that this woman is part of a team working to end domestic violence in their corner of Kigali, within a context where spanking children is relatively normal. I take the occasion to open the circle for a broader dialogue about how we each embody violence in our own lives and how change starts with ourselves. For Drocella, the simple practice of taking three breaths and making room for a more mindful response to her anger has allowed a change in awareness and behavior that is monumental for her. She herself has felt the trigger toward violence and faced the challenge of making a different choice in a single moment. As a result, she has cultivated a new compassion for what it takes to really change behavior. We talk about how this might influence her organization's approach toward addressing domestic violence and what it takes to help a perpetrator become more mindful of their patterns so that they can transform them. On that steamy day in August 2008, a practice of breath, time, and space transforms the way one mother approaches not only raising her own children but also engaging other couples in addressing violence within the family.

The second capacity of conscious social change is becoming whole. Becoming whole involves going beyond the process of contemplation, self-awareness, or just noticing, which I explored in the last chapter. Instead, we must go deeper and proactively address our own stuff—our wounds, fears, limiting beliefs, compulsions, and shadows that can distort our perspective and/or cause us unconsciously to harm others while protecting ourselves. Where we previously asked, *What is happening?* to help us notice our inner and outer landscape, here we now ask, *What is true?* Our key question helps us get to the root of what underlies our unconscious patterns of behavior and what is arising that needs attention, so that we can integrate our deeper understanding and act from a place of clarity as well as wisdom. This process begins with our ability to bear witness to not only the suffering of others but also the unconscious patterns of action within ourselves. When we inquire into the nature of our own suffering, we can better understand where it comes from in others.

We have probably all had experiences when we snapped at someone and later wished we had been more kind. Through mindfulness, we come to recognize those automatic patterns in ourselves and take time to understand why they happen. With practice, we can integrate a new way of handling our emotional material and work to respond with wisdom in the future. When you realize how your own reactivity, stress, fear, or anxiety can unintentionally harm others, you can work on changing that behavior. In addition, you are more likely to understand the destructive behaviors of others and find a solution that will get at the roots of their pain, not just the symptoms of their actions. Further, when you understand how change is difficult from your own personal experience, you are more likely to have compassion and patience when trying to get someone else to change. This form of more conscious leadership results in decisions that have a higher likelihood of being transformative. In this chapter, I look at the most common unconscious patterns of behavior that can distort our work with others if we are not mindful.

Emotional Reactivity

Conscious social change invites us to look more deeply at the wounding that causes us to react to our emotions in unconscious and possibly harmful ways. We can repeat conditioned or learned behaviors if we are not conscious of them. But even in milder ways, those who think they are doing good may still create harm from unconscious reactivity. In experiences where something has affected us emotionally in some way, we can easily let that emotion run away with us, and before we know it, we have reacted in ways we later regret. The results can be harmful to our relationships and distort our efforts toward optimal transformation.

In *The Engaged Spiritual Activist*, Donald Rothberg (2006) observes that often our habit is to "pass on the pain"—we feel terrible, so we lash out or otherwise take it out on another. Our pattern of action looks like the one shown in figure 4.1.

Before we let those emotions drive us to react impulsively, we must pause, just as the woman from Rwanda who raised a hand to spank her children paused. The key to transforming our unconscious reactivity is simply to lengthen the space between our feelings and response. The first step is to recognize when we feel an emotional "charge." This can be a rush of fear, anger, irritation, embarrassment, defensiveness, and so on. If, through our practice in cultivating presence, we can pause long enough to notice what we are experiencing, then we can stop ourselves from immediately reacting. The second step is taking three breaths. The same breath that served us as an anchor in cultivating presence, now serves as a doorway to deeper understanding and transformation.

Conscious social change starts with a state of mind, and then affects our speech and actions. First along our pathway, we ask, *What is happening?*

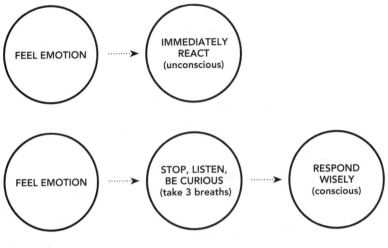

Figure 4.1

Then we look deeply and listen. We explore what emotion is arising. Using mindfulness, we are more able to shift to the inner observer. From this vantage point, we not only recognize our emotions but also see that they do not define us. We do not need to let them run away with our attention or drive our action. Instead, we can be curious about what is arising. By doing so, we disengage automatic pathways and use present moment integration to regulate our emotions as well as minimize unconscious reactivity.

Next, to go deeper and understand where these emotions are originating from, we ask, *What is true?* Is the emotion in response to an injustice? Are we trying to protect ourselves from being vulnerable? Are we too attached to wanting something to be different, or are we acting to avoid pain or change?

Then we go even deeper. We examine our intentions in this moment. Is there part of myself that wants to be liked, seen a certain way, or feel strong? We allow ourselves to feel compassion and gratitude for our underlying instinct to protect ourselves. We take responsibility for our own pain. Then we ask what response is needed to avoid doing harm so that we may transform any underlying issue or suffering for ourselves and others. From here we can respond and act with consciousness as well as wisdom. The more we engage in mindfulness, the more we will come to recognize and alter our unconscious patterns, and the more we will be able to shift from passing on our pain to creating real transformation.

To practice working with reactivity and transforming reaction into wise response, turn to the practices at the end of this chapter.

Attachment and Aversion

Much of our instinct to pass on our pain comes from trying to resist things as they are. Every person suffers to some extent, mentally, emotionally, and physically. For many circumstances, our deepest discomfort or anxiety comes from simply wanting things to be different: we want what we don't have, and we don't want what we do have.

In the first case, there is what we call "attachment." We are always seeking what we do not yet have—whether that is greater influence, personal relationships, or more economic security. These desires can even be rooted in our positive change work—a desire for more success, publicity, or funding for our work. We can easily become convinced that our happiness hinges on obtaining that which we want. And yet it is this grasping or attachment to something itself that causes our discontent. Through self-awareness, we discover our ability to withstand our anxiety, and begin to discern between what it is that we desire and what it is we actually need.

Toward the end of 2008, with the financial crisis and leading up to the presidential election, Global Grassroots began to lose significant funding as people reduced their giving or shifted their resources toward other priorities. I remember the moment that I realized with dismay that I could find no other way to replenish our cash reserves, which would only sustain us for two more months. I chose to go without pay and had to lay off all my staff except for one person in Rwanda who had worked with me since our initial founding. For months, I remember going through a major identity crisis, feeling like a complete failure, that my ideas must have no value, and that I must have no capacity as a nonprofit leader if I could not keep my work afloat. It was excruciating. I was completely attached to needing the funding crisis to be different. I thought my entire happiness, sense of self, and future depended on having the resources to continue my work. I ruminated in misery until I finally went on retreat. With stillness and an investment in self-awareness, I finally realized that all my suffering and angst was tied up in resisting the reality of the situation. Instead, I could accept things as they were and simply consider what choices I might have in that moment: I could close down my organization and take another job, or I could ride out the economic downturn and wait until I could raise funds again, and perhaps become more innovative and resourceful in a time of limited means. I chose the latter. Just as I had worked creatively to ensure all my staff found other job opportunities, I found new ways to support myself through speaking engagements and workshops, which catalyzed my early work bringing the concepts of conscious social change to students and other change agents in the United States. With patience and in response to local demand, I rebuilt Global Grassroots over time, emerging as a much more frugal, nimble organization that could withstand other fluctuations in funding.

The Guest House

This being human is a guest house.
Every morning a new arrival.

A joy, a depression, a meanness,
Some momentary awareness comes
As an unexpected visitor.

Welcome and entertain them all!
Even if they're a crowd of sorrows,
Who violently sweep your house
Empty of its furniture,
Still, treat each guest honorably.
He may be clearing you out
For some new delight.

The dark thought, the shame, the malice,
Meet them at the door laughing,
And invite them in.

Be grateful for whoever comes,
Because each has been sent
As a guide from beyond.
—Rumi, as translated by Coleman Barks (1997).

Pema Chödrön (2001) says that with meditation, "you begin to realize that you're always standing in the middle of a sacred circle, and that's your whole life. ... Whatever comes into the space is there to teach you. ... Our life's work is to use what we have been given ... to let the things that enter into the circle wake you up rather than put you to sleep." Consider what it is you prefer in life—physical comfort, economic security, happiness, or good health. When we seek something we don't already have, we can easily become too attached to getting what we want and think that unhappiness comes from not having it. Yet we never know what life is going to hand us. As conscious change agents, rather than getting caught up in the anxiety of wanting things to be different, we can practice acceptance, and still find choice and innovation no matter what circumstances we face. Being mindful of attachment does not mean we avoid trying to change things, but we do so with compassion and an acceptance of reality—what is true right now. Certainly we want peace or health. We want happiness for ourselves and others. Of course there are things we want to change for the better. But in so doing, we can also better withstand reality, be with it without it causing us so much distress, and work with more clarity to transform it with consciousness, not with selfish urgency because we think our happiness hinges on having things be different.

The flip side of attachment is aversion, also known as detachment or avoidance. In addition to grasping at what we want, we all go to great lengths to avoid what we don't want, especially pain and discomfort. Whether we fear failure, inadequacy, a loss of power, or another unwanted condition, our efforts to protect ourselves are often at the expense of another. Here it is the aversion to the situation—the "I don't deserve this" thought—that is the root of our difficulty.

Through self-awareness, we come to realize we actually do have a choice in every situation: we can either accept the things we cannot change, or identify the things we can change and make an effort to do so. But frequently, instead of making a choice, we spend our time wishing things were different and being upset that they are not. We get stuck in rumination and reactivity. It is in this way that attachment or aversion itself causes us suffering.[1] As we take time to learn to reflect on what causes us pain and where we have choices for action, this helps us see more clearly the ways in which anxiety and fear may cause us to react. When we let go of our resistance, it frees up mental energy to consider more creative options. It also leads us to greater resilience because we are no longer operating under as much stress. Through our own direct experience and understanding of these unconscious patterns, we can recognize when others may be reacting from a place of attachment or aversion too. This leaves us empowered to pursue a path of change with greater resourcefulness and resilience, rather than spending all our time in a place of reactivity trying to grasp at or push away our circumstances.

Mindfulness in Action

The concepts of attachment (wanting) and aversion (not wanting) have implications not only for our own happiness but also for how we work in the world, especially as change agents (see table 4.1 below).[2] Let's look at both in turn.

Attachment in Social Change

Just as in the personal domain, attachment in the realm of social change includes the thoughts of "me" and "mine," the anxiety that comes from

Table 4.1

Attachment, Detachment, and Consciousness

	Attachment/desire	Conscious social change	Detachment/ aversion
Motivator	We want what we don't have.	We acknowledge reality, yet we can also hold a vision for change. We commit to live from the highest place (what is right, good, truth, just, and fair). We are motivated by compassion, our inner values, and wisdom.	We don't want what we do have or we are afraid of experiencing something.
Feeling	Greed, craving, obsession, and grasping.	Peace, equanimity, grounded, balance, curiosity, open-minded, discernment about the needs of others versus our own wants, passion, and energy.	Fear or discomfort with what is or what may be.
Attitude	My way or the highway, me, mine, my solution, my success, I'm right, or I want it this way.	Sense of responsibility, or I care about this.	It's not my problem, I don't deserve this, I don't care, or I just can't do it anymore.
End point	A perception that our happiness hinges on getting what we want and being stuck on own agenda.	Sense of well-being, clarity, and wise action.	Disillusionment and burnout.

wanting something, or the belief that everything will be better if I just have that one thing. In fact, it is even possible to become too attached to doing good. The pitfall that change agents often fall into is in thinking that their way is the right or only way to proceed. This can cause competitiveness between groups with a common purpose that may be able to collaborate better. Overattachment to a means to a specific end can cause great disappointment if it does not arise or even blindness to the other unexpected benefits that might arise. If you expect you will win a race and you don't, you often feel this attachment. If you are leading a group and you think everyone in it needs to agree with you, then you are attached to your viewpoint. If you are emotionally placing all your sense of possibility in achieving a particular goal or obtaining a grant, your anxiety is originating from your grasping at that outcome. Individuals can too closely wrap up their identity with their work, experience an overattachment to their solutions, and believe success is due only to such efforts.

Aversion in Social Change

Aversion or detachment, the opposite extreme, is also quite prevalent in the social sector, though it can frequently grow to overwhelm you subtly. This is where people gradually come to think, "This has nothing to do with me" or "I can't deal with this." In the service professions, we typically see burnout or disillusionment when people feel they cannot create the change they wish to see in the world, and that the issues that exist are too great for them to manage. In these cases, people can reach burnout and simply detach entirely from their efforts, declaring they no longer care or just cannot deal with the problem out of a sense of overwhelm. In other cases, people can focus too much on their own inner world, going so far into themselves that they are no longer engaged with the external world, rejecting or denying the reality outside themselves. In the next chapter, I will explore at greater length the tools and practices that can work to build resilience and well-being through self-care. For now, we should note that practicing mindfulness not only strengthens our capacity to recognize when stress and overwhelm have moved us out of balance but also works to help alleviate that same stress.

Conscious Social Change: Being with Reality

The conscious social change paradigm provides a middle way. It is driven by a willingness and commitment to live with integrity. Actions are not driven exclusively by personal preference and there is an acceptance of reality—being with what is. This does not mean that we stop all effort to end injustice, inform people, or raise more money, but that we accept our current situation as the reality in which we will operate. We invite and hold a vision for what is possible, which can guide our actions in alignment with what is needed in each moment. We recognize truth, and act from a place of inner understanding, compassion for others, responsibility for a higher possibility, and what is truly needed by all.

Conscious social change involves healthy engagement with ourselves and the world. Conscious change agents work to embrace reality with curiosity while making choices about change. Walking this balanced path means continuing to invest in self-reflection and using mindfulness to make sure we are clear about our intentions. Creating change with presence allows us to clear the mind so that we can achieve not only an intellectual understanding but also a deeper wisdom or insight about what is and is not needed in each moment. We realize that what is needed is constantly evolving, so we do not get attached to only one way of acting. As we move underneath all the walls that separate us from others, contacting who we are at our deepest level, we may come to see the ways we are all similar and even connected. We discover that the anxiety that I may feel can cause you to suffer, and vice versa. This allows us empathy for our opposition rather than an inclination for blame.

Through consciousness practice, we train ourselves to be with our discomfort and pain. We notice the discomfort, but we no longer react to it because we know that most pain is impermanent—it eventually goes away. But we also do not try to push it away and ignore it, because pain teaches a lesson. With practice, we are more able to handle discomfort, realize we are not alone, and are less likely to experience exhaustion or overwhelm. Conscious engagement allows us to notice when we begin to move to one extreme or another of attachment or aversion. With the mindfulness facet of observing, we can better assess where our intentions are coming from and what we may need to move back into well-being, including taking time to restore ourselves. Conscious social change is thus a transformative process driven by self-understanding and direct experience.

Understanding the signposts of this framework of when we are off-balance and driven by attachment or aversion, as illustrated in table 4.1, helps us find our way back to the middle path of conscious social change.

For practices that will help you delve more deeply into the realm of attachment and aversion, go to the end of this chapter.

Shadows

As we begin to go deeper into our own self-awareness, we may find there are things we dislike in others or that we feel uncomfortable with about ourselves. These are often one and the same, and so are called shadows.

Connie Zweig and Jeremiah Abram's (1991) book *Meeting the Shadow: The Hidden Power of the Dark Side of Human Nature* proposes that "the shadow acts like a psychic immune system, defining what is self and what is not-self." Poet Robert Bly (1991) offers a useful analogy: when we were young and as we grew up, we had people around us telling us not to be a certain way. Perhaps our parents said we should be responsible, so we carried this invisible bag behind us, and put the side of us that wanted to be spontaneous and irresponsible in that bag. Then our community said girls are supposed to be a certain way and boys are supposed to act a different way, and so we put those parts that were not appropriate into the bag. Then friends teased us, and we wanted to fit in, so we put more things that we felt uncomfortable with in the bag. By the time we got older, the bag was big and heavy. And it still holds the parts of us that we find unacceptable or do not prefer. When we come in contact with those aspects in another person, it can trigger reactions ranging from annoyance to disgust. And often we are not willing to recognize the same in ourselves. Our unconscious shadows can work against self-compassion and understanding of others who hold those traits.

For example, we may have been raised to believe in a work ethic and that doing things yourself is admirable. The shadow part that was rejected by us may have been the part that needs the support of others. When we come across circumstances where others have needs and ask us for help, or rely on others for support, we may come to judge that as irritating or needy. On the contrary, we may have been raised to experience the harmony of a supportive family where individual ambition was discouraged if it went counter to the needs of the collective. When we come across someone who is not inclined to help or puts their self-preservation needs before others, we may judge that as selfish. Consider how this is reflected in the differing conservative and liberal political values around small government and individual liberty versus social programs and safety nets.

When shadows run deep, and remain unchallenged by openness or diversity, we may begin to project our revulsion for those unaccepted traits onto the identity of another or, worse, a whole category of people. This feeds aversion and disconnection. Unexamined, intense dislike that arises from our shadow selves may unconsciously lead us to create separation, act with prejudice, and even resort to discrimination and violence.

It is important here to take a moment to look at the context of power structures that can work in conjunction with personal shadows to affect the collective domain. Conscious social change recognizes that we all suffer by wanting things to be different. As a result, we frequently grasp at or use any power we may have to protect ourselves as well as pursue our self-interests.

Power and Privilege

When we think of power, especially in the context of change, we might think of the capacity to influence—the ability to manifest choice and use our will to ensure our desired outcomes. For many, power is something we seek to attain or preserve for ourselves personally, and that we may even consider linked to certain rights, such as the freedom to speak or choose our religion. Power also holds a significant negative connotation when we consider the abuses and harm that come from its misuse.

I tend to see power as arising from two primary sources—our external environment, and inner or personal domain—and both are important to examine. First, let us explore the most visible domain: the external power that is bestowed on us by our particular culture, and how our privilege and efforts position us within that context. Power is most apparent when driven by one's sources of privilege or lack thereof in comparison to others. Privilege is the benefit or opportunity that is granted to certain people based on how their characteristics are regarded by the dominant culture—the predominant set of values representing the majority. This includes values placed on certain characteristics like race or ethnicity over which we have no control as well as those qualities achieved through individual effort like education, leadership positions, or professional accomplishment. Beyond the broader national level of identity, a dominant culture can exist in smaller subcultures, institutions, organizations, or communities defined by place, religious affiliation, nationality, age, and other factors.

Examining power in various societies gives a fascinating glance at how easily our privilege can change depending on where you are standing. In the United States, I have experienced my gender as female at a slight disadvantage, but being white as distinctly privileged. The difference is even starker in some of the East African and South Asian cultures where I have worked and traveled, where my race and nationality hold significant power, but where my gender is considered a substantial weakness. Obviously we all operate at the intersection of many identities that give us a unique experience of advantage or disadvantage within our particular context. When I walk into a training space with my women change agents in Rwanda or Uganda, I have to be aware that by the nature of my being a Western-educated, white woman from the United States who runs an international NGO with resources available for their local endeavors, I have a certain authority. I have to be extremely aware of not utilizing that power in ways that might have unintended negative influence.

Marginalized society is made up of individuals or groups with characteristics that are not valued by society, or fall outside the dominant culture to the "margins." These characteristics, when concealed, can sometimes become our personal shadow or closeted elements due to their perceived inappropriateness, however unfair. But many circumstances that define the marginalized, such as race, disability, age, a lack of language ability, or other outer appearances, are not so invisible. When those with privilege, often driven by their own shadows around what is preferred, assign the qualities they dislike as a generalization on an entire identity and negatively judge the marginalized for those characteristics, they fuel prejudice. This prejudice can lead to mistreatment, including disempowerment, discrimination, or oppression—unconscious or conscious action that causes harm and injustice.

Individual acts of oppression take place when someone uses their power to manipulate or keep others out of power, either consciously or unconsciously. Consider a white storekeeper who accuses a shopper who is a person of color of shoplifting when they are only putting their hand in their pocket. While the store owner may not be aware of any implicit bias, it may be more likely that they accuse this shopper over a white one in similar circumstances because of conditioned racial views. The negative impact goes far beyond the experience of a single transaction or altercation. It has the effect of creating an unfair environment of hostility and discrimination against nonwhite customers. More incidents of prejudice over time, such as frequent accusations of criminality or being assumed to be a negative influence, cumulatively disadvantage those groups on multiple levels. The impact can be felt in terms of both damage to self-esteem and societal obstacles that keep the marginalized person from flourishing in the same ways as others (Long, 2013).

When integrated into the culture of an institution, such as the inequality of pay for the same job or disproportionate promotions among different genders within a company, we call this institutionalized discrimination or oppression. In 2016, McKinsey and Company and LeanIn (2016) conducted a study of gender among 132 companies employing 4.6 million. They found that for every 100 women promoted, 130 men are promoted for the same first step up to a managerial position. At the senior vice president level, only 20 percent of line roles—those positions with profit and loss responsibility along with management of core operations—are women. In 2015, 90 percent of CEOs were promoted or hired from such line roles, 100 percent of whom were men. Looking at race, women of color hold only 3 percent of such C-suite positions. Why is this? This is not simply a factor of performance. In fact, several studies conducted by financial institutions like Morgan Stanley and Credit Suisse have found that across the board, companies with greater gender equity and diversity perform better (Parker, 2016; Keefe, 2016; Dawson, 2014). A Peterson Institute survey of nearly 22,000 companies in 91 countries discovered that firms with a higher proportion of female executives are associated on average with a 6 percent gain in net profit (Marcus Noland, 2016).

McKinsey and Company and LeanIn (2016) found several obstacles responsible for this institutional inequity, including that women who negotiate are 30 percent more likely than men to receive feedback that they are "intimidating," "too aggressive," or "bossy," and women are more than 20 percent less likely than men to say their manager often gives them challenging feedback that would help improve their performance. Furthermore, women in senior management are seven times more likely than men at the same level to say they do more than half the housework at home. Despite some advances in work-life programs, more than 60 percent of employees worry that part-time work will hurt their career. As a result, only a quarter of employees take advantage of work-life balance programs.

The discrimination against women inherent in the corporate institutions mentioned above is multidimensional, stemming from dominant culture's view of how a woman should act, what their needs are, how they should be treated, what their capacities are, and how much can be expected of them. The fact that women stepping up in similar ways to men in seeking to negotiate are viewed with a negative bias is a function of dominant culture's shadow that does not accept that women should show their strength in this way. Similarly, the choices of senior management to go easier on women with less challenging feedback are also driven by perceptions conditioned by the dominant culture of how to treat women (more gently), possibly an aversion to their (presumed emotional) response, and a discomfort with such expected emotional conflict, which they have come to view as unacceptable (a shadow). The broader dominant culture also still disadvantages women in terms of their share of household responsibilities, while the corporate culture does not as a whole accept taking time for work-life programs that would allow women greater balance to navigate such family responsibilities. Granted, the leadership of the corporation may feel work-life balance is important and may have instituted such policies, but that is not enough to shift the underlying culture that drives inequity. Working toward the transformation of power structures within institutions and society requires a deep understanding of the historical impact of the dominant culture on the inner domain of our perceptions, values, expectations, presumptions, and behavior as much as the external realm of policies, opportunities, obstacles, and needs across difference. Wendy W. Williams (1991), professor emerita at Georgetown Law School, asks, "Are we clinging, without really reflecting upon it, to culturally dictated notions that underestimate the flexibility and potential of human beings of both sexes and which limit us as a class and as individuals?" Transformation begins by deconstructing these elements on a personal level with great mindfulness and a willingness to understand our own blind spots. We cannot lead change effectively or with any real integrity if we do not first acknowledge the historical systems of unequal privilege, and then actively alter the ways we contribute to the status quo.

Eula Biss writes about "White Debt," describing the acceptance by white people of their advantage as normal. She contends that whiteness is less about race or culture than a moral problem of privilege built with now-forgotten debt on the disadvantage of others (Biss, 2015). She explains that when laws treat different people differently within the same community, it undermines the fundamental basis of that community. Biss describes a school district where white students made up only 22 percent of the student-body demographics but 81 percent of those selected for the gifted program. Rather than accepting this as an accurate representation of student capability, the school board was willing to question whether their selection practices were fair and to make adjustments to ensure a more just and inclusive process. This willingness to question the status quo, even when one finds oneself in a position of benefit, is essential for overcoming any form of blind complicity that blocks the pathway for real transformation. Mindfulness demands that we wake up to our own participation in systems of inequality and then take action toward justice.

Just as I explored on an organizational level, societal institutions that exist system and society-wide can also oppress and discriminate. Consider the disproportionate number of black men that are incarcerated in the United States. Black and Hispanic men make up two-thirds of the incarcerated population, while they represent just under 20 percent of the broader national population (Long, 2013). A black man is seven times more likely to be incarcerated than a white man, and 84 percent of convicted killers experience severe physical or emotional abuse as children (Enneagram Prison Project, 2017). Moreover, a study of three hundred thousand prisoners from fifteen states showed that over two-thirds of prisoners are rearrested within three years, and over half go back to prison (Lanagan & Levin, 2002). Is life behind bars actually working to prevent crime? Is the action of the perpetrator all there is to blame?

If we are interested in getting to the root of the issue to understand *what is happening* and *what is true*, we cannot attribute the whole of the issue simply to the actions of the offender. Nonwhite men are overrepresented in nearly every stage of the justice system, both from the disparities in offenses and disparities in opportunity and treatment. The disparities in offenses among these men can be attributed to a large range of other disadvantages including disproportionate levels of poverty, inequitable access to high-quality education, low self-esteem and negative social behavior from racial victimization, a lack of family support due to economic challenges and criminality, the influence of drugs and violence, and/or abuse as a child. The disparities in treatment include racial profiling and bias among arresting officers, larger numbers of arrests, decreased access to quality legal counsel, more frequent and higher sentences, and lack of access to rehabilitation programs that provide greater access to education and job skills training, among other issues.

The Enneagram Prison Project, founded by Susan Olesek, is getting at the root of these structural issues to combat high recidivism rates and help prisoners actually heal through personal transformation.[3] Working in San Mateo County jails and San Quentin State Prison, the project blends meditation and mindfulness practices along with deep personal inquiry facilitated by a particular framework for self-understanding called the Enneagram. The program works to help prisoners come to terms with their crimes as well as transform any childhood trauma, abuse, or neglect that underlies their life choices. Inmates learn the reasons for their anger, how to regulate emotion, and ways to manage emotional stress. By working comprehensively with inmates' inner pain, the societal failures they suffer, and their current justice system treatment, the Enneagram Prison Project is simultaneously intervening to stop the cycle of violence and move the culture of prisons from exclusively punitive to one of greater compassion and care.

There is significantly more to delve into here on power and privilege than can be adequately accomplished in this particular book, as is the case with any social justice issue. What is important to understand is that applying a conscious social change lens to any social issue at any level of society necessitates a deep dive into understanding the individual, circumstantial, institutional, and structural impacts of power dynamics as well as inequity fueled by the dominant culture. Even those of us who work for greater social justice and equality may be unaware of the ways in which we uphold conditioned beliefs around qualities of privilege. And we may grant power and authority, or experience superiority/inferiority, based on dominant cultural values. For example, in the nonprofit world, donors and philanthropists are often treated with certain deference and respect not similarly shown to the beneficiaries of aid, or even the practitioners working on behalf of change, largely because of the value we place on money in our society. Funders mostly determine the procedures and criteria that lead to the investment of resources into certain solutions. This is understandable, as anyone who "spends" money wants to know what, exactly, they are buying. Yet it sets up imbalances and inefficiencies in the sector, including competition among beneficiaries with similar missions. It can also mean a donor emphasis on certain metrics of success that may not align with the work of the organization or particular timing of funding, and required reporting procedures that may create a greater than necessary burden on the venture. Furthermore, the responsibility for the cultivation of that relationship usually falls to the recipient. It is in rare cases that the relationship is built from a sense of equitable status, despite favorable intentions on all sides.

Instead, what if we looked at the donor, practitioner, and beneficiaries as equal parts of a single entity, playing different yet unique roles? Three legs of the same stool. Buddhist teacher Thích Nhât Hanh (2008) presents an interesting analogy. As a right-handed person, most of his writing and other tasks are conducted with his right hand. His right hand does not have an ego that looks down at the left hand as being useless. The left hand does not see itself as inferior. They both have different roles that collectively make up a whole. Yet when we all have a unique contribution to make toward a shared mission, we can often blindly apply the values of the dominant culture in treating one role as more important than another. This is crucial to recognize in working toward equity in power relations because it has the potential to distort intentions, methods, and outcomes when a party with privilege drives choices for the collective.

Opportunity Collaboration, an annual conference focused on poverty alleviation, conducts itself differently. From the beginning, it establishes its own culture as one of collaboration. Potential participants are recommended by previous attendees and then invited to apply, asking what they have to give along with what they wish to gain and learn from the convening. Once accepted to participate, a deliberate process is used to prepare attendees through assignment to a mentor, advance readings, and conference calls to explain the intentions of the gathering as well as what to expect. The core of the conference is its Colloquium for the Common Good. Participants are assigned to a small cohort of twenty or so other attendees, none of whom are distinguished or treated differently as funders or practitioners, where self-promotion is discouraged. Each morning, the cohort convenes to discuss different topics, guided by a skilled facilitator. The space is reserved as a sacred container in which to talk about the challenges of poverty alleviation, and build connection and possibilities for working together around new ideas. The attendees then cocreate the remainder of the conference. They offer to hold lunch discussions or workshops on various issues of shared interest, often coleading with other attendees. Donors are more accessible and practitioners more open to learning from rather than competing against each other. The conference website explains,

> Predicated on the powerful idea that out of fragmentation can come collaboration, from diversity can come unity, and from cross-fertilization can come innovation: the power of collaboration does not presume a single outcome. Rather, it draws its power from the conviction that people of good will forge their own solutions, directions and alliances, and uncover new ways to contribute and leverage resources. (Opportunity Collaboration, 2017)

Over the nine years it has been operating, Opportunity Collaboration's participant feedback has been promising. Ninety percent of the delegates report professional outcomes adding to their organization's impact on poverty, including capital relationships, operating partners, strategic advisers, suppliers, employees, and even mergers. Moreover, delegates regularly proclaim personal outcomes along the lines of "I no longer feel alone. … [It] felt like coming home!" or "I completely reconfigured my leadership style." It is not that we completely discard hierarchy for distributed leadership or consensus in every situation, but the conference demonstrates the possibilities of removing the conventional, frequently distorted ways of relating dictated by existing power dynamics to allow for deeper human understanding, connection, and collaboration.

As much as we must be careful of the ways we grasp at or use our power, on the flip side we must also be careful of judging power itself as inherently bad or letting guilt over privilege drive our actions unconsciously. Eula Biss warns,

> Guilty white people try to save other people who don't want or need to be saved, they make grandiose, empty gestures, they sling blame, they police the speech of other white people and they dedicate themselves to the fruitless project of their own exoneration. But I'm not sure any of that is worse than what white people do in denial. Especially when that denial depends on a constant erasure of both the past and the present. (Biss, 2015)

With mindfulness, power and privilege can instead be a tool for broader liberation. Regardless of our place within the larger dynamic, we must first examine the complexity of the existing system that has determined value, how certain parties benefit from it, and the sacrifices and suffering of those who are limited by it. With greater insight and awareness we must then play a role in shifting it toward greater equity. We have each been given a set of circumstances to work with in this lifetime. What will we each do with ours, or despite ours? What are our particular lessons to learn, experiences to leverage, or gifts to offer? What change can we inspire? We will always have some level of power to move toward transformation. This power includes that which is inner driven, the second context that is critical to explore.

In addition to the forces of the dominant culture that determine power, this second context is the power we source from within. I have found this is shaped by two primary sets of influences. The first is our conditioned perspective on power, largely driven by our personal experiences. If as a child, I was given the space to speak my mind and was valued for doing so, I would likely have a greater sense of personal power that came from my voice than if I were expected to be silent around authority figures. If I grew up in an abusive environment, I might have learned that to exert your power requires physical force, a threat of harm, or manipulation. While these orientations may be influenced somewhat by the dominant culture, it is more circumstantially based on our unique life experiences. It is worthwhile for us to examine our own personal beliefs about power. This helps us identify our own blind spots and the ways we may unintentionally contribute to unequal balances of power.

The second influence that drives power from within is our sense of connection to our wisdom and inner experience that form our sense of empowerment. This includes our faith, confidence, morals, vision, passion, integrity, quality of presence, and so on, that allows us to harness and manifest our potency. This is what allowed Mohandas Karamchand Gandhi, Martin Luther King Jr., and others to advance nonviolent movements that helped dismantle oppressive regimes when their own societies did not value them within the dominant culture.

When I teach my course in conscious social change to university students and other change agents, we meditate on the times when we have felt most powerful. The responses include things such as when I'm surrounded by family, when I am using my body (dancing, exercise, or extreme physical feats), when I accomplish something challenging, when I'm helping others, when I speak my truth, or when I pray. We then step back and marvel that not one of these experiences is driven by the qualities of privilege valued by the dominant culture. This is extremely important in cases where we feel disempowered by our external environment. While there are always influences of privilege at work that determine individual opportunities, I find that these inner experiences of power from within are not reserved for those who have had such opportunities, and indeed many come from circumstances of challenge and hardship despite a lack of opportunity. Regardless of the ways that power is granted or limited by the dominant culture around us, we always have the ability to draw from our own sense of inner power. We can always choose to be a change agent.

While we tend to look at power in reference to something else—what gives us power, or how we wield power over or with others—power at its most pure, essential quality can be defined as energy or potency. Consider that power is simply a force within nature and humanity like love or joy. Take a moment to conduct a mindful walk around the room with a sense of being peacefully powerful. And then try powerfully peaceful. See how this feels different than any concepts you may be holding about what power should look or feel like as defined by society. We all have inherent power and potency when we are able to connect with what fuels us. This inner source is a constant, and never circumstance or other dependent. We just need to know how to access and use it effectively. Mindfulness is again our most effective tool.

Nhât Hanh (2008) says, "When you practice mindfulness well and you radiate joy, stability, and peace, you acquire a much deeper authority. When you speak, people listen to you not because they have to but because you are fresh, serene, and wise." If your power radiates from the inner domain, you are much more likely to inspire long-term transformation from those who want to follow your direction, and have faith in your wisdom due to your authentic equanimity and insight. And from this place, you can utilize the power that comes from the dominant culture, or overcome the limits of the dominant culture without violence or harm. But if you rely only on your power from external sources, and use that to manipulate or force others to comply with your demands or expectations, then the likelihood of longer-term, real transformation is limited, as people will revert back to their original orientation or strive to overcome your power as soon as they are able.

We operate within both the inner and external realities, and both contexts are important to understand; we have to recognize the power that our external environment allows us so that we remain mindful of both how to use it and when we become attached to keeping it. It is also critical that we understand the system—the privilege it affords certain people, and limitations it places on others—as well as our place within that system so that we use our power differently while working toward dismantling oppression and advancing equity. Power can become a tool for social good. And when we let our inner power drive this work, we have a greater capacity to connect with and inspire the higher conscience of others.

Without self-awareness, our emotional states, shadow material, and reactivity drive us. We are powerless over their influence. We truly have no freedom. We are always at risk of grasping for more or abusing what we have. Furthermore, our natural instinct when we feel powerless is to want to change things with whatever power we have or obtain more power to overcome those who we perceive to have power over us. Here we are working toward change starting from a place of division. In the process of becoming whole, just as we look at the roots of our emotions, we must also consider the roots of our intentions, explore our attachments to power and aversions to powerlessness, and act from a place of wisdom and consciousness.

Certainly we each have the potential to be a change agent, and this is the ultimate invitation for how to direct our power. One of the greatest calls to action for each of us is to embody our potency, allow it to flow toward the highest possibility for equity, and make space for every other person to be able to do the same. When channeled for the greater common good, collective power can support significant transformation, even if driven by outrage. But action must still be conducted from a place of mindfulness and awareness. When shadow-driven fear becomes collective, it can be extremely dangerous.

This inner work around power is not always easy, even when we approach it from a place of consciousness and intention. As we begin to strip away the unconscious patterns that try to protect us from feeling vulnerable and increasingly dwell in a place of mindfulness, we will face the gradual dissolution of the ego. The ego with its self-preservation instinct tends to compensate for a fear of powerlessness through attachment to power substitutes, such as control, success, energy, being right, or winning. There can be resistance to letting go of these ego comforts, or a sense of being weak, lost, unsuccessful, or not enough as they drop away. We have to be fiercely aware of the ways we compensate so that we recognize when we are triggered and can avoid grasping at our familiar crutches. Here, mindfulness again plays a critical role. We recognize the emotional flavor of any anxiety, attachment, or aversion, and pause to explore *what is happening* and *what is true*. Mindfulness allows us an opportunity for greater insight so that we may attend to our own needs and act wisely for the benefit of the whole.

What is your personal slant that may distort how you approach issues of power? What are your blind spots? It is vital to explore where you hold an emotional charge. If it is indeed related to areas of injustice you must look at how you can build understanding and compassion for those involved in upholding unequal cultures of power and oppression, even while you resolve to change them. We must examine our own role in the system, look at ways we have fostered division, explore our implicit bias, and scrutinize how we have avoided connection with others who are different or turned a blind eye to systems that do not seek the well-being of all citizens. With greater awareness, we are less likely to act unconsciously and more able to serve as effective agents of change.

For several exercises that can help you deconstruct the power dynamics that you operate within and explore with mindfulness your sources of inner power, see the practices at the end of this chapter.

Us versus Them

In addition to the shadow material that creates an inherent and conditioned dislike of certain characteristics in others different than ourselves, and the dominant culture that determines privilege and power structures that uphold the inequity of the marginalized, there is a third force at work that can limit change: the tendency of groups to self-organize, and then define, stereotype, and demonize an "other" against which we orient our efforts for change.

The extreme political rhetoric surrounding the 2016 presidential election, especially that articulated by the Trump campaign and certain supporters, posited an other as outsiders who were threatening the "best" of the United States. This included widespread negative generalizations against immigrants, people of color and non-Christians, including Mexicans and Muslims. Despite the fact that the United States is built in many ways by immigrants from nearly every nationality, and our predecessors seized land from indigenous nations and built our institutions and infrastructure with enslaved labor, there exists an increasingly explicit resentment among some that seems to suggest that the country belongs to only one subset of people, largely white Christians. Despite our original founding principles of equality and freedom of religion, fear of terrorism and crime is driving many to discriminate largely against all Muslims and US-born, naturalized citizens or legal immigrants of non-Caucasian ethnicity, who are treated as unwelcome outsiders. The Trump campaign catalyzed and then leveraged this fear against outsiders as fuel to advance its agenda, which simultaneously inspired acts of aggression, discrimination, hate speech, and violence. In 2015, violence spiked against Muslims by 67 percent, the highest total in hate crimes against Muslims since the year of the World Trade Center terrorist attacks in 2001 (Lichtblau, 2016).

We often feel a part of something when it is in reference to an other that is viewed as bad or less (less sensible, knowledgeable, right, normal, etc.) than ourselves. When someone speaks directly to our ego and shadows, we can become easily caught up in the delusion that it is who we are. We want to feel like we belong, especially when we may have previously felt not good enough, not heard, not represented, left out, or that we deserve better. This sense of belonging can even include being part of a movement seeking positive change. We grasp at the sense of belonging, which I believe is a distortion of what we really seek: a higher-level, essential sense of interconnection. Unfortunately, our sense of belonging is frequently established at the exclusion of the other. We rally behind a cause to get the other entity to change or to pursue their complete upheaval. When our egos get a dose of validation as a part of our chosen cause, we can stop listening to the rest of those who make up the total ecosystem. This is a slippery slope that can lead to a sense of moral superiority at the expense of another with different experiences and perspectives than our own. In some cases, we lash out to defend and protect our own path, looking at any opposition or differing viewpoint as a threat or proof of their inferiority. It can motivate us to violate boundaries we might not otherwise breach individually when we are part of a larger group mentality.

From torture in the name of national security and ecoterrorism to obstructionist politics and racial profiling, the line between nonviolence and harm is easily crossed in pursuit of what one views as justice or morality, and often driven by our unconscious shadows that lead us to judge or assume things about others. Though it is most apparent among extremists, the rest of us are not immune. Admittedly, activist protests are rooted in a fundamental sense of injustice and vision for a better world. Yet if advocacy campaigns lack avenues for their members to stay grounded in self-awareness, movements can easily demonize their opposition with an us versus them mentality that reinforces a hierarchy of inequality. This completely obstructs our ability to find understanding with our opposition, and reach meaningful compromise or constructive change. As frustration grows, anger at injustice can be replaced by anger at the perceived enemy, and in many cases, can evolve into more and more extreme acts, if not violence.

While there are times when this sense of belonging against an opposing force can feel innocuous and a source of pride to so many, such as the patriotic sentiment that infused the United States after the terrorist attacks of September 11, 2001, it can still come at the expense of our ability to make informed political or strategy decisions, build insightful relationships across difference, and form collaborative coalitions to reach meaningful change. In fact much harm has come to innocent people perceived as "enemies" or a threat, all in the name of patriotism.

While most of us would never engage in violence against another ethnic, religious, or racial group, we are still not impervious to the underlying instincts at work. The minute we find we have lost the opportunity to advance our own agenda, we vow to fight back against the other, until the tables are turned and we have upended the uncompromising forces. Then we can go on to push an agenda of our own, frequently at the expense of the other, repeating the cycle. As a result, we reach places of polarization, obstructionism, and isolationism. Essentially we have adopted everything we thought we were fighting against for the sake of our own gain.

This is not to say that some of these agendas are not valuable. Certainly we want to fight for equality and justice. Certainly we want to upend oppressive regimes. But we have to bring mindfulness to the process by which we advance that change, understand and treat those with differing views, and determine what motivates or resists the change we seek, so that we do not unintentionally come to employ the same divisive orientation that can cause harm. Without mindfulness, we are unable to look at our own role in a system objectively. It becomes too easy to blame others—another political party, a different socioeconomic class or race of people, or a certain policy—for our experience, and in so doing, abdicate any responsibility for understanding the needs of a complex system.

Sharon Salzberg (2008), cofounder of the Insight Meditation Society, explains, "We often use outrage to escape from helplessness and despair. ... But once we get lost in the anger, saying in effect, 'This is who I really am, this defines me,' we are vulnerable to perpetuating cycles of violence, lashing out reflexively instead of acting consciously, or thoughtlessly giving up." Fernandes Leela (2003), professor of political science at Rutgers University, observes that there are "cycles of retribution which perpetuate multiple and linked forms of oppression so that social movements continually find themselves appropriated by or circumscribed within the very structures they have tried wholeheartedly to resist."

So how do we advance change consciously in light of unconscious shadow instincts, the dominant culture, inequitable power structures, orientations of us versus them, and divisive, self-interested group instincts? Here we employ the mindfulness and deep inquiry tools we have used for cultivating presence. Starting with ourselves, we look at our own blind spots and ask, *What is really true?* And the only way to do this is through open, curious, and nonjudgmental inquiry in both contemplation and dialogue with others.

There are five areas related to this unconscious material that are valuable for individuals and organized groups to investigate:

Identify our shadows: It is essential that we take the time to explore our own unconscious shadows—places where we hold any emotional charge, sensitivity, vulnerability, or resentment that can fuel our judgments of others. We need to ask whether there are (rejected) aspects of ourselves similar in any way to those we conceive of as different or other. And we need to explore if we harbor any unfounded fears or assumptions of others that are based on the ways we have been conditioned to believe. Understanding increasingly how our unconscious material may have created barriers against the unknown or presumed known, we can open ourselves up to exploring what we need to learn to grow and the possibilities of connection across difference.

Map dominant culture: We should understand how the dominant cultural context in which we are operating gives us or limits our power based on privilege. Once we understand our experience within the larger system, then we are less likely to abuse any such authority we may be granted, we can be more informed and deliberate in raising awareness of or dismantling its inequities, and we can remain mindful of how to use power as well as when we become attached to obtaining or keeping it.

Understand our blind spots and role in the system: We must examine our own role in the system, look at ways we have fostered division, explore our implicit biases, and scrutinize ways we have avoided connection with others who are different, or turned a blind eye to systems that do not seek the well-being of all citizens. With greater awareness, we are less likely to act unconsciously and more able to serve as effective agents of change.

Seek the roots: We need to look deeply at the ways in which our dominant culture marginalizes certain qualities in us as well as others, and then vow to use that awareness to correct for disadvantage, prejudice, and inequality. We must also work toward building understanding of those involved in upholding unequal cultures of power and oppression, which will make us more effective in changing it.

Find power from within: We should explore the qualities that give us power from within, that we can foster in ourselves and others, and leverage that power to work collectively against the systemic issues.

For a set of conscious social change practices that can help us scrutinize each of these five areas to ensure we are aware of and can work with our unconscious shadows along with power dynamics to avoid contributing to systems of oppression and discrimination, see the guided practices at the end of this chapter.

Limiting Beliefs

In addition to our shadows, we are often influenced by unconscious limiting beliefs that stem from the messages we have received throughout our upbringing and culture, or that we have come to assume to protect ourselves from vulnerability. These limiting beliefs need to be surfaced, named, and actively released to allow us to bring our full courage as well as clarity to our work with others.

I have always had great difficulty asking for money—which is unfortunate for the founder and director of a nonprofit organization that depends on the donations of others to do its work. I felt great discomfort especially asking people that I knew for contributions to Global Grassroots, as if I were begging. I had a sense of shame around this.

When I meditated on the discomfort, I recognized that I preferred to be self-sufficient and earn my resources. This felt like a more fair and just way of operating. It also made me feel more successful, less dependent, and more capable. Going deeper, I realized I had a need to feel that success was my own making, and that I did not need to ask for help. My role was of the helper, and as such, I needed to be self-sufficient rather than dependent. Somewhere deep, I felt I was not worth a gift, and there was a fear of never being able to reciprocate such donations, so I couldn't fairly ask for them. Though my organization depended on the resources of others, fund-raising gave me a severe pain in the center of my shoulders and left me feeling paralyzed. I knew I needed to go even deeper.

So I did a breathwork session on my fear of asking for help. Breathwork, as I have mentioned, is one mind-body modality that uses a particular deep breath practice to help shift stuck emotion. During this session, I was immediately transported to a memory from when I was two years old. I was alone in my bed, and it was nighttime. I was extremely afraid that something was going to come in the window and get me. I remember lying in bed, my covers pulled up to my chin, furiously glancing from window to window, keeping watch. I reasoned that if I could see the window, then nothing would be able to enter, but if I looked away for even an instant, something could come and attack me. I was also aware that I was not allowed to call for help from my parents. They had told me to stop calling out to them at night (probably after the umpteenth time of me calling them), that I was fine, and that I needed to be quiet and go to sleep. So here I was—terrified, paralyzed, and unable to call for help, plus the position of my hands holding my blankets up to my chin was causing my shoulder muscles to squeeze together right in the place where I usually felt pain when considering fund-raising. Somehow my inability to ask for help around money had been linked to a time in my past when I was told I was supposed to be self-sufficient and not ask for help during great fear. This is an example of the condensed experiences that Holotropic Breathwork pioneer Stanislov Grof had observed in his work with therapeutic patients. Through my session, I was able to begin to unpack and delink these experiences, thereby releasing the fear, emotional charge, and limiting beliefs I had around asking for help.

I am still working on this, but I have released a lot of my challenges around fund-raising. I know our work is worth a gift. I know that if someone says no, it is not because they don't like me or don't care about my cause. I know that if I ask for help and they say yes, it does not mean I am not self-sufficient. This has made fund-raising so much easier, and my ability to ask for and receive support in all other areas of my life so much less charged.

Our limiting beliefs might be about money, self-worth, image, success, or something else. None of us have grown to maturity without inheriting some form of a hang-up, so rest assured there are traps, both subtle and obvious, somewhere in every single consciousness. The best that a mindful change agent can do is expose, understand, and release these emotional obstacles as a means to see more clearly as well as move more freely. True needs are intelligence that will lead us to our unique path of meaning. To explore and transform your own limiting beliefs, see the practices at the end of this chapter.

Unconscious Compulsions

I am sitting in an audience of about three hundred women participating in a wellness conference at a well-known retreat center. The inspirational lineup of speakers has provided a range of methods designed to instill empowerment and self-realization. We spend the afternoon engaged in partner work, journaling, and meditations that reach deep inside to surface our greatest needs and possibilities. One speaker has just led the plenary in an activity of self-inquiry and is now asking for a few volunteers to speak about their insights.

A woman sitting a few rows ahead of me raises her hand, and the mike runner brings her the microphone. She stands and begins to speak, immediately choking on her words. Her efforts to contain herself only result in an eruption of tears, as she sputters to continue. Turning to share what she is saying with the whole room, she reveals a face shiny with both tears and a runny nose. Then I notice the woman sitting next to her madly rifling through her things as though searching for something vital. Looking around at her feet, she locates ... a box of tissues. Then she purposefully grabs a big wad of them in one hand, and reaches up to wipe the nose and face of the woman who is speaking. Midsentence! Startled, the speaker stops for a moment, murmurs thanks, and then continues with her emotional share. The tissue lady sits down, satisfied.

Observing the exchange, I recognize the good intention as well as courage to act. The tissue lady wanted to alleviate her neighbor's suffering. But her well-meaning maneuver was driven by a hasty assessment of the situation and her internal, unconscious compulsion to fix a perceived problem. As frequently happens, this change agent was caught interpreting a problem from her own sense of discomfort and viewing a solution based on her personal priorities. To her, the awkward emotional distress of the speaker was clearly a situation that needed fixing. The end result, unfortunately, was more of an intrusion, interruption, and distraction, as opposed to a mindful solution that provided care, support, and respect for the person in need.

The impulse to fix may be one of the most seemingly innocent threats to social service, but acting on that compulsion is often driven by an unconscious discomfort with what is happening in front of us rather than a conscious awareness of what might be most useful. The knee-jerk response might help us feel better, but at the cost of leaving our intended beneficiaries feeling railroaded, misunderstood, and even further disempowered. Again, our proverbial three breaths can assuage this well-intended impulse. Our ability to notice and sit with our own discomfort, and then inquire about the unconscious impulses that are triggered, prepares us to listen to what is truly needed and then act without distortion.

Consider why people volunteer or give philanthropically. If you have ever taken on a volunteer experience or contributed financially to a cause, consider why you were first compelled to do so. Did you help others because it made you feel liked, useful, or powerful? Was it because you felt it was the right thing to do, or thought you had expertise or knowledge that could be useful? Then again, maybe you were motivated by a sense of meaning or the chance of accomplishing something that would distinguish yourself as an individual?[4]

All these intentions can be authentically sourced from a deep commitment to making the world a better place. But they can also be driven from a place of ego that wants to prove a belief about what is right, demonstrate knowledge, or further a sense of accomplishment. There is nothing inherently bad with wanting to advance justice or accomplishment. None of these motivations, though, may have anything to do with what the people you aim to serve actually need. If intentions are not conscious, they may drive us to act in ways that are self-serving and blind to, if not in misalignment with, what is needed by another. And that can be disempowering.

It is possible that there are unconscious drivers to even good acts that are important to be aware of as we engage in social transformation.

This is true not only of individuals but of groups of individuals, organizations, and institutions too. For example, on an organizational level we can ask whether we are acting in support of our core mission, or making decisions that position us to achieve publicity or funding at the expense of those we serve, or in opposition to or outside our mission. Organizations should always review their intentions and decisions in light of their overarching mission statement. On a societal level, we can examine the ways the structures we endorse uphold hierarchy and exclusion. If intentions are set consciously from the ground up, it is more likely that the resulting actions, structures, and systems will support the optimal path for the common good.

To surface and clarify your underlying intentions for the work you do, or wish to do, in the world, turn to the practices at the end of this chapter.

Relevance of Mindfulness in Becoming Whole

We have explored the implications of mindfulness and deeper self-awareness in helping us in becoming whole. Now it should be clear how the brain training and its corresponding capacities correlate to this process of personal transformation. This includes how enhanced present moment integration, increased response flexibility, and the ability to disengage automatic pathways allow us to take those three breaths so that we can disrupt any unconscious patterns of reactivity, and instead respond with conscious wisdom. Furthermore, we can see how the ability to disengage one's ego while letting go of attachments, aversions, limiting beliefs, and shadow material allow us to evolve and grow with less anxiety. As we drop our defenses rooted in our shadows and ego, we are less likely to foster division to prop ourselves up or protect ourselves from vulnerability. Rather, we listen with empathy and foster a much greater understanding of the drivers of behavior. This results in better relationships, better decision making, a greater degree of learning, and fewer fear-based choices. Finally, mindfulness can lead to an enhanced experience of interconnection, compassion, and gratitude, which allows a change agent's problem solving to be more relevant to beneficiaries. The outcome is a greater capacity to work for the wholeness of ourselves and all members of our community.

Aqeela Sherrills and the 1992 Bloods-Crips Truce

Sherrills grew up in the crime-infested Jordan Downs Housing Project in Watts, California, and was soon drawn into the South Central Los Angeles gang world, identifying with the Grape Street Crips (Stoltze, 2012). In 1988, he escaped the violence for college at Cal State Northridge, where he had a transformative experience one night reflecting on his own actions of infidelity that infected a girlfriend with an STD. He decided that he was meant for more, and chose to come clean about his actions along with his childhood of violence and sexual abuse (Sherrills, 2016). He realized for the first time in sharing his story that he had never questioned the violence around him growing up because it would have meant questioning the pain of his own childhood. Instead he directed his outrage outward. He realized gangs were "a surrogate family when the nuclear family has been broken" (Healing Works, 2016). This epiphany compelled him into a deep inquiry about justice, racial discrimination, and his own experience, and when Sherrills returned to Watts, he was instrumental in bringing about a twelve-year cease-fire between rival gangs, the Bloods and Crips. Working with his brother Daude, former football player Jim Brown, and rival gang members willing to talk, Sherrills gradually transformed gang member perspectives from one of retribution to forgiveness and reconciliation. "We'll never get rid of gangs, but we can instill morals and values in that structure and shift their purpose" (ibid.).

The historic cease-fire was formalized in a written peace treaty in 1994, based on the 1949 cease-fire agreement between Israel and Egypt as a template (Stoltze, 2012). But that was not all. In 1999, Sherrills and his brother formed the Community Self-Determination Institute, which provided counseling, emergency violence intervention, and education programs. Sherrills was committed to working to alleviate the underlying societal and individual challenges that fueled violence, addiction, and crime. Prior to the cease-fire, the LA murder rate exceeded a thousand deaths per year. In the years following the peace treaty, gang violence and murder rates declined significantly, and now Los Angeles has the lowest homicide rate in nearly forty years (Transform, 2010). Sherrills has been asked to consult on peacemaking in Belfast, Ireland, the Balkans, Russia, and Holland,

and is now actively working in the Newark, New Jersey, and New York City areas.

Sherrills has since built a movement around his success called the Reverence Project. Founded in 2007, the Reverence Project integrates intentional dialogue, restorative justice, art, music, dance, and wellness to transform cultures of violence and fear into those of compassion and forgiveness.

> That ability to forgive oneself is what I understand as Reverence. To forgive doesn't mean to condone, nor does it mean to forget. It's a creative exploration and analysis of the circumstances that happen. ... Reverence is not what we see or experience, but how we choose to see the experience. I call this type of seeing "beholding." Beholding is the capacity to hold space for the highest possibility and probabilities of good to emerge from the experience because we are not our experiences. (Sherrills, 2016)

Becoming Whole Collectively

Claudia Horwitz (2008), community organizer and founder of stone circles, a nonprofit retreat center for activists, remarks, "If we engage in the collective without some practice of individual consciousness, we're more likely to get caught up in group think and only use a fraction of our human capacity. Without consciousness, there is no choice." It is only by investing in deeper self-understanding that we can effectively turn toward the societal level. Just as we do in our own process of cultivating presence, we ask, *What is happening now?* This allows us to look deeply and listen not just within ourselves but in all corners of our external environment too. We engage as many viewpoints as possible in helping us understand what is really going on with a particular issue—recognizing that every individual has something to contribute to our deeper, human understanding. We know from our own experience how we grasp at or avoid change, and how hard change actually is, so we approach others with greater levels of compassion.

Then we work to see clearly and understand the underlying roots of the issue by asking, *What is really true?* We need to avoid division and instead use presence to understand the entire system, even engaging those who oppose our views and values, even those who are perpetrators of violence and hate. How did they come to those actions or beliefs? How did our society fail them such that they have chosen those harmful actions, so that they have come to believe in ways that limit tolerance and inclusivity? What role can we play in breaking down barriers and boundaries to help foster deeper understanding? How can we understand and heal these unconscious behaviors so that we can work toward common ground and eventually a deeper sense of interconnectedness?

Conscious social change honors both the unique wisdom of our conditioned experience and essential similarities we all have at our deepest levels. Employing mindfulness is crucial for advancing social justice so that we do not re-create hierarchies of power over others but rather eliminate the fear-based prejudice and abuse of privilege that underlies suffering and oppression. A conscious approach to social change fosters understanding of and compassion for the roots of suffering in ourselves as well as those who oppose us. It embraces self-reflection to examine our fears, insecurities, and the rejected parts of ourselves such that we can more easily accept or at least understand others. It scrutinizes power structures in the dominant culture, including our own standing within them, and works to dismantle oppressive institutions. Without denying reality and its historical wounds, we speak truth, listen deeply, bear witness to the experiences of others, and contribute toward a vision for transformation.

Practices

Reactivity: Transforming Reaction into Wise Response

Find a partner with whom to conduct this exercise.

Consider a time where you overreacted, and did or said something you regretted. Now tell this story to your partner, but tell it in the third person. In other words, instead of saying, "Once I snapped at my friend … ," use your own name. "Once Jane snapped at her friend … " This facilitates your taking a step back from any emotional reactivity and becoming your own observer. When you are finished, switch with your partner.

As you tell your story, notice how it feels to share and hear your own experience as a third-party story. What would it sound like to you if someone were telling this story to you not about yourself but instead about themselves? Would you be as hard on them as you might be on yourself? Or would you be less forgiving than you have been of your own missteps? Do you find any humor in your experience now that you are looking at it from a different perspective? What insights do you gain from listening and sharing about reactivity?

Now close your eyes and imagine yourself in those same circumstances. Take three breaths, and then invite yourself to explore how you would have handled it if you were able to pause, take three breaths, and respond mindfully with a full understanding of your own emotional charge, how it affects your heart, mind, and body, and what unconscious material was being activated. Share any insights.

Consider the implications of any insights you may have gained from these activities to your work in service to others.

Attachment: We Want Change

Think about the things that cause us suffering or anxiety in our daily lives. Take a moment to write down all the things that bring you stress in your life or you want to change. Finish your list before reading the next set of instructions.

Cross out all items that you know you cannot change. With self-compassion, we must do our best to accept these circumstances and let go of wanting them to be different, even when they are painful, such as loss or illness.

Now look at the remaining list. Which of those items are things you wish you had, but don't have right now (things like more money, a better job, or a good relationship)? Make a small x mark next to the things you wish you had, but don't.

Now which of those items are things you wish you could get rid of (things like pain in your body or an abusive relationship)? Make a small o mark next to the things you don't want, but you currently have. Is there anything left on the list that does not fall into the two categories?

For the items we can change, we have two choices: accept that this is how things are and let go of the wanting it to be different, or decide to act to change it, in which case you also can let go of the anxiety of wanting it to be different, because you are now acting, not just worrying.

Cross out those items you are going to work to accept. Take a deep breath. Pause to meditate on that commitment and the process of letting go of the anxiety that comes from attachment/aversion.

Circle the things you have control over and are willing to act to change.

For each of those circled items, make a commitment to take one small step toward change.

Notice any changes in the body, any release, or where any remaining anxiety lies. What still has an emotional hold on you? Here is where we continue to practice with curiosity. What is true about these circumstances? What do they have to teach us?

When we choose to accept or act, we no longer need to hold on to the suffering that comes from wanting something to be different. Mindfulness practice helps us with the patience and self-compassion necessary for transformation.

Aversion and Finding Inner-Driven Compassion: But Change Is Hard!

Find a partner with whom to conduct this exercise.

Consider the most challenging thing you've had to adapt to in your life, where you successfully changed. Share your story with your partner, using the following instructions:

- The partner will practice deep listening, noticing both the self (survey your three centers: mind, heart, and body) and state of the other. (To remember how to listen with fifty-fifty attention, go back to the noticing the three centers and fifty-fifty awareness practices in chapter 3. The listener is only to listen. Do not respond, do not offer advice or similar experiences, and do not ask a question or even make a verbal sound or physical response like touching their arm. You may only respond with your eyes. Just listen with fifty-fifty attention and be silently present with them. Notice what arises in you as a compulsion to fix or comfort the other person.

- For the speaker, share your experience and see what it feels like to have someone simply listen to you with complete presence. Once you have finished, switch, and the listener becomes the speaker.

When you are finished, discuss what it felt like to hear your partner's story and share your own. Did you feel heard? Did you have similar experiences or emotional responses to those experiences of change that you shared? What have you learned about change, the drivers of change, and how we respond to change? What relevance does this insight have for the change you hope others to make? What did it feel like to listen? What was your emotional response while listening to each other? Were you able to stay present? Did you feel any unconscious desires to respond in a certain way to improve your connection, share your experience, or ask questions? In what ways do these compulsions help or hinder your ability to listen, or the speaker's ability to share? How can you bring greater mindfulness into your conversations? What other insights have you gained about the difficulties of change from your or your partner's experiences? What role does mindfulness have to play?

Identifying Shadows: Who Do You Think You Are?

Think of a person who really annoys or frustrates you. If you could offer them any advice, write it down: "Dear _____, I wish you would _____." Write a full paragraph of a letter to them, with as much kindness as you can. Only when you are finished go on to the next instruction on the next page.

Read your letter to yourself. But as you read, begin with Dear
_____, and replace the other person's name in the letter with
your name. Then transform each of your sentences into a piece of advice
for yourself: "I wish *I* would _____ ... "

Ask yourself if there is any truth in each statement? Is there any part of
yourself that you rejected that now makes you reject that in another? Is
there a way you are judging them because you are not willing to let yourself
be a certain way? How did it feel to get your own advice? Is there anything
you might change in your tone or delivery to integrate more compassion
and mindfulness? Is there any aspects of your advice that would be useful
for you to consider? What is your role in your relationship with them? How
can we better embody the change we hope to see in others?

What new insights or compassion do you have for the other? What kind
of unconscious material might be driving their behavior? What patience
can we have with the process of change in the other? Consider how our
lack of awareness recycles pain and suffering for others.

Mapping the Dominant Culture

Let's now consider your own culture or the culture in which you are working. What are the identities that give us power or make us feel disempowered? Draw a line on a large piece of paper. Above the line is increasing
power, and below the line is decreasing power. This is the definition of the
dominant culture and marginalized society. Those who fall above the line
are valued by the dominant culture, and those who fall below the line are
marginalized.

Map the identities that give people power or limit their power in your
context. Consider every dimension of identity that you can uncover—
gender, race, ethnicity, citizenship status, education, socioeconomic status, age, relationship status, sexual preference, capability, physical health,
geographic location, mobility, knowledge, appearance, family, and so
on. For example, in some cultures, certain qualities might be placed
as depicted in figure 4.2.

After you have exhausted every dimension that describes your cultural
environment (however you may define that—academia, your professional sphere, your community, among your peers, or your nation), circle
all those identities with which you hold some characteristics. It is critical
that we understand where we fall within the dominant culture so that we

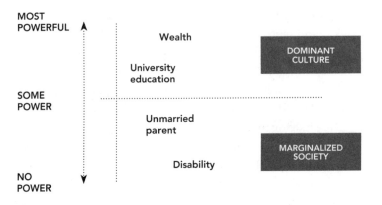

Figure 4.2

understand our power and privilege as bestowed on us from the outside. Some of these characteristics you may have earned, while others you may have nothing to do with. Just note them and notice how you feel about them. It will also be important to be mindful of how this shifts when you go outside your normal cultural context, so this exercise is helping us familiarize ourselves with our current identities as well as give us practice in recognizing societal values more explicitly so that we can quickly assess and understand any new context.

Where do you stand? Which of your characteristics is valued by or given less power by your society? As we can see, we each stand at the intersection of many qualities that have varying degrees of privilege, power, or marginalization. Our complex identities and the ways in which they are treated in one cultural context versus another can shift and change depending on how we identify, what aspects of ourselves we are bringing to the forefront, who we associate with, what we reveal, or what is perceived about ourselves. Again, the importance is to understand that power structures are a reality so that we do not abuse any externally derived power we may be granted. Instead, we must use our sources of power as a tool for positive change, while working to transform the same structures and systems we are a part of to work toward greater equality.

Understanding Our Blind Spots and Role in the System

Meditate on the qualities of power and privilege that your external environment has bestowed on or denied you. Do you feel attached to your position? Do you find yourself averse to or have feelings of guilt or anger around your privilege? Do you see power as a negative force? Notice if there are any unhealed places or emotional charges related to specific qualities. In sitting meditation, invite yourself to go backward again to when you first came to understand or feel this, and what is needed to come into a place of equilibrium.

Once you have an understanding of where you fall within your particular context, take time to do two things if you can:

1. Identify someone in your life that you feel holds more power than you, especially within the dimension that you identified as holding a charge for you. Invite engagement with them about power. Here are a few suggested questions to explore with them:

    *   How does power serve or become an obstacle for them?
    *   How do they view their sense of power or lack thereof?
    *   How have they found ways to inspire others or achieve change despite power dynamics?
    *   When do they feel least powerful?
    *   What do they feel needs to change?
    *   What can you learn from them about your own blind spots and the power structures at work in your society?

2. Engage with someone you know who has an entirely different identity from you—ideally one who may experience greater marginalization than you—even if you feel awkward or ashamed, or uncomfortable with your circumstances. Be aware of all that is arising for you and invite that in as another teacher. Bring your fifty-fifty presence and capacity to relate as one human being to another. Invite in connection. This exercise involves intentionally, consciously seeking out ways to learn and expand our boundaries of comfort as we connect as a human being to another person who is unfamiliar to us. We seek to learn by extending ourselves, being willing to inquire around what feels uncomfortable, and forge relationship around what we do have in common. If they are willing and feel comfortable participating, here are a few suggested questions:

    *   How do power dynamics serve or become an obstacle for them?
    *   How do they view their sense of power or lack thereof?

- How have they found ways to inspire others or achieve change despite power dynamics?
- When do they feel least powerful?
- What do they feel needs to change?
- What can you learn from them about your own blind spots and the power structures at work in your society?

What did you learn about yourself, others who you perceive to be different than you, and the power structures at work in our society? In what ways have you had blind spots? Where have your own shadows been at work? In what ways can you participate in helping to dismantle systems of inequality? What is at the root of human behavior and suffering? In what ways are you called to create change in your life or beyond? Discuss with those whom you have practiced these inquiries or are collaborating with on a social change endeavor.

Finding Power from Within

We also need to know that there is power within all of us, and the ways that we can use our internal power and the power that we have from our various identities to transform inequalities and suffering. As you journal, ask yourself when you feel most powerful. Ask this question again and again until you cannot come up with any more examples or answers. Then wait to see what else arises. Make a list of the qualities that come from within that give you a sense of power and that you can draw on to help you in your work. After building your list, consider or discuss:

- What are the tactics or strategies we can use to overcome the power structures that oppress?
- How can we use our power from within to address imbalances in the dominant culture?
- How do we use power influenced by our aversions and attachments to protect ourselves, avoid fears, or make ourselves feel better?
- How do we use power to fight injustice and protect others?
- How can we use power without judgment, but with kindness?
- How can we use power from within to counteract the ways we feel powerless?

Transforming Limiting Beliefs

Start by making a list of all your fears, beliefs, or assumptions associated with your chosen social issue. Ask yourself what you believe about your ability to do this work, and if there are any reservations? Do you have any worries? Do you have any beliefs that might limit you? Are there other stakeholders involved in your issue who have fears, beliefs, or assumptions that might limit you?

For instance, let's say you want to or are working to advocate among policy makers to raise minimum wages. One example of a limiting belief you might hold about your ability to do this work could be that you do not have the right background or education to be able to convince decision makers to listen to you. Sometimes leaders experience waves of what is often called "imposter syndrome" that they are holding positions they are not qualified to hold. Or you may feel that you are not a low-wage worker and cannot understand their lives enough to adequately represent them. These beliefs may or may not be true, but we need to know what they are to accommodate them into our awareness of self and issue.

Step back and look at your list of limiting beliefs. Ask yourselves if each belief is necessarily true. Pick one that resonates most with you or concerns you most. Then write down the opposite as a positive affirmation or a mantra as an antidote on a new piece of paper. For example,

Fear =	I do not have the right education or background to win the respect of policy makers in order to convince them to raise wages.
Positive affirmation =	I have enough education, knowledge, and passion to speak eloquently and convincingly about this issue.

Try to go through as many fears or limiting beliefs as possible, and transform them into affirmations. When you have written all your affirmations on new pieces of paper, place your fears and limiting beliefs in a garbage bag or basket. Ask yourself if you really want to hang on to these beliefs. Take a moment to acknowledge that these beliefs were forged at a previous point in time to protect you from vulnerability. Our ego often strives to keep us from taking a risk rather than risk failing. But these belief systems are frequently outdated, based on old fears. They no longer serve you. If you are ready to get rid of them, let them go. Burn or otherwise discard the limiting beliefs.

You may want to work with one limiting belief or affirmation each week until you have transformed them all. Meditate on your mantra. Take it out and read it aloud before you go to sleep. Carry it with you and refer to it often. Try to work it into conversation and practice by saying it to someone else. The more you can verbalize it, the more it will begin to feel true and transform your perspective of what is possible.

Once you have named your limiting beliefs and started to transform them into affirmations, you will also be able to adapt your communications with greater potency. Furthermore, you can incorporate this work into the ways you address the belief systems of your constituents, as part of your solution.

Intentions

Take the time to look more deeply at your intentions. Start with a few moments of mindfulness practice, allowing yourself to become aware of your breath, then your body, then your emotional state, and then your mind. When you feel that you can contact each of your three centers, ask yourself, What are my intentions for my work or cause? Or why do I yearn to make this (or a) contribution?

Do not worry about editing yourself to come up with an answer that sounds noble. Just write down anything that comes up. Ask yourself these questions as many times as you can until you can think of no more answers. Then ask yourself at least ten more times. Pause and breathe until something arises. There may be multiple dimensions or a diverse range of intentions that may surface. It is important to let all answers arise without judgment so that you can hear both the ego and your deeper truth speaking once the ego is done controlling the conversation. This will allow you to bring to light any shadows as well as your deepest intentions.

For example, some of my answers as to why I invest in my work with women in East Africa include:

- There is a need that is not being fulfilled by other organizations.
- It is the right thing to do and feels good to help.
- The women have so much they want to do, and I want to be able to partner with them to achieve it.

- It is my passion, and I feel alive and energized while I am engaged in this work.
- I can't step away now or the organization would have difficulty fund-raising.
- It feels like a responsibility.
- I am intellectually challenged by the strategy of building and growing an organization.

Then when you are finished, look at your journal and note what feels most authentic. Does it feel right to your mind, heart, and gut? Look at what feels to be coming from the truest self and what may be coming from the ego. Consider these drivers in the context of the work you will be doing. Which may serve your endeavors, and which may distort? Which align or misalign with the needs of those you aim to serve? So long as we begin to bring shadows into the light, we can integrate and utilize them to help us grow.

5 Ensuring Well-being

The third capacity of conscious social change is using presence for self-care, or ensuring well-being. The need to restore balance exists among all who serve and bear witness to deep injustice or suffering, including humanitarian aid workers, trauma counselors, emergency first responders, community organizers, peacekeepers, and others in service on the front lines. Individuals and organizations can embrace contemplative practices that allow them to both foster a healthy balance and discern when it is necessary to take a step back from their social change efforts in order to restore themselves. A consciousness-based approach allows time for personal restoration so workers on the front lines can tap creativity and energy to continue to serve those in need. This ensures we stay whole, grounded, and completely available to do our work in the world.

During the annual anniversary of the Rwanda genocide, for a brief time, relative to the country's now-everyday calm, the trauma of the hundred-day nightmare erupts forth with the force of a volcano.

On April 6, 1994, a plane carrying Rwandan president Juvénal Habyarimana was shot down, triggering ethnic tensions past the breaking point and sparking the swiftest genocide the world has ever seen. One hundred days later, nearly one million Tutsis and moderate Hutus had been brutally murdered by their own compatriots. The United Nations estimates that between one-quarter and one-half million women and girls were raped (Segui, 1996). Of the survivors, 70 percent were estimated to have contracted HIV (Amnesty International, 2004). Countless children witnessed the slaughter of their parents, often by people they had previously known as friends and neighbors. Approximately seventy-five thousand children were left orphaned (Hirondelle News Agency, 2008).

Somehow in mid-April 2006, I find myself one of only three white Westerners surrounded by a mass of nearly seventy-five thousand mourners who have just spent the last week exhuming the bodies of family members in order to give them a proper burial. I have traveled to Rwanda with a dual purpose: we are on a film shoot for our documentary on Darfur, Sudan, *The Devil Came on Horseback*, about my brother's experience there as a military observer, and came during the Rwandan memorial period to explore the long-term impact of genocide on a population.

I follow the funeral procession slowly, feeling absurdly out of place among the mass of Rwandans, as a parade of rumbling pickup trucks lead the way carrying nearly two hundred caskets neatly draped with purple crosses and damp with tears from hovering family members. The remains of up to thirty people, now safely occupying each coffin, had once been hastily hidden in shallow backyard graves or tossed by their killers into local latrines.

Our destination is the Kigali Genocide Memorial Centre, a heartfelt yet painful testament to the slaughter that drenched this tiny country, the size of Maryland, just over a decade before. Massive underground tombs surrounding the memorial lay waiting for this year's burials, offering some token of honor for lives so carelessly lost. Already nearly fifty thousand massacred Tutsi rest below, nine coffins deep.

As we snake our way through village streets, I try to imagine the sheer terror one must have faced as a target of such hatred: nowhere to escape to, and no one to help. The magnitude and speed of the violence that reached every corner of this small but beautiful country is still unfathomable. In the Kigali Genocide Memorial Centre, photographs of happy children hang somberly over small plaques, which read,

Fillette Uwase
Age: 2
Favorite Toy: Doll
Favorite Food: Rice and chips
Best Friend: Her dad
Behavior: A good girl
Cause of Death: Smashed against a wall

Ariane Umutoni
Age: 4
Favorite Food: Cake
Favorite Drink: Milk

Enjoyed: Singing and dancing
Behavior: A neat little girl
Cause of Death: Stabbed in her eyes and head

Patrick Gashugi Shimirwa
Age: 5
Favorite Sport: Riding bicycle
Favorite Food: Chips, meat and eggs
Best Friend: Alliane, his sister
Behavior: A quiet, well-behaved boy
Cause of Death: Hacked by machete

I'm not sure anyone can completely understand what drives such atrocities. Yet what is painfully clear to me after just one day in Rwanda is the devastating emotional impact of violence long after it ends. You might expect it intellectually, but you cannot really *feel* it until you are standing there on Rwandan soil, surrounded by both dead and surviving.

We eventually reach the Memorial Centre, people amassed around coffins; tens of thousands, shoulder to shoulder; a collective body of pain, alive in silent motion. The quiet distress that must permeate every daily action of neighbors living side by side their family's killers begins to flood the senses, standing hairs on end. It is the rainy season, but for now the sky only glares down at us threateningly. Mourners crowd together under tents, seemingly pleading with nature to spare them this time from the same fierce rains that twelve years ago were unable to dissuade mobs from their vicious tasks. Suddenly a woman begins to scream—it is usually a woman, as it is so often the case that the women bear the greatest burden of such suffering, as mothers who lost their children, widows who lost their husbands, and precious souls whose bodies were claimed as the spoils of war by their captors.

Immediately, trauma workers standing by in red first aid vests dive into the crowd with refined skill. In moments, the tightly packed audience gives birth to the shrieking, gasping woman as she is led away arm in arm with her rescuers, dragging her feet, sobbing, and screaming in a language you need not speak to understand. The fragile facade begins to crumble, and the collective wound again expels grief, anger, and sadness as survivors unwillingly relive or uncontrollably release their pain.

Not only does the emotional trauma run broad and deep, but the impact of genocide is long reaching too. Almost two decades later, despite heroic efforts at reconstruction, justice, and reconciliation, some women still suffer from HIV/AIDS contracted during rape by infected attackers intent on producing Hutu babies. Widows struggle alone to support their hungry families, having to sacrifice health insurance or school fees for food. Child-headed households of orphans have grown up without the support of loving parents, and many are now parents themselves. Other sole survivors still exist homeless, preferring to spend a lifetime bouncing weekly between generous hosts rather than reside among neighbors that slaughtered or failed to protect their families.

Each April, during the national mourning and commemoration period, the genocide becomes a focal point of conversations and public events. The nature of April's commemoration period forces survivors to engage directly and repeatedly with traumatic memories, frequently with volatile and troubling results. Intensely afflicted individuals are removed from the event, and some are even taken to local hospitals, where they are sedated. The strategy is meant to guard against mass hysteria and intended to simply "snap people out of" their traumatic reexperiences. When they wake up, sometimes they are encouraged to discuss their experience or seek counseling. There appears to be little systematic, widespread follow-up support in place, however, to provide comfort, transition, or healing after the memorial period ends for the year. During the conflict, the country's public health infrastructure was effectively destroyed. Yet in the intervening years, governmental entities, women's cooperatives, faith-based groups, and NGOs from around the world have increasingly begun to offer a range of psychosocial programs along with human rights–related initiatives. Slowly, Rwandese are becoming more aware of trauma as an issue, despite lingering stigma.

On a visit to the ladies room during the memorial event I attend that April 2006, I catch a glimpse of a back room full of the same women who had been extracted from the crowd earlier. Most are sitting slumped against the wall on grass mats. Attendees fan them or sing softly while the women sob. Others have surrendered to sleep. I ask a museum staff person standing nearby what will happen tomorrow to support these women. "Nothing," is the answer. "They go back to normal life. Like everyone else."

Many of us are called to work in similar environments that involve service to the traumatized, including war or disaster survivors, survivors of all forms of gender-based violence, torture victims, abused children, and other survivors of traumatic events. Others experience chronic stress from the demands of our jobs. We need to recognize that even as we may study and employ a diverse range of techniques and modes of service as professionals or volunteers, our exposure to chronic stress and others' traumatic experiences can affect us just as powerfully on the physiological, mental, and emotional levels, as if we had experienced the traumatic event ourselves.

I have seen burnout a thousand times among the aid workers of the Darfur refugee camps I visited in Chad, the first responders after Haiti's earthquake, activists, caretakers of the injured and traumatized, and development professionals working with the most impoverished and vulnerable survivors worldwide. On the border of Darfur, people were so fed up with their inability to make a difference in the crisis that they would leave their position within six months. At the war zone in Sudan, the nightlife was where they obscured their stress, imbibing the little packets of black market alcohol smuggled in to soothe their nerves in a largely dry, Muslim country under Sharia law. In the United States, activists seemed on the boiling point, frantically seeking the next extreme tactic they could use or celebrity they could engage to get the attention of the international community. At just about every disaster, you could find aid workers bantering competitively in local watering holes each night about who had the least sleep as they tended to the traumatized. Stress levels were high, disillusionment seeping in, and the intentions underlying their services increasingly confused.

The third capacity of conscious social change is using presence for self-care for ensuring well-being. After we have cultivated presence by asking, *What is happening?* and used our increasing level of self-awareness to proactively attend to our own needs for wholeness by asking, *What is true?* we can move forward with vigilance about and stewardship of our own needs for restoration. Our key question now is, *What is needed?*

Horwitz (2008) asserts, "Individual freedom is the seed of collective liberation, the building block. ... Freedom is the spaciousness that allows us to stay and sit and listen when things get hot." Reverend angel Kyodo Williams (2008), founder of the Center for Transformative Change agrees: "It is the practices of *being with and bearing witness* to that most avail themselves to birthing and sustaining action and activism tempered by compassion." The more we use mindfulness to help us endure what discomfort we experience in our own lives, the more we can show up fully present for the suffering in others' lives without it overwhelming us.

As I explored with the last capacity, a common pitfall of change leaders is falling out of balance to either side of the attachment-aversion continuum. We can get stuck on our own vision, or think attaining whatever we are pursuing is the right and only course of action. Overattachment to a single agenda or way forward can cause competitiveness between groups with a common purpose, diluting resources and rendering leaders blind to opportunities to collaborate. It can further lead to rigid organizations unable to examine changing priorities at the root level of their chosen issue.

On the other hand, the more of a burden we hold and longer we manage it without some investment in renewal, the more we are prone to burnout or disillusionment. There are many contributing factors to burnout including dangerous working conditions, lack of resources to conduct work, repeated exposure to horrific scenes, stories, and experiences, moral anguish, overwork, and separation from family. Individuals who experience or witness traumatic events, especially war, genocide, and sexual violence, often undergo deep psychological stress, including PTSD.

According to the American Psychiatric Association (2017), PTSD "is a psychiatric disorder that can occur in people who have experienced or witnessed a traumatic event such as a natural disaster, a serious accident, a terrorist act, war/combat, rape or other violent personal assault." PTSD includes an entire spectrum of symptoms such as hyperarousal, dissociation, insomnia, nightmares, startle responses, amnesia, reliving experiences, suicidal tendencies, a lack of emotional regulation, self-blame, disconnection, and depression, among others. Even hearing the stories of others' traumatic experiences can result in symptoms of PTSD. Called vicarious or second-hand trauma, early indicators include experiences of overwhelm and survivor's guilt—the sense that it is unfair you have survived or that similar circumstances have not affected you. A report conducted among relief workers six to eight months after the September 11 attacks in the United States revealed that acute PTSD existed among more than 6 percent of those with direct exposure to the disaster site, but also among nearly 5 percent of those with indirect exposure just through survivor narratives (Zimering, Gulliver, Knight, Munroe, & Keane, 2006). The Antares Foundation (2012) and Center for Disease Control collaborated on a series of studies looking at PTSD among various groups working in high-stress environments, and found that 30 percent of humanitarian aid workers, 25 percent of search and rescue personnel, and 28 percent of war journalists experienced significant symptoms of PTSD, while between 46 and 80 percent of health and human services workers faced severe emotional exhaustion. The impact of such stress can be broad, including not only high turnover rates but also higher rates of illness, poor decision making, increased risk taking, and lower effectiveness (ibid.).

In October 2006, six months after the memorial period, I return to Rwanda to offer my first program in conscious social change to the group of women I had met with in April. This first set of Global Grassroots participants in Rwanda are a group of 62 women who are widowed genocide survivors living with HIV, many of whom were sexually assaulted during the genocide. They are collectively caring for 227 children, their own and orphans. A local pastor has helped them form an association to serve as a support group, and they gather regularly to conduct activities in support of their members' needs.

They invite Global Grassroots to bring its first pilot curriculum to assist them in establishing social ventures that will advance their economic well-being while solving some of the social issues faced by their community, including malnutrition. Over the course of two weeks, I plan to help them identify their own assets and capabilities that can be leveraged to create social change, share practices in self-awareness and breathing, and guide them through various social entrepreneurship tools to design their own social ventures. Though I begin my work in Rwanda incorporating some level of self-awareness for leadership, it isn't until I recognize the numbers of women suffering from PTSD that I think about how mind-body work could be critical for trauma healing, individual and community rebuilding after war, and self-care for service professionals too.

One day during our two-week course I am midsentence when I see a thin and wrinkled woman lay down a grass mat and curl up in the corner to sleep. This is not blatant disregard for my class; this is a woman who is seriously unwell. Over the next few days as we go through activities that involve planning the futures of their social ventures, it becomes clear to me that many of these women are incapable of thinking beyond the day-to-day life. Not only is this a reflection of their lives at the bottom of the socioeconomic pyramid, living on whatever they make selling vegetables or handicrafts each day, it is also a core symptom of PTSD. As I explore their other symptoms in conversation, I find women experiencing digestive issues, insomnia, paranoia, hypervigilance, and several other ailments related to stress. I realize how critical wellness is to a change agents' ability to lead and how integral individual healing is to community rebuilding. If these women, whom society failed during war, could recognize their value to community and go even further to realize their ability to change that same society, such an experience could be not only deeply healing on a personal level but also essential in rebuilding community in the wake of the genocide. Job number one was to start the healing process from the inside out.

Overview of the Stress Response System

Let's explore briefly what happens to the body when we experience a form of trauma. As I discussed previously, the autonomic nervous system regulates all the automatic functions of the body including breathing, heart rate, blood pressure, digestion, and the internal glands and organs. Our autonomic nervous system is made up of two parts. One is the sympathetic nervous system or stress response system that activates to protect us from danger (fight or flight), and produces adrenaline, cortisol, and other chemicals to support whatever actions are needed. The other, the parasympathetic branch, is what calms us down and helps us relax. Normally our body regulates between the two as necessary. The stress response system, however, usually stays partially activated even after the stimulus that caused its activation has ceased. In fact, most of the time, the sympathetic nervous system maintains a state of alert or readiness, resulting in an elevated heart rate, higher-frequency breathing, a level of muscular tension, and some anxiety (Elliott & Edmonson, 2006). Many ailments are exacerbated or driven by sympathetic dominance, including hypertension, digestive problems, insomnia, headache, and an inability to concentrate (ibid.). Furthermore, autonomic nervous system dysfunction is related to many psychological symptoms, including depression, PTSD, attention deficit disorder, and anxiety disorders (Gerbarg & Brown, 2016).

During and after a crisis, our sympathetic system can become overly activated. This system burns a lot of energy, and when it stays on for too long, it leads to exhaustion, overwhelm, and illness. When this occurs—for example, in high-stress service positions—people can get burned out, depressed, disillusioned, or angry about all the suffering to which they are bearing witness. When we have a traumatic event or are exposed to repeated stresses, the stress response system can get stuck on overdrive or react erratically. When the stress response system gets stuck on high, it can lead to a range of symptoms such as difficulty sleeping, nervousness, headaches, paranoia, flashbacks, muscle tension, overreactivity to certain stimuli, feeling over-emotional, feeling numb, or depression. The stress response system requires significant levels of energy to maintain, and when it stays activated for too long, the body can become depleted like a battery that has been completely drained of energy and can no longer hold a charge, leading to exhaustion, depression, and illness. Any and all of these things can be experienced at different times as well as at different levels of intensity.

While conventional Western psychiatry can offer prescription medications to treat the overactivation of the sympathetic branch, they have not found medication that treats the underactivation of the parasympathetic branch (ibid.). The good news is that there is a simple practice to stimulate the parasympathetic branch and help bring our nervous system back into balance. It is the breath. The same breath that serves us in mindfulness.

Breathing for Stress and Trauma

At five breaths per minute, what is called Coherent Breathing has been found as the optimal pace of breathing necessary for most people to reset the autonomic nervous system, allowing it to once more self-regulate. Coherent Breathing requires that we breathe gently at a slower pace than our natural breath frequency, which requires focused attention. When we breathe more slowly, the breaths become deeper naturally without making any effort to expand (fill the chest with air) or copress (expel the air). Conducted with equal six-second inhales and six-second exhales through the nose, Coherent Breathing's three facets of slow, gentle, and conscious breaths have multiple impact. In addition to the many benefits of mindful, conscious breathing discussed throughout the book, breathing at a slower pace helps to bring into balance the sympathetic and parasympathetic branches of the nervous system, resulting in cardiopulmonary resonance and maximum heart rate variability, discussed earlier as markers of cardiovascular health (Elliott & Edmonson, 2006; Gerbarg & Brown, 2015). At this pace, the breathing rhythm is synchronized with the heart rate variability rhythm at the frequency of resonance. This means that the electric rhythms of the heart, lungs, and brain are synchronized (Brown & Gerbarg, 2012).

Coherent Breathing has also been shown to decrease beta brain waves—the brain waves associated with normal waking consciousness—and increase alpha brain waves—the brain waves associated with wakeful relaxation (Elliott & Edmonson, 2006). In essence, Stephen Elliott asserts, "Coherent Breathing *results* in meditation."

As discussed earlier, Brown and Gerbarg studied the effects of Coherent Breathing along with several ancient practices from Indian yogic traditions, Qigong, Zen Buddhist practice, Japanese and Chinese martial arts, and a form of breathing done by Russian Orthodox Hesychast monks. After several years of scientific study and practice, Brown and Gerbarg (2012) distilled the practice into a four-part program they call Breath~Body~Mind (BBM).[1] The program has been used to relieve stress among sexual violence survivors in Sudan, 9/11 first responders, Hurricane Katrina survivors, Haiti earthquake survivors, and combat veterans with significant success.

BBM includes simple movement and breathing practices that help restore balance to the nervous system, resulting in greater calm, energy, and resilience. It rapidly relieves stress, sleep problems, and other PTSD symptoms. BBM incorporates four main parts: Qigong movements as taught by Master Robert Peng, Coherent Breathing (using the "2 Bells" track on the *Respire-1* CD by Elliot), Breath-Moving Meditation and Open Focus Meditation by Les Fehmi, and bonding as well as reconnecting with oneself and others.[2]

The practice begins with four Qigong movements, which help synchronize the pace of breathing with slow movements of the body, supporting autonomic balance. The movement also helps relieve the outer levels of tensions held in the body, and supports trauma survivors in becoming more grounded and less dissociated from their bodies. Next, participants practice Coherent Breathing lying down with eyes closed for between five and twenty minutes. Coherent Breathing, practiced in and out of the nose at five breaths per minute, sets the optimal pace of breathing necessary to enable your body to rebalance the autonomic nervous system. The practice integrates a form of resistance breathing called Ujjayi breath, or ocean breath, where a slight constriction of the throat during the exhale, while the mouth remains closed, produces an audible, almost-sighing sound. (Imagine you are trying to fog up your sunglasses to clean them, but do that with your mouth closed. Some think this makes you sound a bit like Darth Vader.) Third, Breath-Moving Meditation, which imagines the breath moving through parts of your body, supports self-awareness as well as respiratory and circulatory resonance. Open Focus Meditation performed with Coherent Breathing is an advanced form of meditation on space that can dissolve physical and emotional pain as well as restore to normal trauma-related misperceptions of the body. One of the symptoms of PTSD is disconnection, the loss of any sense of meaningful connection to oneself or others. The BBM practice can restore the sense of connectedness (Gerbarg & Brown, 2015). Finally, bonding activities such as dialogue, singing, and journaling help groups connect and integrate their experiences. When we use this special breath practice, our body is telling our mind that we are safe and can relax. These messages from the body reach all levels of the brain including the primitive autonomic regulatory circuits, emotion regulatory centers, and higher thinking centers in the frontal lobes (ibid.). Evidence suggests that Coherent Breathing could turn off defensive reactions and turn on our social engagement system (Brown & Gerbarg, 2017). By practicing this program up to twenty minutes twice every day for at least two months, according to Brown and Gerbarg's prescription, the body is able to convince the mind that it is safe to turn down the stress response system and turn on the healing, soothing, recharging systems. Over time, the practice helps reset the autonomic nervous system so that it can self-regulate. Participants have found significant elimination or reduction in PTSD symptoms through BBM practice. Global Grassroots utilizes BBM as our core practice for trauma healing with our survivors of war, genocide, and gender-based violence in Rwanda and Uganda.

It is important to recognize that the stress of our work has a negative and measurable impact on our stress response system. Mindfulness and mind-body practices like BBM that support nervous system balance and self-regulation serve as an antidote. Change agents and service professionals engaged in high-stress operations must make their own emotional preservation and stress resilience a priority in order to be of greatest service in their ongoing endeavors to help others. Take time to learn about practices like BBM, and invest in regular mindfulness and mind-body healing practices proactively for your own long-term resilience. As a bonus, such mind-body practices are safe, and easily taught across cultural, religious, and language differences. While they require some skills training, they do not depend on a long-term therapeutic relationship to be able to practice and share. In environments like post-genocide Rwanda where the sheer scale of enacting justice and rebuilding a nation's core institutions take precedence, the struggle to attend to the welfare of individual citizens can be met initially with simple mindfulness and mind-body practices that are scientifically proven to have a positive impact on health as well as emotional well-being.

Coping with Stress and Trauma

Now that we understand how trauma and chronic stress affect the body, we need to recognize the more harmful coping mechanisms we employ to manage our stress unconsciously. Just as we utilize presence and mindfulness to recognize our own unconscious patterns of behavior that distort our intentions, we must use our practice of cultivating presence to recognize our indicators of and typical responses to stress as wake-up calls for investing in our own restoration.

Each of us has our unique ways of managing stress, some of which are healthier than others. We may find that we consistently procrastinate or get irritable as stress increases. Under pressure or anxiety, we may withdraw from social interactions or drown ourselves in entertainment as a distraction. Exercise may become a lifeline to sanity, or alcohol consumption might become a crutch. Sometimes we are barely aware of the impact of stress except for a nagging headache or back pain, until one day we find we are in the middle of burnout.

Exposure to traumatic events, chronic stress, and secondary trauma through our work environment can also manifest in ways that are disguised as part of the culture of our particular industry. From caffeine consumption to limited sleep, to feelings of cynicism and disillusionment, these indicators of imbalance may pervade the workplace as accepted badges of honor for one's commitment, sacrifice, and perseverance in the face of hardship. Unfortunately, these indicators of stress and our associated coping mechanisms can distort our effectiveness, and lead to other chronic health and relational challenges. Critical to employing a mindfulness approach to social change is investing in our own capacity to notice ourselves slipping into one of these patterns so that we may take time out to rebalance ourselves.

In her book *Trauma Stewardship*, Laura van Dernoot Lipsky (2009) explores more acute coping mechanisms of long-term stress and trauma exposure. One of the first signs of imbalance is the sense that you can never do enough, followed by an experience of helplessness and hopelessness.

Though you may be a part of a successful program or organization, at some point the needs and suffering of others feels too big. You may feel overwhelmed, as if there is nothing you can ever do to help. You may feel personally responsible in a situation for which no one could reasonably expect you to be responsible. This feeling of not being enough is a form of perceived inadequacy. You may cope by striving for an idealized lifestyle so as to feel enough, imposing what you believe to be right or wrong on others, or compulsively trying constantly to do more, feeling that if only you could help enough, be smart enough, or "man" enough, then maybe you could manage more easily.

Guilt may also come on returning to your own environment after working in a traumatic situation. You may feel guilty about your ability to leave that environment when others cannot. You may feel shame about the imbalances in resources, inequity in suffering, and disparities of privilege. This may lead to a sense of comparison of suffering. Guilt leaves you unable to form authentic connection because you may unintentionally diminish yourself to try to establish greater equity. When you feel guilty about your sense of privilege, you may attempt to minimize your own circumstances, undermining your own wellness. You may even take up more space in seeking to have your guilt assuaged, diverting attention from communities of need who are suffering from disadvantage or violence. Guilt brings your own emotional responses into imbalance, including pity and avoidance, rather than authentically being present to reality. You may feel you are unable (or that it is inappropriate) to feel any pleasure or happiness. This reduces your ability to nurture yourself and others. It also begins to numb your ability to stay present with suffering when it does occur.

When you are exposed to a traumatic event or bear witness to another's severe suffering, you may become less sensitive to other forms of discomfort or pain. You can likely relate to the experience of returning home or spending time with friends or family who have angst over seemingly insignificant things, leaving you feeling completely irritated or disconnected from their pain or complaints. After one particular trip to Africa early in my work, I was visiting a family member who asked if they could see my photos. I was excited to share until about three photos in, when this family member shifted their attention unapologetically to a situation with the swimming pool that took all their attention, completely forgetting to revisit our conversation for the rest of my time there. I felt intentionally ignored. I was left stewing with judgment about the concerns of the privileged over the "real" issues of the world, unable to find any empathy.

Over time, it may take more and more to shock you, or elicit an empathetic response. This can lead you to trivialize certain pain as less important or less authentic than that of others. This is an experience of losing compassion and empathy by creating a hierarchy of pain, and judging others based on that hierarchy. This may lead to conflict or competition, where you seek out or stay fixated on the extreme in order to feel you are on top of that hierarchy.

You may also find yourself deliberately avoiding people as opposed to engaging, and withdrawing from social functions, avoiding activities that once brought joy. Or you may isolate yourself, talking with only those who "get it." A colleague once told me she found herself constantly conversing about the sexual violence she was researching in the eastern Democratic Republic of Congo, catching herself only when her fellow attendees at a wedding either walked away or stood there with mouths agape in shock.

Soon you may find a sense of boredom, a feeling of being stagnant, or that work no longer holds interest or inspiration. Before you know it, you may find yourself exhausted in every cell of your body. As the stress response system remains turned on over time, the chemicals it secretes like adrenaline and cortisol become toxic, including to the immune system. The circumstances can be further exasperated when you push yourself to work beyond your limits. Physical ailments may result, including migraines, back pain, high blood pressure, and other body aches. This is not helped by the culture of certain work environments that accept these symptoms as "part of the job."

When your discomfort becomes too much, you may actively medicate yourself to impose a sense of numbness, including through alcohol, recreational drugs, or prescription drugs. Coping can also happen through addiction to work, caffeine, chaotic environments, dangerous behavior, or exercise. Addictions begin as a way to numb out, and become an attachment so strong it persists despite recognition of its harmful impact on yourself and others. It is important to look at those attachments that help you numb out. The danger is when you hit a point where everything emotional you have tried to avoid comes bursting forth, and you find you are less equipped to handle it than you once were. Such coping mechanisms that induce numbing or aversion undermine your own capacity to experience authentic presence and peace even in the face of suffering.

In other instances, you may attempt to maintain a sense of adrenaline high to avoid time for reflection. You can also become addicted to the high-stress environment in which you work or the experience of being of service to others. The rest of the world feels boring compared to the high-intensity experience of working in life-or-death situations or circumstances of significant trauma. Some have called it the "knight in shining armor" syndrome, where you become overly identified with your work and must feel needed to be relevant.

Self-Care Practice

As a conscious change agent, perhaps the single most important tool you can carry with you is an ever-evolving self-care practice. This includes not only the personal transformation and self-awareness practices that we have already explored but also the awareness and active nurturing of our well-being. When we are not whole, we are doing a disservice to our work. While this would appear to be a no-brainer, conversations with activists and aid workers globally indicate this is the easiest to ignore, and first thing that is sacrificed in advancing their work.

Our first step is identifying our negative coping mechanisms. Using mindfulness, we notice when we have fallen out of a sense of well-being. We examine our moods and behavior, looking for any of the red flags discussed above. Even a suspicion of unhealthy coping, cynicism, or feelings of exhaustion should serve as a signal for renewal. But it is also crucial to maintain self-compassion. We are not superhuman, and it is normal to get out of balance.

The second step is to develop a proactive self-care plan. Self-care takes many forms, and it is essential to aim for a holistic balance between our physical, mental, and emotional centers. Like a plan for physical fitness that works all major muscle groups, the self-care plan is a maintenance regimen for holistic balance, and should be utilized both as a regular, proactive investment in well-being and emergency resilience plan to protect from or treat burnout. For a guide for mapping your stress response habits as well as developing your unique, comprehensive self-care plan that touches on well-being of the mind, heart, body, and spirit, see the exercise at the end of this chapter.

The most important tool to support self-care is some form of regular, contemplative practice so that we can find clarity and insight, and so that the nervous system can regulate itself. We also need emotional experiences of peace, joy, and gratitude to help us remain grounded and whole. Mindfulness can help counter our feelings of hopelessness or helplessness, because we are not as easily overwhelmed and can ask for what we need. Instead of minimizing others' pain or numbing ourselves, we can be more present and respond from a place of attunement instead of alarm.

We must be aware of any guilt we feel about investing in our own restoration, especially when working in organizational cultures that do not prioritize well-being. In fact, conscious change agents must embody the values we hope to support in others. Others will look to us to see how we are modeling effectiveness and managing stress. Those of us in positions of leadership may need to change the system, dissolving constructs that are not supportive, and putting in place different structures that allow for and encourage self-care as integral to the work itself.

For example, Jeremy Hunter, founding director of the Executive Mind Leadership Institute at the Peter F. Drucker Graduate School of Management at Claremont Graduate University, studies mindfulness as a critical driver of productivity and happiness within organizations. He explains that what makes knowledge workers effective is different from what makes industrial workers effective. Yet we still adhere to organizational practices such as a 9:00 a.m. to 5:00 p.m. workday that were put in place to ensure the speed and tempo of all parts of a manufacturing process (Hunter, 2013). Instead, in the knowledge economy, the worker is the asset, and so how workers relate to each other along with their social-emotional competencies directly affect their ability to concentrate, innovate, and strategize. It takes on average twenty-three minutes to reestablish one's concentration after an interruption (Pattison, 2008), and as such, many workers these days find they do their best work at home after the workday has ended. If more workplaces honored the different needs people have for both focus and restoration, we might invite greater creativity and productivity, which in turn benefits people's morale.

Finally, we must recognize that the heightened stimulation of our culture and increasing demand for multitasking is damaging our capacity for mindfulness. I will be the first to admit that I am too plugged in; I have been known to check my e-mail on my iPhone at a red light. In the West, we too often emphasize multitasking, analytic thinking, and "doing" over presence and "being." Yet multitasking actually limits us. Stanford University researchers have shown that multitaskers actually perform worse on tests for managing distraction, memory, and task switching (Ophira, Nass, & Wagner, 2009). Furthermore, the Brain, Mind, and Consciousness Lab at Case Western University has found that when you think analytically (mechanical reasoning), you diminish the part of the brain that allows us to empathize (social reasoning), and vice versa (Begany, Cesaro, Bary, Ciccia, & Javk, 2009). While critical thinking skills may be essential for problem solving and design, we must also integrate an understanding of the human experience in that same solution. We need a balance of presence in action.

This reality is a rich and dynamic arena. On the one hand, we are offered a world in which injustice, inequity, and tragedy abound; opportunities are nearly endless for those who wish to engage in social change on the front lines. On the other hand, our culture, power structures, and even own conditioned selves provide obstacles as well as traps to bringing our full potency to the fight. Fortunately for us, we have the tools and capacities of mindfulness available. They are built in and accessible to all. And they are ours with a simple, conscious breath.

Richard Goerling and the Mindful Badge Initiative

One particular conscious change agent, police Lieutenant Richard Goerling, founded the Mindful Badge Initiative to bring mindfulness-based resilience training to US police.[3] He first entered municipal policing in 1997, and quickly recognized that the culture of policing along with the stress and trauma officers experience on the job set officers up for a high risk of performance failure and poor health. Historically, police are hired and trained as capable people, yet are placed into a profession rife with violence, trauma, perceived injustice, and chronic and acute stress, and then expected to manage the impact largely on their own. Some internal programs provide peer support after a critical incident, but limited training that might supply the skills for developing resilience proactively. This conventional, reactive approach is not at all sufficient in addressing the severe stress and its impact on law enforcement officers: police officers are at higher risk of PTSD, chronic sleep deprivation, obesity, type 2 diabetes, alcohol abuse, sudden cardiac death, and clinical depression, and are more likely to die of suicide than in the line of duty (Christopher et al., 2015; Hartley, Burchfiel, & Violanti, 2008). These stressors are more likely to contribute to anger, which is negatively correlated with ethical decision making, and positively correlated with interpreting actions as hostile and the intent to punish harshly (Bergman, Christopher, & Bowen, 2016). Without a formal program in or leadership emphasis on the importance of resilience, stress manifests in the shadows of cynicism, addiction, illness, burnout, and aggressive reactivity, degrading police decisions as well as interactions with each other and their broader community.

Goerling underwent training in MBSR and, profoundly inspired, spent two to three years studying mindfulness along with its impact through his own experiential practice, conversations with elite performers in a variety of areas using mindfulness, and a review of the available scientific research. He became convinced that mindfulness training would not only improve resilience but also help police officers open up to their greater humanity, cultivate compassion, and build social-emotional intelligence to navigate the high-risk challenges of their job.

In Oregon in 2013, Goerling first piloted his own programs, called Mindfulness-Based Resilience Training (MBRT), which involves an eight-week program adapted from MBSR. The ultimate mission is whole system reform toward a resilient police institution along with a culture of awareness and compassion. Goerling sees a need for change not only in the well-being and mind-set of individual officers but also among police leadership in order to ensure a system-wide cultural shift. He works with both officers in the field and police department leaders through programs customized to address their unique stressors. His programs are taught by a police veteran or first responder alongside a community member not only to avoid insular trainings with those only "in the club" but as a check on biased community perceptions of police too. The diversity of trainers is a spark for greater relationship building that extends beyond the training.

One of the core teachings of his training is the difference between judgment and discernment. Goerling (interview, February 1, 2017) explains that it is easy to pass judgment, say, when you answer a call from a sex worker who has been beaten by their pimp for using their money for drugs. Cops are naturally going to be driven by a range of thoughts about whether the sex worker is to blame or not based on their addiction and choice of profession. These biases and judgment come from the need to make sense of their world of violence, abuse, neglect, and crime. Add a dose of cynicism, toughness mentality, stress, and burnout, and they may be unable to make the best possible decision. Instead, mindfulness practice can open up a police officer to their own humanity and that of another individual. They are then more likely to be able to recognize their own internal biases through the capacity for self-observation (as opposed to trying to follow a department policy to not be biased), set aside moral judgment, and show up with compassion. This allows for discernment to determine the wisest response.

Goerling's work is beginning to reach a tipping point. As of 2017, he has been invited to train three hundred officers in the Dallas, Texas, police department, and has other programs under way in police departments in Bend, Oregon, Cambridge, Massachusetts, and Menlo Park, California. Moreover, as a faculty member at Pacific University, he is collaborating with Richie Davidson's lab at the Center for Healthy Minds at the University of Wisconsin at Madison on training officers at the Madison Police Department. Early outcomes have shown positive impact, including increases in the mindfulness facets of nonreactivity, nonjudgment, and acting with awareness as well as improvements in mental health, physical health, emotional intelligence, resilience, anger, fatigue, and stress (Christopher et al., 2015). Increases in acting with awareness and nonjudgment were also shown to correlate with a reduction in anger (Bergman, Christopher, & Bowen, 2016). In a stressful job, Goerling's mindfulness-based training empowers officers to take better day-to-day care of themselves as well choose the wiser path when actions can have real or even lethal consequences.

We know that meditation and awareness training supports empathetic thinking and stress reduction. We know that self-awareness and mindfulness practice support self-regulation of emotion, conflict resolution with others, and increased ability to connect and understand with compassion. We know that breath can help regulate the stress response system. And we know that stress and trauma exposure is the leading cause of burnout. As such, we must employ mindfulness and self-care as essential components of our work, just as an athlete would undergo physical rehabilitation for an injury. Without well-being, we are at risk of distorting our efforts, minimizing our potential contributions, or worse, creating harm. Change must begin from within.

Practices

Three Steps to a Self-Care Plan
Mapping coping: The first step in developing a self-care plan is to note the ways we normally and unhealthily cope with stress or trauma. Using the exploration of negative coping mechanisms for chronic stress and trauma above, make a list of which ones resonate with or feel familiar to you, and list any other ways you typically deal with stress, fear, and trauma. For many of you, you may find you have not yet experienced any of the more severe signs of trauma exposure, but you know well your typical mechanisms for dealing with stress. These might include having one too many glasses of alcohol, procrastinating, snapping at your loved ones, staying up late watching television, eating poorly, and so on. These will become your signals to invoke your self-care plan.

Mapping stress: For one week, each night, before you go to sleep, take an inventory of how well you were able to be present throughout the day. Ask yourself these eight questions and keep a log for the week:

1. Rate your stress level for the day on a scale of one to three (one = low, two = medium, and three = high).
2. Did you use any of your typical coping mechanisms during the day? If so, when, and in response to which level of stress?
3. Consider whether you were more connected to your mind, body, or emotional center during the day—which was driving you today, especially at moments of high stress, and which were you disconnected from?
4. Note any moments where you felt peace and calm. Was this authentic peace where you felt present with what was happening in your life, or due to numbing/avoidance? What were you doing or what did you do to evoke that feeling of peace?
5. Before you go to bed, scan your body. If you have any tension or stuckness, note where that is located and how you would describe it. Note if there are parts of yourself you cannot feel.
6. Note your emotional state at the end of the day—what is your mood and what are you feeling?

7. Note the state of your mind at the end of the day—are your thoughts now swirling about the past or the to-do list of what's to come? What are you preoccupied with? Are there any messages, fears, or limiting beliefs present?

8. Ask yourself if you feel completely alive. If so, how do you know? If not, why not?

Designing a self-care plan: Next, use the following map to make a commitment to at least one practice that nourishes each of the three centers of mind, body, and heart that you analyzed above. Take into account which of your three centers seems to dominate or go off-line during stress, and nurture yourself so that you feel balance between all three. Notice any experiences of stuckness, pain, or disconnection as well as where your mind spends most of its time. You will invoke your self-care plan when you recognize yourself investing in any of the more harmful or less helpful coping mechanisms you identified in the first step.

A self-care plan is well served by having a daily mindfulness or contemplative practice, but we want to consider a whole range of holistic choices to support our mind, body, heart, and spirit:

Nourishing the body: Our bodies are the vessels we need for being able to bring change into the world. It is critical that we take care of them so that we can draw on their strength when we need to. This includes:

*   Exercise, such as aerobic capacity, flexibility, and muscle strength. Consider activities that you may find meditative (such as swimming, running, or yoga), feel are invigorating and enlivening (such as certain sports, dances, or activities that involve nature), and help support physical strength and well-being.
*   Nutrition, including eating whole and well-balanced foods to give us the nutrition we need to stay well.
*   Deep rest, especially for more than seven hours per night.
*   Health, including taking care of our bodies when they are ailing and striving to prevent getting ill.
*   Drinking water along with limiting caffeine, alcohol, sugary drinks, or drinks with artificial chemicals.
*   Being outside in the fresh air.

Nourishing the heart: Our emotional center is what drives our desire to support others in need and help them reach their greatest potential. It provides us with a sense of harmony, interconnectedness, love, forgiveness, and compassion. It includes the ability to bear witness to another's suffering and discern when to abstain from trying to fix things. Our emotional health requires that we attend to imbalances in our own relationships, learn how to give and receive gratitude, make room for creative expression, remember to embrace joy in our lives, and find the space and serenity to experience ourselves, our feelings, and our natural surroundings, and that which is beyond us.

- *Love and connection:* Find ways to express love with those closest to you, including hugs, deep conversation, writing letters, being together without distraction, or providing help or support to another.
- *Serenity:* Find the space and freedom to experience yourself and your surroundings. Often spending time in nature is supportive of emotional well-being and physical well-being. Find a space that feels restorative to you to visit when needed, or a place in your home where you can meditate or spend time quietly without distraction. Remember a time when you felt serenity and use a visualization of that experience for a meditation on peace.
- *Loving-kindness:* This involves the intention and capacity to create or offer happiness to oneself and others. Consider the loving-kindness meditation shared previously.
- *Compassion:* This is about the intention and capacity to relieve or transform suffering in oneself and others. Activities that support compassion include volunteering, reading about other's lives, or engaging in mentorship or support groups.
- *Boundless joy:* This concerns the feeling of joy in oneself and for others when they feel joy. Cultivate joy by surrounding yourself with people or animal companions who you enjoy, engaging in activities that include laughing, giving, or receiving hugs, watching and providing support for others, joining in celebrations, and participating in other actions that foster joy and awe.
- *Gratitude:* It is crucial to experience the grace, gifts, and beauty we have in our lives. Gratitude can be cultivated through meditation, direct expression, sharing blessings, or writing letters of thanks.

- *Emotional well-being:* This involves feeling your feelings without aversion or attachment. Consider ways to support your own emotional well-being through conversation with supportive friends and family, journaling, therapeutic work, and crying or other emotional expression that can be done without creating harm.
- *Creation:* This revolves around the expression of emotion and ideas. Creation can be done in many ways including fine art, dance and other movement, sculpting, design, storytelling, other performing arts, music, and writing.

Nourishing the mind: The mind can help us discern the truth and keep us open to new possibilities. It can also block these same abilities when we cling to the past, worry about the future, and pass judgment on ourselves as well as others. Caring for the mind includes living with integrity in the present moment, investing in our accumulation of knowledge, and yet also viewing our experiences as opportunities to learn.

- *Education:* This concerns learning new things intentionally. Take a course, read a book, travel to experience a new environment, teach yourself how to do something new, attend a lecture or arts performance, or engage in new experiences alone or with others to broaden your mind.
- *Perspective:* Here, we see our experiences as opportunities to learn. Any experience or person, no matter how challenging or joyful, can serve as an opportunity to learn if you are open to what is arising for you and what it has to teach you. Be willing to have difficult conversations, invite differing viewpoints and consider the perspectives of those who think or believe differently for greater insight and to release judgment or attachments.
- *Peace and equanimity:* This involves nonattachments, seeing things as they are, and having a stable or quiet mind. Cultivate peace and equanimity through meditation, mindfulness, and journaling.
- *Discernment:* This is the ability to tap into intuitive wisdom and truth.

Nourishing the spirit: For those who have a sense of spiritual practice or religious tradition, this realm may represent a fourth dimension to invest in nourishment. This may include:

- Spiritual practice
- Attending religious services or worshiping

- Prayer
- Being in silence with community
- Fasting or other sacrifice
- Celebrating specific rituals
- Making offerings
- Creating a sacred place for honoring spiritual beliefs
- Pilgrimages
- Reading religious texts

Consider whether you invest adequately in care for all aspects of the self. Where do you need more attention? What ways have you found to nurture the body, heart, and mind, and if appropriate for you, the spirit? Your self-care plan will represent what you will do if you come to recognize yourself slipping out of balance and into your unconscious patterns of coping with stress. Once you have developed this plan, share it with a coworker, friend, or family member who will support you in recognizing the need to invoke your self-care plan for restoration and greater future resilience.

As you develop your plan, take time to ask yourself the following questions either with a partner or through meditation and journaling:

- When do I most feel peace?
- When do I most feel joy?
- When do I most feel alive?

Envision these occasions, and think about the qualities of the spaces, people, and circumstances that support these feelings. Sometimes just reflecting on such an experience along with how you felt emotionally, physically, and mentally in those moments can bring back the same states. It may also help you define where you need to go and what you need to do to find well-being:

- What are my deepest intentions for my work?
- Why do I do what I do?
- What brings meaning in my life?
- What do I really need?
- What do I really love?

6 Engaging Mindfully

The fourth capacity of conscious social change is engaging mindfully. Having begun to invest and apply mindfulness in our own life, now we look to integrate mindfulness into each phase of our solution design work for social innovation. Employing a conscious social change approach means using our personal insights about the change process and its difficulties to find compassion and understanding for others' experiences. We deliberately work to forge connection as well as foster the participation of others in diagnosing an issue comprehensively, developing a collective vision and theory of change, designing an intervention, and evaluating our impact—all while staying attuned to the changing needs of those we aim to serve. We investigate our own role in upholding the status quo, examine our deepest intentions, and then focus on how we can best alleviate the underlying issue rather than advancing our own narrow agenda. We avoid demonizing our opposition, and limit our use of rewards and punishments to force compliance. Instead, we seek avenues to support deeper individual transformation through enhanced human understanding.

Tools applied with a participatory approach such as mindful issue diagnosis, stakeholder analysis, and assets mapping allow new ideas to be based on a shared understanding of what works. Here, in examination of our broader issue, we employ the first three questions: *What is happening? What is true?* and *What is needed?* Next, we look to identify the unique perspectives, gifts, and other assets that each party has to offer and leverage to form the optimal solution. We ask collectively, *What is helpful?* This is more likely to bring us to an innovative and systemic intervention that has been reached with the insights and ownership of as many as possible who either suffer from or shape the problem. We are now prepared to prototype, test and assess our endeavor with as much intention and mindfulness as it was created. We use deep listening practices in our process of implementation and evaluation. This will support us in maximizing our learning and responsiveness for greater impact and sustainability over time.

Conscious social change is a method steeped in self-awareness along with compassion for the needs and perspectives of all people. It is an approach that unites, not divides, and one that is driven by a desire to alleviate suffering at its roots and across the system, not just to benefit the interests of one particular group. It is a method that sets aside blaming and defensiveness for a process built on human connection to maximize social innovation.

Often when people of privilege work with communities that have experienced relative disadvantage, they may come in with a whole host of unconscious assumptions about what the community needs, thinks, expects, and values. This is also possible between those working toward change, those involved in the underlying issue, or the perpetrators of harm. We have to be aware of our presumption that we know better or are more ethical. Our implicit biases and expectations may well be exposed and turned on their heads. This is a chance to remain open to and learn from others. We must listen, not impose, and accept and be accountable for the ways we misstep. By cultivating the capacities of mindfulness that involve observing, nonjudgment, and nonreaction as well as an orientation that every circumstance or person has something for us to learn, we deepen our understanding and connection to others. From this place, we are able to participate in making meaningful, collaborative choices that draw from and honor all. I have come to this perspective from my own misguided assumptions.

Ever since leaving the arena of international investment banking and completing my masters in business administration, I had been exploring the world of social entrepreneurship. Inspired by the world's leading social innovators, I first went to work for Ashoka, a global pioneer in advancing the profession of social entrepreneurship, but soon felt compelled to start my own endeavor. I have always been fascinated with why social ideas do not spread more quickly. Given the extreme nature of poverty, disease, and violence plaguing the majority of the population, why do social entrepreneurs struggle to establish and scale their ideas, even those that are radically revolutionizing systems like health care or education? Why don't pattern-changing ideas spread as fast as news of a disaster or viral tweet? Perhaps more business investment in the work of leading change agents can both enable social ideas to reach new economies of scale and have a positive impact on the business investor's bottom line. Drawing from my background in international project finance, I hypothesized that if I could find a strong enough value proposition, perhaps companies would be willing to underwrite the expansion of the work of the most effective social entrepreneurs. In 2004, there was no issue where social purpose and business profit motives were more aligned than HIV/AIDS, which was straining company health care, recruiting, training, and retention costs as workers fell ill and died rapidly from the disease. And there was no place where the issue was more acute than in South Africa.

In January of that year, I find myself sitting in a tiny, windowless metal shack owned by a woman named Zolecka Ntuli in a township outside Cape Town. The intensity of the summer heat radiates inward from the corrugated metal roof, as Zolecka moves a single light bulb from its socket in one of two connected, windowless rooms to a single socket in the second space so that we can see each other in the relative darkness.

I am here to learn as much as I can about the HIV/AIDS epidemic in South Africa. I came to interview the Ashoka Fellows and other social entrepreneurs engaged in the issue in order to comprehend their radical innovations. I want to understand firsthand the impact on businesses whose workers are dying so quickly that they hire three people for the same job since two will be dead within the year. I hope to learn from academic experts, social workers, and health care professionals, and visit the clinics and orphanages that are managing the heart-wrenching aftermath of the disease. I am here with two good friends, the remains of my emptied-out bank account, and a homemade brochure for my new hastily conceived Social Project Finance Initiative.

My first trip to the continent, I find South Africa in 2004 one of the most unusual places on earth—where the greatest wealth meets the most tragic poverty, where racial divisions still run deep, where democracy is fresh and new, and where indigenous cultures intersect with modern industry. To my new eyes, South Africa appears to have an almost completely developed infrastructure—water is good, there is power almost everywhere, and the communication and transportation systems are first class. There are malls that make you swear you are back in the United States, and the wealthy (albeit almost entirely white) enjoy all the same conveniences that most of the United States enjoys. When I first arrive, I don't even feel like I have left the West.

On the other hand, as of 2004, apartheid has only been extinguished for ten years. During apartheid, I learn, blacks were prohibited from living or even entering the main cities without proving they were employed by a white business or residence. So when apartheid ended, they began moving back toward the cities from their rural villages for work. They set up temporary settlements, called townships, which then became semi-permanent slums during the transition. The townships consist of whole cities of one- or two-room shacks made of corrugated metal, brightly decorated inside with salvaged bottle labels and newspaper for wallpaper. These townships sometimes stretch as far as the eye can see. Many have no public services like sewer, water, or electricity, although some communities tap into the electric systems illegally. Gradually, as these townships grow larger and more permanent, they are being supplied with water and power. Stores, bars, schools, restaurants, post offices, and so on, are springing up to serve these areas too. But poverty is still widespread. As of 2004, many people make less than eighty dollars a month, and unemployment is nearly 25 percent across the country and even reaching close to 40 percent in some places.

As for HIV/AIDS, it is a sad story. South Africa has had the highest prevalence rate of HIV compared to anywhere else in the world. In 2004, of the nearly thirty-seven million adults and children living with HIV/AIDS in the world, two-thirds live in sub-Saharan Africa, and one-third of all global cases are in the epicenter of southern Africa (UNAIDS, 2006). Fueled by ignorance, stigma, poverty, and customs, HIV is spreading rapidly.

Perhaps the biggest issue is the enormous stigma surrounding HIV. There are stories of people being beaten to death because they go public with the status of their disease. Others commit suicide after learning they are HIV positive. Most will not even get tested, and if they do, they will not tell their families, spouses, or significant others out of shame, ... and instead go on having unprotected sex.

Even more serious than the stigma are the terrible myths that plague the prevention of the disease. It was not so long ago that the government itself was saying that HIV does not cause AIDS and antiretroviral drugs are toxic (Specter, 2007). The most disturbing myth is that having sex with a virgin will cure a person of HIV. Already at this time, the incidence of rape in South Africa is one of the highest in the world among countries not currently at war. Horrifyingly, there are incidents of young children, even infants, being raped so that men can be certain they have found a virgin. There were 52,733 *reported* rapes in South Africa in 2003 and 2004, half of which involved children (Cox, Andrade, Lungelow, Schloetelburg, & Rode, 2007).

Going deeper, I learn that men have enormous power over women in South Africa. Among the black communities with which I speak, women share that unprotected sex is simply expected of them as a duty. While women are expected to be monogamous, men frequently engage the services of sex workers, among whom the HIV prevalence rate in urban areas of South Africa was just over 50 percent in 2000 (UNAIDS, UNICEF, & World Health Organization, 2004). Women are biologically more susceptible to contracting the disease, and in 2004, represent nearly 60 percent of South Africa's population infected with HIV over the age of fifteen (UNAIDS, 2006).

Economic vulnerability in a society with high unemployment only exacerbates a woman's lack of negotiating power. Often when a woman becomes pregnant, the man will provide some monetary contribution to help cover the costs of the child, so some women explain they feel pressure to find a man and have a child in order to ensure some living support. But then when men die of AIDS, the women are left to raise their children alone, competing for jobs at the bottom of the barrel, with relatively little education or skills.

Toward the end of my journey through South Africa, I am asked the vital (and obvious) question, "Have you gone into the townships and spoken to anyone actually suffering from AIDS?" I have to pause. Despite my confidence in meeting with executives, academic experts, and political leaders, I do not know how to go about learning at the truly "grassroots" level. How would I even enter the townships or find someone willing to talk with me about these taboo topics? One of the social entrepreneurs I know offers to arrange it.

I meet Zolecka at her home in the Crossroads township outside Cape Town. We sit with her friend Ana, who is suffering from AIDS, Ana's little boy, and a few other neighbors in her one-room shack. Zolecka tells us how she was fed up when a twelve-year-old neighborhood girl was gang-raped by young boys who thought it was their right to have sex with her because she was their girlfriend.

This incident catalyzes Zolecka to start a support group in her community, just six months prior to my visit. Zolecka is unemployed and has no personal reserve of funds. But for her first meeting, she found some loose change to buy some bread and invited fifteen women to come together to start a dialogue about the issue of child rape. She now has sixty people meeting together three days a week (forty-five women and fifteen men) to talk about these issues. During the meetings, she tries to provide food, which is sometimes the only meal her members have that day. She has raised her own money through income-generating projects like selling beadwork and HIV ribbons. Zolecka uses the funds to put herself through training programs as a sexual violence and HIV/AIDs counselor so that she can educate her community. She tells me that men think that women carry HIV, so when men get sick, they do not want a woman caring for them. Thus, Zolecka is working to start training men as caregivers. She also sees the advantage of training men to become educators, because somehow other men see information from fellow men as more credible.

Zolecka knows what she is meant to do to help her community. And the startling thing is that she is only twenty-five years old.

What I discover among those most deeply impacted by the HIV/AIDS crisis is that the women already know what they need to do to protect themselves from contracting HIV. But they do not have enough economic freedom, sexual rights, or personal voice to decide when, where, how, and with whom to have sex. It is a woman's powerlessness that strikes me as the single-largest obstacle in the fight to prevent the spread of HIV—that is, until a woman has the courage to step forward to address such issues head-on, like Zolecka.

I know then and there that it is not merely greater business investment, Western innovation, or philanthropy that is needed to advance social change (although it can always be of support). Radical social change is already taking place outside the boardroom in rusty shacks with only a few coins and an enormous level of dedication. These change agents simply need some additional skills training and seed funding, and change will be fostered from the grassroots level up.

Since that moment, I have dedicated my work to helping change leaders within these marginalized populations of women advance their own ideas for social change. Rather than impose my own assumptions about what communities need to thrive, I support those most deeply impacted by a social issue in determining and initiating change for themselves. On my return from South Africa, I shelve my Social Project Finance Initiative, and found Global Grassroots to provide the training, funding, and advisory support for grassroots change agents, like Zolecka, working to advance social justice for the world's most vulnerable women and girls. I had found my purpose.

Stay Attuned to the Need for Conscious Action

Let's look at the difference between conventional change and conscious social change. Refer to table 6.1 below, which I first referenced in chapter 2.

In *Change the World: How Ordinary People Can Achieve Extraordinary Results*, Robert Quinn examines the patterns of change agents who advance systemic change. He proposes that most of society embraces a transactional model that is other driven and inner focused. In other words, individuals are driven to accomplish and attain what outer society values (e.g., prestige, knowledge, power, or material wealth), and are focused on results that benefit the personal good or good of the group's limited self-interests.

In contrast, Quinn (2000) notes, extraordinary change agents work from an opposite, transformational orientation. They are inner driven and other focused. They are driven by their own internal sense of purpose while focused on serving the larger common good beyond themselves. Here is a comparison of our two paradigms again.

Conscious social change advances the possibility of innovative and long-term transformation by disrupting our conventional patterns in four ways: it encourages an inner-driven/outer-focused paradigm; it is built on unity and deep human understanding instead of divisive and punitive measures; it looks to understand change at the roots, and explores systemic levels for greater effectiveness, longevity, and impact; and it uses participatory models to surface and engage the assets of all parties. Let's go deeper into each of these four aspects of engaging mindfully to understand why this conscious social change method is effective.

Table 6.1

Conventional model of change	Conscious social change model
Outer driven: we try to achieve what society says we should have—wealth, status, or beauty—or seek approval and direction externally.	Inner driven: we are driven by what we feel most passionate about and called to do in the world.
Self-focused: we look at what's in it for us.	Other focused: we look at how we can benefit the common good.
To create change, we tell or force people, and are motivated by our needs. This creates a sense of division: us versus them. We use threats of punishment or rewards to get people to comply with what we want.	To create change, we begin with self-examination to understand how much of the problem is our own, develop compassion for others, seek the insight and participation of others in designing a solution, stay attuned to the changing reality, and look to collaborate to optimize social value creation.
The results are incremental change within the norms of behavior, often without people changing at a deep level; instead, they are just complying to avoid punishment or get the reward.	The results are systemic change at the root levels and individual transformation that lasts longer term.

Inner-Driven, Outer-Focused Paradigm

First, let's look at the personal and societal potential of inner-driven change—meaning much of what guides our actions comes from our sense of purpose and self-understanding, as opposed to our own agenda or reactivity. Research shows us that conducting work for the benefit of the common good leads to a sense of meaning, which translates to a greater likelihood of success. I speak frequently about the importance of investing in one's own self-awareness for its influence on the way we carry out our work in the world. But the reverse is also true: selfless investment for the benefit of others has a significant impact on our own sense of well-being and success. Several studies have demonstrated that individuals who act on internal motivation rather than external incentives find more meaning in their experience, and are more likely to succeed in any such endeavor. A study of 11,300 West Point cadets showed that those motivated primarily by external motives, such as a desire to get a leadership position after school, performed worse than those who were internally motivated, such as wanting to be trained as a leader or to serve their country (Wresniewski &

Schwartz, 2014). They were less likely to graduate, be commissioned as an officer, get an earlier promotion recommendation, and stay in the military after their five years of mandatory service. In another experiment, college students were asked to work on a puzzle, and half of them were paid. Those paid stopped working on it immediately after the experiment had ended, while those unpaid continued working on it and reported feeling more enjoyment in their experience (Brooks, 2014). One distinguishing feature of conscious social change is that change agents' efforts are inspired by their inner sense of commitment to a larger social need. Drawing meaning and a sense of purpose from the work as well as the path of personal discovery inspires change agents to invest their full capacity in seeking a viable, impactful solution. As mindfulness allows us to let go of judgment, and inspires awareness, compassion, and interconnectedness, we are more likely to set aside our culturally biased presumptions of what a solution might look like. From this perspective, we are more open to radical wisdom from unexpected sources.

Unifying and Deep Human Understanding

The second area where conscious social change diverges from the conventional change model is in its collaborative versus divisive or forceful nature. Conventional change is often oriented around a philosophy of us versus them. A self-determined group targets those whose behavior they wish to change, and then uses incentives or punishments to try to push forward that change. In almost all cases, the traditional paradigm involves judging and faulting, if not demonizing, the opposition while working to advance the solution. This creates division and separation, driving participants to identify with a side at the cost of understanding the other. Furthermore, using tactics to tell or force change only creates incremental shifts in the face of that pressure. Such changes are unlikely to last when the incentive or punishment is removed, or the opposing party comes back into power. Without working with an understanding of what motivates real transformation in human behavior and belief systems, and without working in ways that engage people in feeling ownership over that change, interventions will likely be only temporary. Yet it is natural that we find the conventional model of using sticks and carrots to enforce change so familiar. For most of us, we have been immersed in this model since childhood.

I am the mother of a young daughter. Raising her has been, and continues to be, the most extraordinary journey of personal transformation in my life. I am reminded constantly of the monumental task in front of me. I am not only nurturing, guiding, and supporting the growth of this little being. I am the first to be influencing her conditioned sense of self. On the one hand, this is the self that is raised to understand how to coexist appropriately in community: what societal expectations are for our behavior including manners, what values should guide us, and how we should treat other people. On the other hand, this is also the self that will absorb all the (often-unintended) negative messages we get about how to look, how to fit in, and how to cope—all the stuff that our work in becoming whole helps us undo. That responsibility terrifies me.

In my exploration of parenting philosophies as a new parent, I found a resource that led to profound insights on not only parenting but also how we tend to approach social change and why. I discovered the work of Alfie Kohn, author of *Unconditional Parenting: Moving from Rewards and Punishments to Love and Reason*. As he sees it, conventional US parenting tends to place the adult's needs at the forefront, with the expectation that the child's needs will accommodate adult life. We expect, for example, young children to be able to stay quiet and sit when they eat, when every cell of their bodies wants to jump up, wriggle around, flip upside down, and hoot and holler with overflowing natural energy they cannot contain. As they get older and their basic needs are supplemented with other wants, we manipulate for compliance by offering treats, toys, fun, entertainment, or whatever is desired if the child responds as we wish: "If you do _____ right now, I'll let you do _____ or I'll give you _____." Or we withhold things or enact punishments if they don't. We feel that control and compliance are of priority, and are afraid that without such enforcement, it will result in out-of-control, spoiled, or disobedient children who lack discipline.

But Kohn effectively dismisses both punitive measures and incentives as ineffective attempts at behavioral compliance. Both sticks and carrots have the unintended consequences of teaching children a focus on outcomes for themselves (self-focused) and an orientation toward external systems of rewards (other driven). They are not necessarily learning the underlying lesson intended but instead what will happen to them if they do or don't do what their parents want, and how not to get caught the next time (Kohn,

2006). For instance, I can't tell you how many times I took away a toy when my child was using it as a weapon. Her only concern was how to get that toy back, rather than acknowledging the underlying lesson of whether or not to hit things and people with it. There was no room for any other lesson when she was exclusively focused on her own self-interests: that doll now held captive on top of the refrigerator.

According to Kohn, conventional parenting revolves around behavioral changes, parental control, and compliance. Again, an admission of guilt—I too require a few more bites of veggies before ice cream. This is how we've been taught by our own upbringing and culture to do parenting. This is our norm. Instead, Kohn contends, we need to be looking more deeply at what the child actually needs in each moment. Perhaps they are lashing out and hitting with a toy because they are flooded with frustration and don't know how to handle their emotions. Or perhaps they have had a drop in blood sugar, and don't yet realize they are hungry and are acting out of desperation. Certainly there is no reason to ignore the harmful activity in the present, but we also have to be diagnosing what is really going on (*what is happening, what is true,* and *what is needed*) so we can more effectively attend to needs and change behavior patterns.

I was struck by how closely his theory of unconditional parenting aligns with conscious social change: that the key to real transformation is working on the root causes of a situation and seeking to address what a local population really needs from a place of inner understanding versus imposing a top-down solution. Conventional change in its telling, forcing, and incentivizing mirrors the predominate mode of parenting, and defines the outer-driven, self-focused orientation we have around change.

As we become school-age children, we learn again that there are rules established by both our school and the culture of our peers, and face some form of punishment (shame, isolation, or ridicule) if we do not comply or rewards (acceptance) if we conform. Not only do we try to disown those parts of ourselves that we believe are unacceptable; we also are internalizing the process of responding to an external authority to dictate our behavior and identity. Policy and culture within our professional environment sets forth further sticks and carrots. As a society, we have built our institutions with the same tendencies toward a paradigm of authority-leadership, top-down decisions, penal code enforcement, and market-based incentive structures. This is not an argument for discarding the rule of law. But we can see that we have few culturally sanctioned opportunities to listen to the inner wisdom that once guided the formation of intentional societies—whether an indigenous community or the authors of the US Constitution. And so when we seek change, we do so most often under the same paradigm of punishment and rewards with which we are so familiar. As a default, our conventional approach to creating social change starts with wielding the power to reward or punish.

Conscious social change is a more compassionate approach. We recognize that sticks and carrots are sometimes useful, but rarely lead to long-term transformation on their own, as they more frequently force temporary compliance just so long as they are in effect. Rather than seeing the world as two sides of a battle, and working to win by using our power or privilege over others, we know we are all connected and cannot consider a community to be well if change is at the expense of another stakeholder group. Instead, we look for common ground and avenues to support deeper individual shifts that are based on greater human understanding.

This process begins with self-examination. Through mindfulness of our own direct experience with change, fear, and reactivity, we gain insight into and compassion for the way others react to challenges. Next, we connect with people and listen to understand their needs and perspectives. We do not see opposition as the enemy; we see divisiveness as the obstacle. As opposed to competing for our agenda, we seek the highest benevolent outcome through compromise. Conscious social change involves collaboratively forging solutions that speak to people's underlying essential nature as human beings, fostering real and effective transformation rather than incremental, temporary change in response to a stick or carrot.

Root and Systemic-Level Change

The third way in which conscious social change represents a departure from conventional change, is that it works at the root and systemic levels of an issue rather than applying a Band-Aid to the symptoms. In conscious social change, the same principles of deep inquiry used for self-awareness and personal transformation are applied to identify, understand, and transform underlying social concerns. Where the conventional approach may simply address the symptoms of the issue—"People are going hungry and malnourished, so we will provide meals"—conscious social change considers and targets the root causes, such as why food deserts or malnutrition exist, how to fix distribution networks so food does not get wasted, or how to elevate people above the poverty line into self-sufficiency. It strives not for just at a onetime fix but instead for how change can happen in a way that transforms individuals, groups, systems, institutions, and whole societies for the long haul.

In looking to understand the issue at a root and systemic level, conscious social change invites us to examine our role in those systems that uphold the status quo. For example, in this case, How are we contributing to food waste or supporting businesses that do? In every moment that we act, we can do so with intention.

By employing mindfulness, conscious social change requires that we are driven by a mission to alleviate the underlying social issue, not simply advance or grow our own programs. Many service-based organizations, for instance, feel the pressure to demonstrate impact in terms of ever-increasing, concrete outputs such as the number of meals served to the homeless. Progress is measured by increasing size and scale—how many more meals, say, were served to the homeless this year compared to last year. This drives the need to keep the nonprofit engine funded and constantly growing. We can define this conventional orientation as being *activity driven* or focused on the program delivery as opposed to the transformation created by the program. It may be the case that a program is serving ever-larger numbers of homeless, but that does not necessarily mean the program is having a measurable impact alleviating the issue of homelessness or hunger. Instead, what would the program look like if it were focused on growing its impact at the root level and not just scaling its programs? In contrast, conscious change solutions are *issue*, not activity, driven. Conscious change works to answer the question *why*—why does this issue exist?—and then aims to solve it, creating social value first and foremost. We must be careful not to blindly push our *what*, knowing that it is easy to get caught up in scaling a program while falling short of maximizing effectiveness.

Conscious social change also necessitates that we stay attuned to the underlying needs of those we aim to serve. Through mindfulness, we can better recognize our attachments that are not optimal or helpful. Organizations must closely evaluate their effectiveness and regularly rediagnose their issue collaboratively. Otherwise, they may advance their solution without noticing changes in the needs or challenges of their target populations. Deep examination of program impact and an understanding of problem roots will help refine program offerings to achieve transformation more effectively over time. Though organizations may still work to replicate or scale effective solutions, ultimately conscious social change ensures organizations exist only for the common good, not for their own survival. Outcomes that emerge from this collaborative process result in greater personal transformation for those involved as well as solutions with greater innovation, longevity, and impact. To achieve this, we must come together with our stakeholders and collectively ask, *What is needed?* From there, we can determine our common mission and set a vision of what we want the community to look like when we succeed. This serves as our guide.

Participatory and Bottom-up Models

The fourth way in which conscious social change diverges from conventional change is in how it uses participatory models to surface and engage the contributions of all parties. The participatory development methodology, complemented by the realm of human-centered design, provides an example of how working from a collaborative, bottom-up versus outside-imposed approach has value.

In the international development and humanitarian aid realms, local citizens often have little representation or participation. They are the subjects of aid, not the cocreators of their destiny. They are rarely asked about their priorities. At the same time, there is also a lot of talk about "empowerment." Yet empowerment still implies something someone does to another. The marginalized and disadvantaged have inherent power, ideas, and solutions. They have preferences, deep cultural knowledge, and wisdom. But too often good intentions to help result in outsiders imposing their view of what *they* think others need, while denying the local community or "beneficiaries" the right to lead or even participate. And that is disempowering. Furthermore, each time an NGO comes in and decides what the population needs, it misses the hidden issues, which may not be spoken of openly with outsiders. As a result, the NGO loses the local wisdom that is vital in understanding the particular cultural context and developing appropriate solutions. Change will happen more efficiently and quickly in addressing social ills if citizens are fully participating in leading that change.

According to Robert Chambers (2009) in *Whose Reality Counts: Putting the First Last*, the goal of global development should be the sustainable well-being for all, including quality of life along with economic, social, mental, spiritual, physical, and material well-being, as defined by the person themselves. Participatory development aims to ensure that the vulnerable, marginalized, and exploited should come first, and lead the process of achieving well-being for themselves.

The participatory development approach reverses dominant power dynamics. Outsiders might facilitate and listen, but not lead the discussion. Participatory development relies on open group dialogue where all members of a community join in creating a substantially more accurate picture of the whole (ibid.). Methods and tools are shared as well as inclusive, as communities articulate their ideas and vision. Frequently, participatory development tools utilize visual methods to ensure participation from all parties including the most marginalized, who may be illiterate. This method embraces self-sufficiency and dignity as two critical qualities of the process, and involves constant shared experience, where learning happens in all directions. It requires a relaxed and patient approach that builds rapport and trust, and flips the normal expectation that outsiders come with answers. This ensures a more comprehensive understanding of social ills among the broader population, cultivates deeper connection between facilitators and stakeholders, and leads to more culturally relevant ideas that are sustainable because they are locally designed with ownership and buy in.

In working with a group in Rwanda to understand its assessment of local poverty, for example, I could have utilized a survey with questions determined by an international institution, such as how much people earn, which might vary daily for subsistence farmers. Instead, I used a tool called "poverty diamonds" developed by Linda Mayoux, an international expert on participatory and gender action learning tools.[1] Now most of us have heard the impoverished described as living at the "bottom of the pyramid," but Mayoux asserts that most communities do not look that way. Instead, they tend toward a diamond, where the bottom point represents a small minority that experience the greatest extreme in their economic circumstances, and where the majority fit within a middle to lower range. Using drawing tools like the poverty diamond, I invited the women to develop their own representation of their community. The drawing looked like figure 6.1.

When I asked them to explain the different strata and stick figure drawings, they said that at the bottom of the diamond were people who were homeless. These included people who voluntarily chose to be homeless

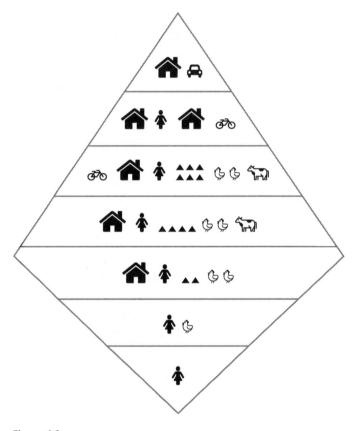

Figure 6.1

rather than go back to their communities and live near the neighbors who murdered their families during the genocide. These people were considered to be living with the greatest need. The second stratum was differentiated by the presence of a chicken. When I asked how much it cost to purchase a chicken, they told me a chick costs approximately $1.50. In their eyes, $1.50 separated the most impoverished in their community and one-level higher of socioeconomic status. The next level included people with one more change of clothing (a triangle representing a dress). As an outsider, I could never have expected this or even designed survey questions to surface this without handing over the reigns to the local community to determine how to represent themselves. These tools involving pictures to establish each grouping, checkmarks to count the number of people from

the village in each category, and arrows to define future goals (by indicat-
ing how many of each grouping might move upward one level) can be
conducted anywhere—even in the dirt with sticks—thereby ensuring any
community with scarce resources and limited education can participate in
its own self-determination.

A complementary theory is human-centered design (HCD), made popu-
lar by the work of IDEO, a nonprofit design and social innovation organization. At every phase of the design process, HCD is driven by empathy and
understanding of those for whom you are designing solutions. It involves
immersion in one's environment to understand local needs as comprehensively as possible, generating ideas, then prototyping, testing, and refining
solutions, and finally seeking ongoing feedback from the end user.

For example, when I was operating in Haiti after the 2010 earthquake, I
was involved in doing trauma-healing work with one particular tent city in
the Bourdon Valley of Pétionville, a community just outside the capital city
of Port-au-Prince. There, we came across a set of new latrines built hastily
by an aid group. When I investigated further, I was shown that the latrines
were built on a relatively remote and dark area of a hillside, without doors
or locks, and with large holes that were risky for small children to fall into.
The women simply did not feel safe using the latrines, and so the toilets
stood there untouched.

HCD would require a deliberate process of engagement with the tent
city inhabitants to incorporate local needs into the ultimate design and an
understanding of how they would use the toilet. After testing and refining, the final product usually eliminates most of the obstacles that arise
with top-down, imposed solutions. This ensures a product's or service's
viability and impact, and in more commercial circumstances, its ultimate
marketability.

The conscious social change methodology complements HCD and the
participatory paradigm in its trust in the value of each individual's contribution to the whole. It uses a learning methodology of direct experience to
draw out local wisdom with compassion and respect for the experience of
others. Diverging from HCD, rather than primarily consulting with local
users, conscious social change acts to support local users in designing their
own solution, such that investment and ownership of the change is held
by the local community. Unlike participatory development theory, and its
focus on taking a hands-off approach, we actively facilitate input from any

and all interests, both from within and outside the larger ecosystem, recognizing that every individual or entity may have a role to play, including
outsiders as partners. The key is using mindfulness to ask *what is needed*,
and work collaboratively to understand how best to support the needs and
vision of the broader group.

In addition to the mindfulness practices shared throughout this book
for cultivating presence, I have included tools that you can utilize to apply
mindfulness to your process of engaging with others within a community,
listening deeply, diffusing conflict, and cultivating compassion that will
help you identify *what is needed* for solving your issue at the end of this
chapter.

Leveraging Assets

In the Byimana Sector of rural Rwanda, just over 60 percent of the female
population is illiterate, lacking the skills to inform women's knowledge
of laws that protect them and their families. Without these skills, these
women are essentially excluded from development and are unable to participate fully in society.

One of Global Grassroots' teams began a social venture to teach almost
thirteen hundred women how to read. They were teaching the women at
night in the primary school where their children attended during the day.
The team knew the women were poor and could not afford to pay a fee. But
the project had no source of income, and after their start-up grants were
spent, they would need to find a way to pay their teachers' salaries on an
ongoing basis.

They engaged the women with a participatory approach to explore their
collective ideas and assets, and used one of our financial sustainability
teachings about leveraging waste. Looking around their community to see
what could be resourced, they saw a lot of unused sticks, rocks, and broken
bricks on the ground—what most would consider useless. So they said to
the women, "We know you can't afford to pay a monetary fee, but instead
we want you to bring a stick, rock, or brick with you when you come to
class as your payment. And if your children go to school here during the
day, have them bring one with them too." After about two weeks, the program had accumulated such a large pile of sticks, rocks, and bricks that
they were able to fill a dump truck, and sell the rocks and bricks as building

supplies to a construction company. Then they bundled the sticks, and the women sold them as firewood kindling locally, earning new resources for teacher salaries.

When I begin my work with a new community of vulnerable women, especially genocide survivors, many of them think they have nothing at all to offer the world. And then we initiate the process of mapping out their internal and external assets. One woman might say, "I have a spoon." Another will chime in, "I have a hoe." "I'm good at telling jokes!" one will add with a giggle. Soon they are accounting for every personal capability, gift, and object they can use. You should see their faces when we complete the exercise, and large sheets of flip chart paper are filled with lists and taped all over the entire room. They never knew they had so much to draw on to create transformation.

Ironically similar, when I work with Western groups, they sit paralyzed with those first few questions I ask them about what they have and what they are good at doing. We don't even think about things like our mobile phones and cars as assets anymore because everyone has them. But as I share the stories about how women are creating change with sticks, rocks, or bricks, their faces light up in recognition of the resources swimming around them.

Once we list all the assets we have from our passions, know-how, capabilities, equipment, spaces, people of influence, and things that have been wasted, we pick a few randomly and brainstorm creative ways to leverage that one asset to solve the issue at hand. I love to ask our Western participants, for example, how they would use a wheelbarrow to fight domestic violence—one of the challenges successfully envisioned by one of our cohorts. They joke about carting away abusive partners in the wheelbarrow or using it to affix messages that can support community awareness. One group of Rwandese women recommended using the wheelbarrow as an alarm system—setting it up next to a house when it is apparent a woman is being beaten and banging on the wheelbarrow with sticks until the violence stops. One venture actually went on to incorporate this method using pots and pans into their domestic violence prevention program.

What might an application of this process look like on a larger scale in the social sector? Well, how might you use soccer balls to solve HIV/AIDS? Sound far-fetched? Consider Grassroots Soccer, an international NGO founded by a professional soccer player and doctor that has used the game of soccer to connect nearly two-million at-risk youth across the global south to the education, resources, and mentors needed to learn about HIV and other health issues. How do you use merry-go-rounds to solve clean water access? The PlayPump is a less successful innovation created by Round-about Water Solutions in South Africa that used the power of kids' play on school merry-go-rounds to operate the water pumps for village wells.

While you can creatively challenge yourself with each individual asset, the truth remains that you are not looking for the single-best asset to engage but rather how, when, and in what way you might use all the relevant assets of the collective community available to you. This is where innovation takes shape, and where the innovators find meaning in leveraging the gifts and capabilities about which they are most passionate.

To explore how to leverage the assets of your team in creating social innovation, use the frameworks and exercises at the end of this chapter for guidance. This process, in conjunction with the tools of mindful social issue diagnosis, target population engagement, and stakeholder analysis that are shared in this book, will contribute to a powerful set of innovative solutions that invite the ownership, partnership, and collaboration of all involved.

As a point of comparison, let us now take a look at what unfolds when a privileged entity uses its power to try to force change without a mindful or participatory approach, as is seen in the case of Johns Hopkins University's expansion into the Middle East community of East Baltimore.

Marisela Gomez and the Save Middle East Action Committee

Gomez speaks with a serene calm and sharp intellect, and exudes the wisdom of a seasoned monk. Born in Belize, a woman of color and daughter of immigrants, Gomez has reached the pinnacle of success, as defined by the dominant culture, despite a childhood of poverty. Her impressive list of academic distinctions includes a master of science from the University of New Mexico along with a doctor of medicine, master of public health, and PhD from the prestigious Johns Hopkins University. Yet this would not be how she would define her success.

In early 2001, while still at Johns Hopkins, Gomez gathered with a group of about a hundred people in a church in the Middle East area of East

Baltimore in response to a massive university development project, which threatened to relocate 750 households by eminent domain. The school's aim was to build a residential area and biotech park across eighty-eight acres just north of its medical campus (Jacobson, 2013). For years, Gomez had watched structural and institutional changes take place across the city dictated by white paternalism that fueled development as well as the abandonment of Baltimore's way of life as a historic black city. She explains that visions for real estate development, urban development, and community development are usually defined by the predominant white lifestyle, and assumed by those who design and implement such projects to be what every person should or does ascribe to. Gomez (interview, January 31, 2017) declares, "Development *is* gentrification, as opposed to gentrification being an outcome of development, when existing residents are not decision makers." The development driven by large corporations and institutions, such as Johns Hopkins, has continued to uphold the inequities of pain and discrimination experienced by its original residents. Gomez observes that in spaces of conflict, disparity, and inequity, people internalize the message that their lives are not acceptable because they are not representative of mainstream US culture. This leaves people feeling isolated, and they turn inward in their suffering. The social cohesion in these environments is not one that brings people together but instead alienates them in their perceived "otherness," affecting their ability to build social capital together (ibid.; Gomez & Muntaner, 2005). When development projects move forward without community engagement, it only exacerbates these disparities and separation.

This time was different. Gomez and her community of one hundred residents sat down to share with and listen to each other. In some cases, this was the first time neighbors were talking with neighbors. People were afraid. Most had first learned about the likelihood of being displaced through the newspaper. Developers were persistent and intimidating, pressuring homeowners to sell their houses at below-market rates (they were initially offered a mere $22,500 for their homes in 2001 during the growing real estate bubble) (Jacobson, 2013). They had no idea where they would go, what they could afford, or how they would handle changes in schools and work without access to public transportation. Their coming together to talk about their pain for the first time was extraordinarily healing and provided the energy that seeded political action.

An organization was created, the Save Middle East Action Committee (SMEAC), which Gomez went on to direct in 2003. It was designed to operate with deep values and intentional protocols to uphold with mindfulness as well as integrity the process of participatory engagement in opposing Johns Hopkins. The organization committed to total honesty, transparency, deep listening, and respect so that it could remain solid in the face of the goliath without falling prey to people's anger. Gomez is clear that if activists do not embody and abide by such inner values, they are at risk of adopting the same divisive and aggressive tactics abused by their counterpoints. Even so, she recognizes that engaging anger is effective. Those who would suggest otherwise may not have spent time on the ground in these environments. Often circumstances have real consequences that may require urgent action fueled by outrage—people will be ousted from their homes, shot by police, or denied opportunity. She does not take a black-and-white, reductionist view that approaches must always appear peaceful. Nevertheless, what is important is that tactics must be driven not by hatred but instead by an ethos of integrity, ethics, compassion, and peace. It is mindfulness that teaches us the discernment that serves to identify the appropriate action in each moment.

SMEAC worked tirelessly to challenge the university's development process and bring local community needs to its attention. They were able to push back, holding up the project until developers agreed to pay market value for properties as well as not demolish houses next door to existing residents until there was adequate mitigation of exposure to lead and other contaminants in the dust. Community members raised public awareness in the media to expose inconsistencies and when developers treated them in ways that were demeaning. Under pressure from SMEAC, the city passed a law that required people to have a third source of affordable housing before being asked to relocate. The group realized it could not halt the entire project, but SMEAC wanted to ensure that the development was carried out as equitably as possible. In the end, the project was implemented and 750 people were displaced (most final relocation packages averaged $250,000), leaving less than 15 residents still remaining (Jacobson, 2013). But the process was conducted differently than it would have been without SMEAC's influence, and as such, SMEAC built substantial social capital that helped to begin to heal long-standing neglect and inequity.

While SMEAC has disbanded, Gomez continues to consult with other local efforts through her organization Social Health Concepts to encourage the process of deep dialogue for healing and community-driven change. She is now working with East Baltimore residents to acquire a church hall and a dozen row houses to start rebuilding the "Beloved Village," a collectively owned, intentional community focused on black and brown people involved in justice and love. It will include incubator spaces, a community event space, and living residences. Gomez (interview, January 31, 2017) states that the project, which invites outside involvement, allows "historic residents to become shareholders and coowners in the redevelopment process, and encourages real access to wealth building. Love in action!"

Four Steps in Applying Mindfulness to Social Change

Conscious social change begins with one intentional breath. From a place of clarity, a change agent can proceed to harness the greatest collective wisdom toward the most powerful and creative good. Revisiting the key questions, tools, and practices of conscious social change, let's look at how a more mindful problem-solving process might evolve for the whole. In using the topic of illegal immigration in the United States, I hope only to provide an example for the *process* of applying a conscious social change approach, and not an expert-level understanding of an intricate and dynamic issue. And then, in considering how conscious social change might manifest in sustainable *outcomes* of transformational change, I will tell you the story of a Global Grassroots venture in Rwanda.

Cultivating Presence: *What Is Happening?*

We begin by applying the same inquiry tools that we used to cultivate presence within ourselves to our work on a societal level. First, we become aware of our present state, inside and out, with curiosity and nonjudgment. We ask *What is happening?* as a means to gauge what is arising within and recognize any charged emotion. With intention, we listen carefully to ourselves and become intimately in tune with our three centers, or whole self. We breathe into the present moment, and by so doing, tap into our own wisdom to inform our work with others.

Next, in the same way we looked internally, we ask *What is happening?* as we examine our social issue. This is the step of simply noticing reality as it is. With equal devotion as that which we hold for our personal practice, we can deliberately apply a mindful lens to both the complexity of the issue itself and dynamics playing out around it. We bring intention to how we listen to our community with openness and curiosity. We become aware of any fear or thought patterns that might distract us, and try to set those aside. We identify who has a stake in the issue, and notice the actions, emotional intensity, beliefs, and messages of those who are vocal as well as those who go unheard. We notice the role that fear and opinion play. As we inquire, we strive for a deep understanding of the stresses, suffering, needs, and resistance around the issue. Now let us explore the application of this approach to the issue of illegal immigration in the United States.

Increasingly, Americans are concerned about the numbers of immigrants who have illegally entered and remain in this country—currently estimated at eleven million. Much of the apprehension stems from a fear that these immigrants may be terrorists, will take jobs that would otherwise employ US citizens, and are bringing drugs and crime into the country. Conventional change, which posits immigrants as the threatening other, is driven by the US voices of self-interest and frequently prioritizes punitive measures to address the concern. These might include enforcing borders to prevent illegal immigration, changing immigration policy to limit entry among those of certain characteristics or nationalities deemed a high risk, and identifying and deporting existing illegals. While this approach does have a concrete impact on the people entering and living in our country, it is also important to recognize that a narrow focus on ridding our country of unauthorized immigrants may not get at the underlying drivers of terrorism, crime, and economic well-being that motivate these policies. Furthermore, solutions that address primarily the symptomatic level or are imposed without broad vetting may have a range of other unintended consequences as well as inefficiencies that may not immediately be seen without a more mindful inquiry.

What would it look like if we were to engage in a process of conscious social change? We begin by letting our capacity for presence help us notice the larger dynamics surrounding the issue, asking *What is happening?* At the surface we observe an intense level of strong opinion, polarization, fear, and resentment. And as the arguments grow more heated, so too does the perception of sides. We must also identify the deeper emotions that are present and fueling action, including outrage, mistrust, or victimization at the hands of an other. This may exist among residents fearing foreign-born migrants and illegal aliens fearing law enforcement. Other dynamics we may notice include xenophobia, a sense of entitlement, and racism as well as pleas for compassion, generosity and acceptance. With presence, we must check ourselves for similar feelings when and if they come up within us, so they do not become unconscious drivers of action or judgment. Gaining insight into our own resistance or leanings allows us to better understand as well as see through the reactivity we hear from other stakeholders.

Right behind the emotional stances and polarization lie a swarm of arguments along with their supporting evidence. This too must be noticed as a means to understand the emotional investments across the spectrum, facts, and assumptions they rely on as well as to help identify other stakeholders. And so we go deeper in our noticing, engaging specific voices and exploring *what is really happening* from a desire to understand the direct human experience. We extend our inquiry to a representative sample of all parties impacted by the issue, or interested or influential in it. This might include a town hall–style meeting within a border community or series of consultations with a broad range of actors. With mindfulness, we listen, reflect, and inquire.

Why do illegal immigrants come to and stay in the United States? What is happening in schools, and with social services and law enforcement, as pertains to illegal immigrants? What is it like to get deported, or live in constant fear of being deported? What are illegal immigrants leaving behind? Who profits off illegal aliens? Who employs them? Who is being taken advantage of by them? What are we afraid of? What violence and discrimination is embedded in the broader system? What values do we hold sacred in the United States, and are these changing? What have been the costs and trade-offs of any given action? As we begin to map out the complex reality with nonjudgment, we avoid any inclination to seek proof for one perspective or another, and employ a willingness to hear all views. Soliciting direct input from the broadest set of voices in answering these questions helps us to understand the entire system and get a better idea of the roots of the social issue. It also allows us to identify the priority needs and values of each stakeholder group. Insights this process may reveal could include that we are facing threats and want to be able to control them; we want to know if our laws are fair, humane, and sensible; and how we define who we are as a nation as well as our obligations to our citizens and the larger world may be changing.

In addition to being present to the emotional intensity, underlying opinions, and stakeholder dynamics, we ensure we are aware of the known facts behind the issue. We explore data about the flows of immigrants, demographics of crime, and trends in employment. We look at the source of terrorist activity and impact of security measures. We investigate the rationale for and effectiveness of existing policies—both opposing immigration and offering a pathway to citizenship—and seek feedback from all sides. We look at the burden on our social services, health, law enforcement, justice and education systems along with the economic contributions of immigrants, and cost of slowing or eliminating settlement. We look at the global undercurrents driving immigration and consider our underlying values that define us as a nation. All before any such action is determined.

Finally, we take into our awareness the proposed solutions, whether they are posited from the halls of government or bandied about in social media circles. Are ideas coming from a place of fear and reactivity, or human connection, understanding and compassion? What best practices exist from other societies? What can we perceive in the arguments of others? As always, we practice noticing what is arising, continue to examine our own emotional response and use our insights to better understand what we witness in others. Once we have an awareness of the broad complexity of reality, we seek to go deeper to understand what is really true.

Becoming Whole: *What Is True?*

Next, as we explored in becoming whole on a personal level, we now ask *What is true?* on an organizational and societal level. As we have invested in our own wholeness, we are increasingly aware of and can detach from our own fears, shadows, and biases when they arise. In looking outward to our broader society, we now similarly examine and separate (if not heal) what is generated by our own collective fears and unconscious material from what is real at the roots of the issue. In this step, we go beyond noticing to *discern*.

We start by asking *What is true?* from a place of nonjudgment to ascertain what is taking place unconsciously beneath stakeholder dynamics. Have passionate arguments been put forth relying more on emotion and false assumptions than facts? Have our prejudices colored our perception of reality? What shadows are present, and how are we resisting or grasping at certain changes? Has fear been used to justify a stance or unify one subset of the population against another? What really concerns us? Are we reactive because we are afraid of losing our culture? Are we resistant because we feel our long-standing values are being altered? Are we suspicious of those who don't look, live, or worship like us? Do we condemn others' concerns without seeking deeper insight? By daring to look at ourselves honestly, we can both better understand the greater human resistance and correct toward truth. We can intentionally find ways to connect more deeply with others as well as forge understanding. And by conducting these analyses through diverse community dialogue, we can humanize the experience of immigration and its impact on all parties.

As we gather information, we question what we hear and put it to the test to discern truth. We engage all vested parties in building a deeper, collective, and comprehensive understanding of *what is true* at the roots of the issue. We operate with open curiosity, not agenda. We use tools for deep listening, conflict resolution, mindful issue diagnosis, and stakeholder analysis (included at the end of this chapter) to ask why again, and again to diagnose the underlying issues comprehensively and try to ensure all parties are listening to each other to optimize learning.

For example, we might explore, What is the real financial liability of illegal immigration? How much will greater law enforcement cost, and what is the unintentional impact? What is the real link between illegal immigrants and terrorist acts? What industries are truly stressed by undocumented workers, and which ones benefit from diversity in their ranks? What is really true at the multifaceted roots of terrorism, drugs, human trafficking, economic trends, and crime? What are the actual motivators driving immigration and its opposition, and what are the human costs to all?

As we engage a diverse range of voices in this exploration, we can then surface ideas and work towards a common vision that will inform a comprehensive, holistic solution. Without confrontation or an agenda of "winning," we can work toward a more objective truth. Though it may be difficult to get an invested party to loosen its grip on a defining argument solely on counterfactual evidence, doing so from a place of mindful facilitation that builds human understanding, defines common ground, honors what is at stake for all parties, and surfaces diverse ideas is perhaps the best chance. By humanizing each of the positions, from an illegal immigrant's hopes to a local police officer's sense of duty, to a state legislator's need to justify spending, sharing real stories emphasizes people over ideology. Suddenly, we move one step closer to experiencing ourselves as part of one ecosystem. And though it may make our perception of the issue exponentially more complex, we want our understanding of the system to be as large and complete as possible. Getting closer to truth means seeking out each voice, encouraging its story, and celebrating its contribution. This drives collaboration, cocreation and innovation. This is problem solving, not ideological warfare.

Ensuring Well-being: *What Is Needed?*

Next we shift from gaining insight toward solutions building. Here we ask our communities, *What is needed?* as we design an intervention that is multifaceted for systemic transformation, works at a root level, involves deeper human understanding, leverages stakeholder strengths, and stays attuned and flexible as needs shift.

What is needed? In order for the community to best deal with such a polarizing issue, perhaps the initial steps toward a solution might include a discharging of the political debate surrounding the subject. Let's encourage a less incendiary level of discourse. Let's scale back the accusations and blame, and unify against all manifestations of harm, from terrorist propaganda to acts of violence against those perceived to be foreign immigrants. This requires mindful leadership. This requires courage. In order for any solution to have a fair chance, calmness, awareness, and compassion are critical. These qualities can be cultivated intentionally through our two previous steps of engaging mindfully in our own internal inquiry and the way we honor the human experience of the parties involved in the issue. By engaging a wide spectrum of stakeholders, and finding avenues through which they can cross-connect and be heard, we might further create an atmosphere where position statements become less volatile. By looking at the issue from many different perspectives, and putting a face and human experience to each one, we have done the best we can to build a shared view of illegal immigration. We have also facilitated an orientation toward problem solving that prioritizes human experience over attachment to one's argument or political stance.

Moving forward, active engagement and connection with each voice within the issue will generate a more comprehensive list of *what is needed* in a solution. *What is needed* to ensure the rights and safety of all people legitimately within our boundaries? *What is needed* to guarantee enforcement is maximally effective while managing its expense? *What is needed* to safeguard the legal path to citizenship along with the treatment of the unauthorized fairly, securely, and efficiently? *What is needed* to ensure our solution is humane, devoid of racial, ethnic, or religious discrimination, and implemented mindfully? And what do specific stakeholder groups say they need? How do we embody the ideals of freedom and celebrate diversity? Across the spectrum of interests in the issue of illegal immigration, this list of needs may be long, complex, and at first, potentially feel impossible to accommodate. But it will also provide insights that may have gone unnoticed, and as such, may have inadvertently fueled resistance or enduring aspects of the problem.

This is also a time to look closely again at the causes of the issue unearthed in our last step, as understanding the roots (and the roots of the roots) of the entire system may inform new, more effective places and ways to intervene. We must look at the parts of the whole, examine every contributing factor to the issue, and see who is involved at each point. We can then entertain creative combinations of partners, resources, and actions. How might illegal immigrants actually work with law enforcement in combating terrorism or reducing crime? How might a legal pathway to citizenship be cost-effective *and* contribute toward a social benefit? Rather than blaming and demonizing all outsiders, and instead of obstructing opposing views to win with our agenda, we work from a place of greater unity to identify the core concerns we all agree on one by one. We examine the costs and benefits of each choice, consulting broadly for ideas and feedback on needs before beginning our design. This allows ownership for more sustainable innovation.

And just as we mindful change agents are aware of our own mental, emotional, and physical health within a stressful as well as taxing environment, so too are we attentive to the health of the collaborative process as we facilitate toward a viable solution. We carefully watch for emotional charge. We maintain the atmosphere that embraces collaboration and compromise, guarding against polarization. Should signs of stress emerge from the process, we tend to our community's health by doing the same as we would for ourselves in the face of occupational burnout. Perhaps scheduled breaks from the process for solitude and reflection are needed. Or maybe a collective practice or renewed investment in fifty-fifty awareness can rejuvenate the effort. Regardless of whether it is for you as a change agent or whole community working toward systemic change, self-care and well-being remains a priority.

Engage Mindfully: *What Is Helpful?*

Finally, to build our solution, our new key question is, *What is helpful?* What is going to work? At which level of this complex issue can we intervene? Rather than imposing one narrow agenda as "right," or using sticks and carrots to compel people to change, we identify and leverage the unique offerings as well as insights of each party to form the optimal solution. We design interventions informed by each perspective, mindful to avoid the dynamic of us versus them or fighting for a majority stake. We realize it is the sharing of power along with distributed ownership and investment that helps ensure a lasting solution. Now we can work toward a synergistic solution that does the most sustainable good for the most people. Stakeholders work not as competitors but rather as cooperatives, proposing solutions while providing checks and insights as the process unfolds.

Returning to the exploration of illegal immigration, by consulting with various interests, we source ideas and participation from those most deeply impacted. Building on our understanding of the motivators for immigration, needs of stakeholders, and impact of immigration, we create nuanced programs targeted at certain circumstances, not just one blanket program without concern for the human impact. Instead of relying on the established power structure, how might we allow parties to help themselves or each other? By working against fear and fostering common ground, communities may be more willing to participate in solutions rather than oppose immigration or other policies outright, ultimately serving as networks of greater oversight and support. From here we transform not only the underlying issue of immigration, security, crime, and economic well-being but also the way we see ourselves and each other as one nation, united in a vision for liberty and prosperity.

Mindfulness can be employed in all phases of the process of social solutions design, though it is impossible to predict exactly what conscious social change will look like after its methods are applied. The solution will always depend on the needs, ideas, insights, and wisdom of each individual concern within the group using this method. Conscious social change is not defined by outcome but instead by process. Our obligation is to be aware of truth, inside and out, and follow where compassion, inclusivity, and wisdom lead. The companion Toolkit for Conscious Social Change (www.conscioussocialchange.org) offers an expanded set of tools for designing a solution with mindfulness so that you can maximize the effectiveness and sustainability of your particular program model.

Conscious activist and author Jay Early (2008) states, "If we truly want social justice in the world, it is not enough to work for the kinds of changes in social, political, and economic structures that are usually pursued by social justice activists. We need a more fundamental transformation of our entire society." Change at a systemic level requires integrating consciousness from individual action through social innovation to structural transformation. We are committed to alleviating the underlying issues and putting ourselves out of business. Conscious social change creates space for the most effective and innovative ideas to move forward, which in turn are more likely to be sustainable because of their informed, inclusive, responsive, and creative nature.

It is hard to know the extent of what might be possible in the realm of immigration until a more compassionate, inclusive, and conscious inquiry is undertaken within community using the key questions along with the tools I have explored in this book. But let me share the potential outcomes of a conscious social change approach used in international development by looking at one success story from Global Grassroots' programs in Rwanda.

One of the first communities I visit the year after implementing Global Grassroots' initial pilot program is the rural village of Gahanga on the outskirts of the capital city of Kigali, Rwanda. Gahanga is a mountainous town, where small mud-brick huts pepper the hillside sloping away from either side of a central roadway. A small marketplace of rickety wooden tables situated under hastily constructed scaffolding provides shade and signifies the center of the community. Here we turn off the main highway. A short drive down a dirt road, ruts cutting veins into the terra-cotta dust, sits a tiny church. Tucked into the small piece of shade lingering alongside the building gather a group of squinting, grinning women, bedecked in multicolored Dutch wax print skirts and matching head wraps. They greet us with embracing slaps to both shoulders or a hearty forearm grasp, and I try to connect with my limited Kinyarwanda, *"Muraho! Amakuru?"* Laughing at my poor attempts to communicate, they reply, *"Ni meza!"*

We have come to Gahanga via a referral from the pastor whose association of widows we last supported in order to understand the needs of this community. I am interested in finding the most vulnerable teams of women who have ideas for social change, especially solutions that eliminate violence as well as advance opportunity for women and girls. We assemble on grass mats and rickety benches to learn more about the women's priorities. These women are mostly subsistence farmers, some widows and single mothers, all living below the poverty level, and mostly uneducated. To our knowledge, they have never been consulted about their needs, and certainly not their solutions to those needs. As I connect with this community, I bring myself to a state of calm awareness, guided by the question, *What is happening?*

The women come to tell us on this first visit that they want to address the issue of sexual exploitation. I ask them to elaborate about it, employing our mindfulness-based deep listening techniques. They explain that women have no water source near their homes, so they must make a three- or four-mile journey round trip down the hillside to collect water at a contaminated, hand-dug well. They can usually only carry one five-gallon jerrican. This is the water that they need daily for their entire household, which might include between four and eight people. This water is used for drinking, cooking, cleaning the house, laundry, bathing, and washing dishes. Sometimes the children are required to bring water with them to school for drinking and handwashing.

I'm astonished by how far a single household must stretch its usage of water. Compare this to the nearly 70 gallons of water used in per person per day in the United States (including 11.6 gallons for a shower, 15 gallons for clothes washing, and 18.5 gallons for flushing toilets) (American Water Works Association, 2010). In 2015, there were still 663 million people who had no access to safe water, nearly half of whom live in sub-Saharan Africa (UNICEF & World Health Organization, 2015). Women remain those most often tasked with daily collection. According to the United Nations, on average women in sub-Saharan Africa travel close to four miles every day, collecting water and then hand carrying it to their homes (United Nations Human Rights, UN Habitat, & World Health Organization, 2010). But I'm not clear about the connection to sexual exploitation. I inquire further.

The women explain that many of those who were left physically disabled by the war, and those who are elderly, blind, pregnant, or HIV positive, are too weak to make this journey. In this area, a service has sprung up where local men will deliver water on bicycles for a fee, as women do not normally ride bicycles. But if a woman cannot afford to pay the fee, as one woman told us, "Your children are coming home from school for lunch, and you have no water to cook them rice and beans. ... And so, you do what you have to do." They explain that many women end up being pressured to exchange sex for water delivery daily, just to feed their children.

I am horrified, and would never have anticipated this dark side of water collection. I feel myself react, outrage simmering beneath my intent to be present and curious. I recognize my first instinct is to fix it; I want to offer to build them a private well. This is exactly what so many well-intentioned development efforts do. With a pause, I also realize that if I had led this convening by offering a solution without asking about their priorities, I would have missed the hidden issues like sexual exploitation. Perhaps they would have gratefully said yes, and then we could have built that well and inadvertently handed over operational control to the (mostly men in) leadership who might be less likely to protect the needs of the vulnerable, and might not even know about the issues the women are facing. Instead, Global Grassroots' method is to employ the skills of mindfulness and deep listening to support those most deeply affected by the issue in defining how *they* want to initiate change.

We invite this group of nineteen women from Gahanga, who have self-organized into a team they call *Abanyamurava* or "Hard Workers," into our 2007 cohort at our Academy for Conscious Change. In the post-conflict communities of Rwanda and Uganda, Global Grassroots goes in search of teams of women like this one that have ideas for social change. We target women who are undereducated, impoverished, and survivors of violence. They have borne the greatest burden of war and conflict, but are still the caretakers of their community. Unfortunately, they are also those with the least access to the training, resources, and opportunities to advance the changes they know are needed to improve their lives. As we did with this team in Gahanga, we visit their villages, and ask them to share their greatest issues and proposed solutions, and then we invite them to apply to attend our academy. The two-year, experiential program incorporates mindfulness-based leadership skills and a social venture incubator to facilitate teams in designing as well as launching mindful organizations benefiting other women and girls. Our training integrates the following:

- Mind-body trauma healing to ensure that all change agents have the opportunity to attend to their own rehabilitation needs before working toward societal change.
- Personal transformation and mindfulness practices, many of which are shared here, that support change agents in developing as self-aware, compassionate leaders who understand change from the inside out.
- The nuts-and-bolts social entrepreneurship skills and seed funding needed to design and initiate a sustainable micro-NGO or nonprofit from scratch in their own communities.

In every interaction with our change agents, we try to employ our own techniques, seeking to model and embody our philosophy of deep listening, nonjudgment, and participatory methods of issue diagnosis as well as design that support self-determination. The women decide their issue, determine their solution, design their organization, and implement their idea in their own community.

During our training, we work with Hard Workers to examine *what is true* about the complex intersection of women, water, and violence. Global Grassroots offers specific tools to facilitate this process of mapping the roots and developing a complete understanding of the system behind an issue. We share frameworks for analysis, innovation and planning, including the ones at the end of this chapter, and facilitate their use in developing a comprehensive venture plan through our experiential process in the classroom. Then we encourage our teams to take these same exercises back to their larger groups and community to engage as many parties as possible in completing their research. This supports teams in understanding change from a more inclusive perspective rather than impulsively blaming an external party.

As they go deeper in their analysis of the roots of the issue, I learn even more. It becomes clear that lack of access to clean water is one of the most critical obstacles facing a girl's education, a woman's economic opportunity, and the ability to live violence free, and that this venture team wants to address all three concerns through their intervention.

According to the World Health Organization and UNICEF's (2010) Joint Monitoring Program for Water Supply and Sanitation, girls under fifteen years are twice as likely as boys the same age to be given the responsibility to collect water. Girls who are tasked with the collection of water in place of their mothers miss part of their school day. Moreover, children who do not have water to bring to school when required may not be allowed to attend that day. Overtime, they can fall behind and eventually drop out.

Women who manage this task for their family give up hours of productivity that might have been spent other ways to enhance a family's economic well-being. Decreased economic power means women are less able to seek independence to protect themselves from abusive relationships. Water collection thus continues to perpetuate the vulnerability of women, undermining the economic and educational opportunities that may exist to advance their well-being.

In addition to the disease and poor hygiene associated with poor water access, even more unfortunate is the violence inherent in the process of collection. Because it takes so many hours to reach and return with water, many women leave before dawn and travel in the dark to get to a natural water source early. Some locations serve hundreds of surrounding households. Arriving early means that they are more likely to collect clear water from shallow creeks or hand-dug wells before it gets muddied with dozens of others coming for collection. Traveling alone through the dark, however, also leaves women more susceptible to sexual assault and contracting HIV. On the other hand, returning later than expected from collecting water is often a trigger for domestic violence as husbands await their morning tea or bath.

In Global Grassroots' trainings, we teach as well as embody how to employ mindfulness, deep listening, and community engagement not only in the process of understanding a particular issue but also in determining the solution. A consciousness-based process facilitates the community in developing a vision, determining the mission of its work, deciding its particular intervention and program model, distilling the theory of change that describes why its solution will work, deciding what outcomes it anticipates, and defining how to measure if it is successful in creating real transformation.

Global Grassroots also believes strongly in our role as a facilitator. When we walk into a classroom, we are mindful of the dominant power structure and our presumed position of authority with respect to our participants. As such, we are careful not to impose our social issue priorities or solutions.

We do not want any input from us to sway our women to discard their own insights or ideas. In interacting with our participants, we frequently use a process we call *inquiry without imposition*, with an overarching goal of catalyzing self-sufficiency. This means we utilize a form of dialogue to ask probing questions, facilitate learning, and invite reflection. It is designed to support a team's agency in coming to its own creative solutions rather than telling participants our answers. We offer design frameworks and help coach each team as it takes these tools to its community to complete its social issue diagnosis, the crafting of its solution, and its organization's development. And we use our inquiry process to help teams address their own weaknesses to mitigate risk and ensure long-term viability.

In 2008, after a year of our training, venture development coaching, and an initial $2,600 grant, Hard Workers launched its own nonprofit water solution. It installed gutters on its community church, which fed a new water storage tank. It collected and purified rainwater from the roof during the rainy season. In the dry season, it paid for clean water to be delivered by truck from the city. For pennies per jerrican, Hard Workers began by supplying a hundred households with fresh, clean water daily. The revenue generated from those who can afford to pay ensures the most vulnerable, including the blind, pregnant, disabled, and elderly, always have water for free. The organization's focus is not just on ending sexual exploitation for water but also educating about hygiene, assuring the elimination of water-borne disease, protecting girls' ability to attend school, and creating new opportunities for women.

Hard Workers is organized as a nonprofit or locally registered Rwandan NGO, so it must reinvest any profits into creating additional social value. After it determined it could operate its water enterprise sustainably, Hard Workers decided to use its profits to pay orphan school fees as well as provide annual health insurance for vulnerable women and their families. Soon it was able to set aside enough to start a small revolving loan fund, so it could offer microloans to the women with greatest need to start a business. Once a woman repays the loan, they loan it out again to another woman. From here, Hard Workers was able to spin off a community garden and establish a brick-making venture. Women from as far as three hours away soon traveled to visit the team to see how it was able to initiate this kind of project alone as uneducated, subsistence farmers. So the team started teaching others the skills it learned from us.

As the venture began to facilitate so much positive change in the community, local men also stepped up to help with the project. The women, some of whom were in their late seventies, normally sleep side by side on the ground next to their water tanks at night to prevent theft. Increasingly, when a team member would fall ill, her husband would offer to take the night shifts instead. Hard Workers, perhaps without intending it, has helped to improve gender relations by initiating a well-respected, women-run program that benefits everyone. In an environment where shared domestic labor between men and women is relatively rare, the wide gap in voice, power, and leadership in the community has started to narrow.

Since its launch in 2008, Hard Workers continues to operate sustainably as a social-purpose nonprofit. It has expanded to two other sites, and by its own estimate, serves nine thousand people, providing safe water for families and protecting even more women from sexual exploitation. Project leader Seraphine Hacimana has spoken on the radio about water issues, was invited to Kenya to share the methods of the team's venture, and was recognized by local officials as an example of women serving other women in the community. The local water municipality, WASAC, which is trying to expand rural water access through its pipelines, now regularly consults the team about local water needs and is interested in continuing to collaborate with it as a local nonprofit.

In 2009, Global Grassroots was selected as a semifinalist for the Kyoto World Water Grand Prize for our model of catalyzing grassroots-level, women-led social ventures, based on a case study of Hard Workers. And in 2015, we began a partnership with the Coca-Cola Africa Foundations' Replenish Africa Initiative to expand our training of and investment in women-led water enterprises to serve another thirty thousand people across Rwanda through the partnership's first cohort.

But most remarkable of all in this work are the women themselves. Of Hard Workers' original nineteen members, only seven are actually literate. And Seraphine, a mother of eight children in her forties, has only a first-grade education. Hard Workers is now seen as the first organization to bring development to its village community.

Again, if we had defined what was needed and imposed our own vision for success, we would have undermined the wisdom, creativity, and capacity of these women to lead with their own multidimensional solution. Think of all the ripples of impact we would have missed that only local women, empowered by their personal unique contributions, could imagine.

Instead, we held back our own agenda. We asked questions as opposed to making assumptions. We had to set aside our own schedules for implementation and patiently collaborate in the ways the women needed most as they drove the pace. Rather than remaining attached to our ideal solution, we made room for new information, mistakes, learning, and innovation. And things did not turn out the way we expected. They turned out better. Conscious social change and effective solution building is driven from within the community itself. But it begins within each individual. It requires self-awareness, letting go of ego, patience, flexibility, compassion, and deep listening—all skills that are fostered through mindfulness.

We employ the same conscious social change methodology when Global Grassroots evaluates and improves our own programs. For instance, over time we learned that we should ask the participants themselves what goals they wanted to see as outcomes of our work, and how we should be measuring those outcomes, rather than using our own misinformed as well as biased goals and metrics. So we set up a local advisory council composed of our beneficiaries to seek their advice. To date, our advisory council has helped us set the goals for our program, identify appropriate metrics to evaluate impact, and design culturally appropriate methods for conducting assessments. It regularly contributes when we evaluate the process and content of our programs.

We discovered that the goals we had for our change agents were not necessarily what they would want to experience as a result of our programs, or the way they would measure those changes. We had been looking, for example, to explore changes in economic well-being among our graduates. But despite our encouragement, in many cases the teams had no need for the venture to drive improvements in personal economic well-being and were satisfied conducting their work as volunteers. Some paid their team members a daily wage for work conducted, but rarely were team members salaried employees of their nonprofits, notwithstanding our encouragement to make their organization their livelihood. Instead, they proudly named themselves *Abitangira Abandi*, which literally means "people who sacrifice themselves for others."[2]

Surprisingly, our advisory council described seeing economic well-being improve in other ways. It was important to council members that they had enough money for health insurance and their kids' school fees. Then they explained indirect economic benefits as a more likely outcome of their work with Global Grassroots. There is the example of Médiatrice Mushimiyimana, a teacher who led another Global Grassroots venture in the rural village of Bryimana, Rwanda, called Think about the Young Girls. A team of teachers designed an intervention to build safe, same-sex latrines for girls to end the harassment and assault they had been experiencing in the crumbling, unsafe, shared toilets at school—something that had significantly affected their academic performance. In the first year after building new latrines as well as implementing a sex education and antibullying program, the passing rate of girls at Byimana Primary School on the national exam soared from less than 15 percent to 76 percent, and then advanced to more than 87 percent the following year. While Médiatrice was not compensated by her venture for her leadership or program delivery, she was promoted not long after to head mistress of a neighboring school—a promotion she credits to the leadership role she played in implementing Think about the Young Girls, and one that came with additional responsibility *and* economic benefit.

Seraphine and Hard Workers exemplify the work of change agents that are inner driven and other focused. They are working at the root and systemic levels to get at the complex intersection of clean water access and gender-based violence. They are leveraging the unique assets of their collective, particularly their water access point and its revenue, to stay attuned to and innovatively address the needs of their community. They have avoided divisive tactics that blame others and misuse privilege to advance an agenda. Instead, they bring self-awareness, a sense of purpose, and mindfulness to the way they continue to engage their community while advancing the lives of the most vulnerable.

If you were to visit Gahanga and glance at Seraphine's life, you would not consider her to have achieved success in terms defined by the dominant culture. She still lives in a small hut with dirt floors with her husband and eight children. She is still a subsistence farmer and doesn't make much more money than she did before she started Hard Workers. But if you speak with her, you will hear her passionate commitment to protecting women from sexual exploitation for water, and will recognize the confidence and demeanor of a community leader.

Seraphine will tell you, "We are not rich because of what we have in our pockets but because of believing, trusting, even having consciousness. ... Consciousness helps us in leaving behind all of our challenges and even all the problems." When we asked those in Hard Workers if they wanted to pay themselves a salary, they said, "No, we are *Abitangira Abandi* and our project is nonprofit. We even give people water to drink for free." If you ask Seraphine what she gets out of this work, she will tell you, "Those blind people, even though they cannot see those of us who have started these activities, they are joyous. Although they don't see you, they say thank you very much, you are good people, you are blessed people."

At Global Grassroots, at the end of the day, we embrace the potency of local initiation and ownership in and of itself, and its power for individual and community transformation, even if implementation may not always be what we envisioned. We honor the women, recognizing that even to be willing to advance social change and human rights in their communities is often a courageous, radical act. We believe in learning by doing. We acknowledge the remarkable wisdom, resourcefulness, and creativity in problem solving among local communities. And we recognize there is usually more for us to learn than for us to teach.

Practices

Cultivating Presence
Deep Listening and Inquiry without Imposition Listening compassionately is the first offering we can provide. Being fully present with the other, breathing deeply, and mirroring their breathing as you consciously slow down your breath rate can help any individual who is experiencing anxiety begin to relax. Sometimes we feel compelled to fix the other, yet we must recognize it is not always our job to alleviate all the suffering of those around us, as much as we may want to. Sometimes simply being present is enough. And it demonstrates to the other that their just being there and showing up, however they are, is also enough.

In listening to individuals who may be seeking your counsel, there are levels of engagement to consider that can help an individual expand their agency and come to their own conclusion—a more empowering and mindful approach than simply giving your advice outright. I extend my gratitude to Jessica Dibb of the Inspiration Community for her teachings on therapeutic facilitation, which I have adapted for use in a conscious social change model:

Mirroring: Repeat back what the person has said word for word, thereby helping someone feel heard. So if they say, "I feel totally lost right now and I don't know what to do." You respond, "So you're feeling really lost right now and you don't know what to do?" It may feel strange to you to repeat their exact words, but the other individual will feel heard and thus encouraged to continue.

Furthering inquiry: If they feel stuck, you can use open questions that enable them to speak further about the circumstances. You might ask, "Is there more?" or "Can you tell me more about that?" Again, this allows the person to feel your presence with them, but does not require you to provide advice or counsel. You can ask, "How does that make you feel?" or "How are you feeling about that right now?" You can also ask how they feel in their body—a technique to help them slow down and focus on the present.

Among a group, you can inquire in the same way: Can you elaborate? Can you tell me more about that issue? What else? Why is that the case? How is your community feeling about the nature of this issue?

Inviting questions: These questions are more targeted and are meant to help the individual move beyond the story and shift to a more constructive problem-solving process to reach their own conclusion. You can ask, "What does it feel like needs to happen now?" "What do you really want?" "What do you feel would help at this moment?" "Have you thought about how to handle the situation?" "Do you have others who can help you think through this?" "What do you know to be true?" Again, you do not have to provide your opinion or a solution. It may be enough that someone has had a chance to speak what they have been keeping inside. Their words may come with emotion that you can be present for without having to do anything specific. Telling people it will be OK is not always the right thing, as it can be patronizing and may not acknowledge their reality.

In a larger collective, you can ask, What have you considered might need to happen next? What else do you need to know that could help us really understand this challenge? What might success look like? What do you think your community really needs? Why do you think this has happened? Where might we go from here? Where are you seeing common ground?

Validation and affirmations: If they answer any of the questions above, you can repeat their response in a form of an affirmation or validation. If they say, "I think I need to drop out of this course." You can say, "So you feel like you need to drop out of this course." Or they may say, "I need to know my husband loves me." You can say, "Of course you do. You need to know your husband loves you. You are lovable, Jean." Again, you are not providing them with advice but rather supporting their own capacity to access their own wisdom. Of course, if they say something like, "I just don't think I'm good enough." You can counter with "I understand you feel you're not good enough, but trust me you are good enough. I have seen your capacity to lead others," or something that can support their connection to their own strengths. Be certain not to just say anything positive but instead to respond with an authentic recognition of who they are and their qualities.

In a community environment, you can honor the impact of the situation, express your acknowledgment of the experiences of all participants, restate the diverging views or common ground, affirm their feelings, and validate what they are discovering by going through this intentional process as a facilitator or fellow stakeholder.

Advice: They may simply want your advice. Be certain never to lead with your advice, especially if it is not solicited. In some cases, asking for your advice may also be a giving up of one's own power to an authority. So you may need to lean into what is happening to recognize whether they want you to solve the problem for them. You may need to say, "I just don't feel qualified to know what is best," or "Only you know what you truly need." In other cases, someone may be in danger or at risk, and you may feel you can reasonably offer advice that will protect them. (Sometimes withholding advice could be neglectful. Use presence and mindfulness to know how best to respond in each circumstance.)

In a group, rather than offer advice outright, you can ask people what might be most helpful, or "How can I best support you?" You can propose how you might think about an issue, offering a framework or suggesting a next step, then turn over the analysis and conclusion to the group again: "Here's how I might look at it," "Would you like to explore this or that next?" or "One thing I think I could offer is _____. Would that be helpful?" Each time, you are allowing the team or group to make the final call, which supports its agency, ownership, and leadership.

In this form of questioning and deep listening, the least intrusive form is more supportive of self-empowerment. So try to stay with the mirroring step above and only move up the ladder to advice as absolutely necessary.

Conscious Conflict Resolution One of the skills that will serve us in our work as conscious social change leaders is the ability to listen not just to ourselves but to others too, including opposing voices. So much conflict is caused by a lack of understanding, unwillingness to listen to the other, and our own need to be right. We spend much of our time thinking of what we want to say rather than being present and hearing what our opponent is saying. Or we try to convince the other of blame instead of solving problems together. Mindfulness of ourselves as well as others will help us not only with any opposition we may face in our change work but also in communicating better with our colleagues or beneficiaries. In addition, it is likely that if we are working on the root causes to suffering, working against the dominate power structure and beliefs, and changing systems that may cause change to the people who depend on those systems for their own power, we will face opposition or resistance. This is the first step of working with conflict nonviolently. I extend my gratitude to our former staff member Jamie Persons as well as Harville Hendrix's Imago Dialogue model of active listening, which influenced this approach.

Previously, I discussed ways to notice an emotional charge and practice a method for avoiding reactivity to ensure the wisest response:

- Recognize an emotional charge in yourself or another.
- Stop and take three breaths.
- Listen and be curious. Go within and notice if there is something that upset you that is unrelated to the other person—a fear, wound, assumption, attachment/aversion, and so on.
- Respond wisely and consciously.

The more that you practice this process, the less slow and awkward it will feel, and the more quickly you will be able to scan your own intentions and develop a wise response. If we can control our own urge to react, then we have eliminated half the conflict. Now for the other half of the conflict …

So what is a wise, conscious, and nonviolent response to conflict? After you pause and breathe, utilize the following next steps, drawn from the path of conscious social change:

Listen and share respectfully: This aligns with the path of conscious change in our willingness to be mindful and present to look deeply and listen. Listening to the other point of view does not mean you agree with it or the person's actions. It gives that person space to explain their perspective and feel acknowledged. Much of conflict comes from not feeling seen and heard. First, make sure that each person involved in the disagreement has the opportunity to share their perspective respectfully and explain what they feel in regard to the conflict, without the other ones trying to argue or defend their position. During each person's turn to explain, they should do the following:

- Name the problem/behavior and its impact, using specific, fact-based examples to illustrate the situation.
- Describe personal emotions about the issue, using "I" statements, not "you" blaming statements (e.g., "I felt disrespected" versus "You disrespect me").

Example: "I felt frustrated and disrespected when you arrived two hours late for our scheduled meeting today."

Clarify to see clearly and understand: After both people have shared their "side" of the conflict, ask questions if you need clarification. This is important so that both sides can fully understand the root causes of the issue. By seeing the conflict from the other person's perspective, we are also able to be empathetic as well as more aware of how our words and actions affect others. This aligns with our commitment to work at the roots and stay attuned. You can use mirroring to repeat their concern, even using some of the same words they chose to ensure they feel heard.

Acknowledge with compassion: After listening to each other to better understand the problem, thank them for what they have shared, acknowledge how they must have felt, and reflect on and claim responsibility for your role in the conflict.

- Do thank and acknowledge: "I really appreciate your sharing how you experienced these circumstances. I understand now that when I showed up late without calling, this might have made you feel disrespected. Did I get that right?"
- Do not jump to your own defense first: "I was late because my car got stuck in the mud, and I had no battery left on my phone. Why don't you ever give me the benefit of the doubt?!"

By acknowledging what they have said and how it may have made them feel, you are helping them feel heard. This still does not mean you agree with them; you are acknowledging what they said, though. You should also check that you understood correctly. Again, we are trying to bring mindfulness and attunement to understanding the roots of each person's experience. We may find that there was a misunderstanding, a limiting belief, fear, or assumption at play, or suffering that is coming from a place of attachment or aversion. Remembering our own experiences with the challenges of change can help us find compassion for the challenges others may have, which often drive conflict. This frequently requires a letting go of ego, which wants to jump to protect and defend our own interests. Mindfulness practice helps.

Set an intention to resolve the conflict: Find common ground and state your intention to resolve the conflict. If you can, clarify what is at stake (explain why resolving this issue is important to both parties). In doing so, you begin to develop an intention, mission, or common vision for a resolution. This is the most critical piece of reaching resolution: rather than rehashing the circumstances and fighting to be right, we make a commitment to find a solution, and let go or compromise where necessary to do so.

- Example: "I want to resolve this conflict so we can work well together. I think it is important that we both show respect for each others' time and effort on this project by following through on commitments we make to each other."

Problem solve together: Just as we work together in getting to the roots of a social issue and designing solutions collaboratively, work together to find a solution of mutual agreement. Make a plan that addresses and respects the needs as well as interests of both parties.

•   Example: "In the future, we will commit to attending our project meetings, as planned. If one of us must be late for a scheduled meeting, they will call the other person ahead of time."

•   Example: "In this case, I meant no disrespect. My phone was without battery when I was stuck, but I will resolve to always charge my phone so I can call you if there is an emergency and I might be more than fifteen minutes late. Would that work for you?"

Employing deep listening and self-awareness while recognizing our role in the conflict will help to shed light on the unconscious material that may be driving our reactivity, inspire empathy for the other's experience, and bring clarity to what needs to happen to reach resolution.

Cultivating Compassion   It is a funny thing, even if you are not practicing our structured inquiries, the relational field will still engage with you whether you like it or not. It is where some of our most powerful learning takes place. If we allow ourselves to be curious about what is arising for us and others, if we engage deeply with what needs attending to, and if we stay open to let it transform us, our intersection with the external environment will move us ever so gently (or not so gently!) down our path of personal evolution.

In this space, we let presence guide us inside and back out again. Presence allows us the awareness to see clearly and deeply. We stop and ask, *What is happening right now?* We look within to see how much of what is arising is coming from a vulnerable place that has colored our perspective, and what resonates with our true self. To know how best to respond, we ask ourselves, *What is needed?* And we do the same with the person across from us. We recognize that, like us, they have a conditioned self that springs from their unique life experience that has built defenses, and an essential or true self that allows access to inner knowing. We lean in with more presence and ask, *How can I learn from this relationship?* We invite curiosity and compassion for ourselves as well as others. Then we ask, *How can I support the highest possibility for myself and the other?* We let our essential wisdom guide us and respond in each moment.

What does this look like in the social change field? Compassion is derived from an understanding that we are all the same in our motivation to protect ourselves from suffering. Through a consciousness-based approach to social change, when awareness of such suffering in others moves us, we can more easily access compassion in our work. We also can see the interconnection between inner and outer transformation, including how we are implicated in social problems through our own unconscious patterns of behavior. Compassion is as important among our perceived enemies as much as it is with the victims of injustice. Knowing that when people cause harm to others, they are acting to avoid their own pain, can help us understand our opposition's motivation. From this inner-directed and other-focused approach, conscious social change supports a diagnosis of society's ills at the most fundamental level. Acting with compassion from this deep understanding, we can more effectively unhinge the belief systems that underlie injustice.

Let's imagine the scenario of a person in a relationship with an addict. Yes, we all would probably agree that the addict "should" end their addiction. How do we handle this circumstance from a place of mindfulness? A series of contemplations can guide our response.

Look to the roots: How do we contemplate the addict and the underlying reasons for their behavior? What are their underlying needs (love, protection, safety, understanding, or power; consider their core wound)? Where are their intentions coming from in their choices? Can we observe without judgment or evaluation?

Cultivate empathy and compassion: How is the addict suffering? Empathy is the ability to feel what it would be like in their shoes, and compassion is the desire to alleviate another's suffering. Can we feel empathy and compassion for the addict's suffering? Can you imagine the addict as innocent as the day they were born? How can you express this empathy and understanding with grace?

Consider our similarities: How can we understand this from within? How are we similar? What has been our hardest act of change? How have we coped in ways that harmed ourselves as well as others? How have we acted out of fear? Is there any way we have contributed to their suffering? How deeply can we accept our interconnectedness?

Consider our needs and accept reality: Though we may want the addict to change, can we acknowledge the reality that this person may never stop their behavior? If we are in relationship with the person, what do we need on a human-values or practical level? Can we ask for what we need and make choices given this reality?

Listening from the essential level: What would be the highest possibility? What needs to be spoken to the other's essential or true self? What does the ego or conditioned self need to hear? What would unconditional love dictate in this circumstance?

Choosing to respond: What is needed most now? How can our needs be expressed from a place of nonblaming or demanding, but also from a statement of truth about essential values/qualities?

This process integrates our work with presence and deep listening, experience of suffering and interconnectedness, experience with change, attunement to needs, and our own self-care.

Practice: Consider someone with whom you are in conflict, or someone in the world that you most despise—those you could never understand or forgive. Then go through the set of six contemplations above about the circumstances. If you know someone who fits these criteria, consider doing this exercise as a kind of "trial run" before engaging them face-to-face.

Consider how this deeper level of compassion for self and other may transform how you approach working with them in an effort to create social change.

Becoming Whole

Mindful Issue Diagnosis   After cultivating presence, and creating space for inner and outer awareness of what is happening, the next critical step to undertake in designing a social venture that will work effectively at the root and systemic levels of an issue is to diagnose your social issue comprehensively. We begin by using a basic problem tree as a tool with the added dimension of applied mindfulness. Problem trees are easy to conduct in a group and allow for the participation of all parties. It is important to conduct this exercise with as many stakeholders as possible, and if you are a facilitator, ensure all voices are heard. What follows are step-by-step instructions for conducting a mindful diagnosis of your issue using a conscious social change approach, adapted from Mayoux's challenge action tree.

Trunk (Problem): Begin by drawing the trunk of the tree. This represents your issue. Place onto the trunk your one central issue. You can determine the size of your trunk to match the size of the issue you are diagnosing.

Roots (Causes): Each of the roots represents a cause of the problem that you marked in the trunk. The first question you ask is, Why does this issue exist? Try to come up with five reasons why this central issue exists, and for each of these reasons or causes for the issue, draw them on five separate roots. After you have made your first set of roots, ask why each of these causes exist and give them their own subroots. Repeat. Continue to draw down from the trunk roots and subroots (roots of roots) that explain each cause. And continue to ask, What causes this to exist?

Continue to draw the roots down at least four or five levels, or until you cannot think of any more causes for each issue (and subroot). The more you expand your analysis, the deeper your understanding of the issue and the entire system will reach. With each added level of complexity in the root system, your opportunities to engage the issue and intervene increases. So too does the diversity of your stakeholder community.

It is ideal if you complete your problem tree with as many members of your team and community as possible to ensure you have a comprehensive diagnosis. Allow all parties, including those involved in the issue, to participate so that all voices are represented.

Working at the roots: We need to know as much as possible about the causes of the problem, so that we can design a solution that works as deeply as possible in the roots. If you change something in a subroot, it will affect all roots or problems above it in some way. The deeper you go with your solution, the more effective and lasting your change will be.

Working systemically: Once you have finished mapping out your roots, consider the whole system. Notice how certain roots work together to create the problem. Using a different-colored ink, include on your problem tree the people, organizations, institutions, or other stakeholders that are involved at each root. Look at where similar stakeholders are involved in more than one root, and be as specific as possible about what classifies them as a group. Consider what institutions or populations are involved— legal system, education system, and so forth. Notice the connections and

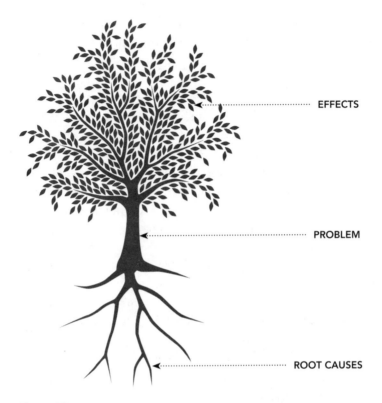

EFFECTS

PROBLEM

ROOT CAUSES

Figure 6.2

patterns that show up within your map. The more subroots you target in your solution and key stakeholders you engage, the greater your systemic impact. The breadth and depth of a solution may be achieved gradually across several iterations or through partnership and collaboration. Understanding the entire eco-system informs the strategic planning and ultimate evaluation of success.

Mapping effects: Though it might seem a simplistic distinction, it is important to explicitly discern between causes and effects. We map causes in the roots, and effects in the branches. Where you ask the following question of the roots, Why does this issue exist?, when you look at the effects, you ask a different question: What happens as a result of this problem? These branches will later become key indicators of whether your problem is changing. You would not want to focus your intervention or solution on the branches, as this only addresses a symptom and does not work to alleviate the underlying reasons for the issue. Yet the more successful you are in solving the problem deep in the roots, the fewer symptoms you will see in the branches. The problem tree will serve as a guide throughout the analysis and design of your solution, as well as help identify metrics for evaluating your social impact.

Analysis: When you are finished mapping out the roots and branches, take a look at your drawing. Consider the following questions for discussion with your team and community:

- What have you learned?
- How extensive is the issue?
- How much of the problem is due to behavior or belief systems?
- Where can you see shadows, attachments, or fear playing out?
- Are certain groups more disadvantaged than others?
- Who is involved (e.g., perpetrators, victims, and/or advocate groups?) at each root of the problem?
- Where are the intervention points you are most interested in working on?
- How many roots might you address, and which stakeholders might you need to engage in your intervention (and how)?
- What voices have not yet been consulted in verifying or expanding the diagnosis?

Target population: Once you have mapped out the issue with as much participation of the community as possible, consider among all your stakeholders who will be your target population—the recipients of your intervention. Looking at your problem tree, consider whom among those most deeply affected by your issue will you be targeting with your solution. Perhaps it is the perpetrators of the issue, or perhaps it will be the victims. Perhaps you will be targeting an institution that you feel needs to change in order to alleviate the underlying problem. Consider those who may hold belief systems that you want to change. You may be working with several target populations.

Make a list of the criteria that characterize the population you wish to address and determine its approximate size. Then consider how you will access your target population. How much influence do they have? What will drive their participation or resistance? Where do they usually convene? When do they intersect with the issue? How do they spend their days? Where do they go when they are in need of something? Who else interacts with them, and where? Will there be issues with safety or stigma in engaging them in your programs? What else do you need to know about them? Consider geographic choices. How broadly or deeply will you be working? Have they participated in this issue diagnosis?

Three I's Stakeholders Analysis   Once you have completed a full diagnosis of your social issue, including beginning to identify the parties that are involved at each root of the issue, you will take your stakeholder analysis deeper. Using the following tool, called the Three I's (pronounced *three eyes*), you will analyze the stakeholders engaged in your issue at three levels.

Take out your problem tree, and look at the roots and where you identified the different people involved in each underlying cause. Using your problem trees to assist you in this exercise, we are going to think about three sets of stakeholders—key stakeholders who are directly impacted by the issue; secondary stakeholders who are indirectly impacted, or who may be interested in the issue and might be able to help you; and external stakeholders who may be able to influence your success positively or negatively. We can think of these stakeholders as occupying concentric circles that go outward. You are in the middle, the stakeholders who are most important to you are the closest, and those who have less relevance are often farther away.

Three I's

Impact: These are the key stakeholders who are directly impacted by the issue, positively or negatively.

Interest: These are stakeholders who may not be impacted, but also have an interest in the issue and may be able to help you or may oppose you.

Influence: These are external stakeholders who may not be impacted or even interested in the issue, but can be influential in helping or hurting your work.

As with your problem trees, it is important to conduct your stakeholder analysis with as many members of your community and target population as possible. Also, recruit their participation to test your initial

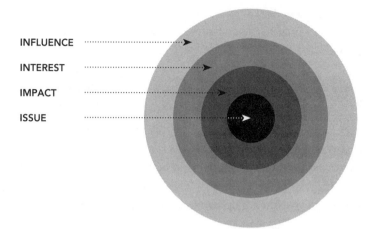

IMPACT:
These are the key stakeholders who are also impacted by the issue, positively or negatively.

INTEREST:
These are the stakeholders who may not be impacted but also have an interest in the issue and may be able to help you.

INFLUENCE:
These are external stakeholders who may not be impacted or even interested in the issue, but can be influential in helping or hurting your work.

Figure 6.3

analysis to ensure it is as fully developed and accurate as possible, and that you are deepening your understanding of their relationship to the issue.

Part I—Impact: Who are the people ultimately affected by the issue? Who are the people who will benefit from the issue going away, and who will be adversely affected by the issue going away? Does gender play a role? Are vulnerable groups included? Are there any new stakeholders who are likely to emerge as a result of the intervention?

Part II—Interest: Who is likely to have an interest in this project even if they are not directly impacted? Who might benefit indirectly from the solution? Who might be adversely impacted indirectly from the issue? Consider all sectors (business, political, civil society, and institutional).

Part III—Influence: Who is not going to benefit or be hurt by the issue or its solution, but who may have some level of influence over your work and situation? Why, and how?

Part IV—Identify stakeholder interests: Go back through each of the three circles and discuss stakeholder interests. Make notes on a separate piece of paper for each set of stakeholders. The questions to consider are:

- In what ways might they be impacted?
- In what ways do these stakeholders have an interest or intersect with the issue?
- In what ways can they help or obstruct your solution, or get in the way?
- What might you need from them, and how might they help you?
- What benefits are there likely to be for the stakeholders if the issue is alleviated?
- What challenges might they face, which may determine how much they may oppose your work?
- What resources or assets might the stakeholder have and be willing to commit?
- What other interests does the stakeholder have that may conflict with the project?
- What do they want, and what ideas do they have?
- How does the stakeholder regard others in the list?
- What are their strengths and weaknesses?
- What might you be able to offer them?

Part V—Value Propositions: Next, consider how to identify common ground, moving as many stakeholders as possible closer to the center of the circle of impact. How can you build understanding, cultivate core supporters, and create relationships with these stakeholders to unleash the ideas and resources needed to advance change? The more a party feels the issue impacts them, the more they have at stake for participating in the solution design process.

For each stakeholder, work to understand their needs, invite their ideas, and consider the drivers for their participation in the solution as well as possible fears, shadows, or belief systems that may be at work. Determine what value you may have to offer them by alleviating the issue. Consider what you may want from them in terms of resources, actions, or partnerships.

Create a value proposition—a proposal that demonstrates the value they will gain from you if they join you in collaboration.

By working collaboratively as much as possible to assess the issue and forge a solution, you are more likely to develop a comprehensive, systemic, and root-level intervention that will be sustainable as well as maximally effective. You may not need to utilize sticks and carrots, but through greater understanding may be able to invite engagement with all actors toward longer-term transformation.

Above all, you as the change agent must work to cultivate presence with your inner and outer environment, and remain open to the highest-possible response at any given time. Keeping aware of your own emotional charges will allow you to ascertain when you need to step back for res-toration (ensuring well-being), attend to a personal need that is arising (becoming whole), or simply be with what is, remaining aware of the shifts in your inner experience (cultivating presence). This will help you disen-tangle your own bias from what is truly needed by those you aim to serve. Your response will be in alignment with the higher wisdom of partner-ship and compassion, while also representing your unique gifts for a better society.

Engage Mindfully

Creative Assets Exercise Here I share an assets exercise to utilize with your social change team, community, or other problem-solving group. The exercise is a simple method to engage teams in reenergizing the creative-problem-solving process. For early stage change agents or communities who have yet to determine how best to intervene, the first objective of this exercise is to help participants recognize their strengths and passions as tools to apply toward positive change. The second objective is to release the creative ideas of the collective.

Identify assets: Begin by guiding your group in making a large list of all the individual and collective assets you have available to draw from. Consider the following:

Internal Passions

What do you love to do?
What do you really care about?
When do you feel truly alive? (e.g., when performing or in nature)
What do you feel called to do?
What do you like best about yourself?

Individual Skills and Competencies

What is your knowledge expertise?

What are key skillsets, core competencies or know-how?

What are your gifts?

What are your strengths?

External Assets

What tools do you have?

What technology do you have access to?

What forms of transportation can you use?

What assets do you have that can be used creatively?

What items have you created or can you create that can be used to entertain, communicate, learn, build, and so on?

What equipment does each person have or have access to or through others?

What raw materials or supplies does the group have that can be used to produce a product, provide a service, or offer in trade or for sale?

What is the most ridiculous item you can imagine offering?

What kind of spaces do you or the people you know have access to?

Human Capital

Who do you know? What people of influence (e.g., state representatives) or people of certain types of professions (e.g., doctor or attorney) do you know?

Who might be available to volunteer?

What connections do you have to other groups or influential people?

What skills, gifts, and competencies do these people offer you?

Financial Capital

How would you assess your existing sources of funds?

What potential sources of funds might exist within your eco-system?

Number each asset.

Identify issues: Make a large list of all the issues you, your group, or your community is dealing with that you would like to change to establish a more conscious, whole society. Number your list of issues.

Creative brainstorm: Now have someone call out one random number from each list, and read the chosen issue and asset combination out loud.

Then ask the group to consider how it can use the selected asset to solve the chosen problem.

Allow yourselves to consider at least three different ways to leverage that asset creatively in designing a social solution. All outrageous ideas are welcome to stretch the group's conception of the possible. Next, pick a new issue and pick two assets randomly. Repeat the process of employing the assets in an innovative solution to the chosen issue. Then pick a new issue and three to four assets. See what ideas can use all chosen assets or as many as possible.

Ideation: After completing the creative brainstorming process, begin the process of crafting your solution to your priority issue using the combined offerings of the group. Together, take a moment to breathe deeply, close your eyes, and meditate on your particular issue and passions. When you open your eyes, discuss what you each have to offer, and how you can incorporate as many assets as possible, an understanding of suffering and compassion, inner-driven power (as opposed to power determined by the dominant culture), and mindfulness to begin to address the underlying core or root issues of your problem, mapped out comprehensively in your problem tree.

Innovation to maximize social value: Once you have an initial vision for how your solution addresses the key issue at hand, optimize it to add greater social value. Looking at your problem tree, how deep in the roots and how comprehensively across the entire system will you intervene? Who else might be helped? How could this program have greater impact in a different location? What other issues might be addressed with this methodology or program? What other levels of intervention might be necessary to alleviate an entire root? Will your solution transform belief systems and underlying assumptions? Will it address behaviors and what drives action? Will you be targeting individual actors, institutional issues or systemic inequities? Identifying one primary stakeholder and utilizing your understanding of how that stakeholder is impacted/interested/influential relevant to the issue, how many ways might you engage them across the roots?

Test, evaluate and grow with mindful engagement: It is essential to test and evaluate each component of the solution with the same level of mindfulness and deep community engagement with which the issue diagnosis was conducted. Much of the complexity of the intervention may need to be implemented over time as part of a longer-term strategy. And as is core to the philosophy of conscious social change, adjustments are made over time informed by the broader eco-system in response to what is needed to alleviate the underlying social issue without attachment to one particular agenda.

The overarching objective of this exercise is to inspire creativity and demonstrate that any one asset can be a tool to leverage for change, though our true list of assets is extensive. We are more gifted and empowered than we might at first suspect. Our potential to create change is virtually unlimited.

Leading from within distinguishes the mindful change agent. It begins by listening for an individual calling and then consciously leveraging it toward transformation. Bringing presence to our deepest intentions is a direct link to our sense of meaning. Bringing this same presence to our social justice work allows for radical creativity, because our egos and personal agendas step out of the way, leaving us open to new ideas that arise from the connection and cross-fertilization that take place within community. Using an inherently interconnected and systemic approach, conscious change leaders ensure those working together are inspired by a common cause, and find a way to marry their unique contributions and passions too. Here we are guided by our final question: *What is possible?*

Early on, I was particularly influenced by the book *Man's Search for Meaning*, written by Victor Frankl, a Holocaust survivor. Victor was a psychologist, and while imprisoned in a Nazi concentration camp, his power of observation led him to a powerful conclusion: those individuals who were able to find purpose in their suffering—perhaps a position of power that gave them an extra piece of bread that they would share, or the memory of a loved one that they were living for with hope of reuniting—were able to persevere. I have seen this power of inner purpose as a distinct characteristic of conscious change agents. Let me tell you one such inspirational story.

Adam Musa

At the same time in 2004 that I was sitting with Zolecka in South Africa, my brother, a former US Marine Captain named Brian Steidle, decided to leave the United States to begin work as a military observer in Sudan. Over the next twelve months, he shared with me via e-mail and satellite phone his firsthand accounts of the Darfur crisis. Each day, armed only with a camera, he would visit bombed-out villages and take testimonies from survivors, including women who had been gang raped and whose husbands had been executed.

I traveled to eastern Chad in the middle of 2005 to launch Global Grass-roots' work, learn more about the Darfur crisis, and start work on a documentary film about my brother's experience during the genocide, called *The Devil Came on Horseback*. We met refugees who had come stumbling into Chad in groups or alone, some with their starving animals, and some barefoot with only the clothes they wore. Enduring up to a three-month journey on foot, sometimes with six or eight children, they told of sleeping under trees during sandstorms with no water to drink except what might be salvaged by digging in a stone-dry riverbed or collecting after heavy rains. But not even the thought of starvation or the hyenas that stalked them at night worried them. "We are facing death both ways, so there is no point in fear," a woman said. Many were forced to step over the murdered bodies of their people as they shuffled past villages recently attacked and burned to the ground. The wounded traveled with the same determination, albeit at a slower pace, and others carried injured relatives on their shoulders. Theirs was a harrowing journey.

Adam Musa is a Sudanese English teacher who I met in Kounoungo refugee camp, which was home to over ten thousand Darfuris at the time. Adam was one of the few refugees who spoke English, so he served as a translator for the International Medical Corps helping treat refugee health issues and was often the one to interact with international visitors to the camps.

Antonov aircraft began terrorizing Adam's village of Tine (pronounced *tina*), Sudan, in the afternoon, returning again in the evening, dropping bombs again and again over his community. Adam and his four children, two of his brother's children (his brother had already gone missing in another attack), and his wife, seven-months pregnant at the time, trembled beneath their beds, terrified. Anticipating the arrival of Janjaweed militia at daybreak, they escaped at 3:00 a.m., fleeing across the border to Chad with nothing but a few belongings. Without money, Adam had to sell a few of their blankets so they could eat for the first three days, while he sought a better solution. Resourcefully, he decided to use his cart and donkey to transport goods in exchange for meager change, often dangerously back and forth across the Sudanese border, so they could continue to survive each day. Facing the near-impossible task of supporting his large family with only occasional odd jobs, Adam did everything he could to save the money needed to transport his family to the newly built Kounoungo refugee camp. To his dismay, when they finally arrived at their new home, they were not immediately allowed to register and had to survive for a further twenty-four days in the desert outside the camp, living on the offerings of other refugees while they waited for the monthly UN registration process.

Once he was allowed to register, he discovered that his family was the only one of the Fur ethnic group in a camp of all Zagawa. Both tribes had been persecuted and targeted by the Sudanese Arabs, but the Fur and Zagawa had long-held tensions, and Adam frequently felt threatened. He tied a stray dog near his tent encampment to protect his home, and his son was isolated and beaten by the teacher at school. Nevertheless, Adam focused on opportunity for his family and hope for his people. When I asked him what I could bring him back from the United States, he selflessly asked for chalk, a chalkboard, pencils, and paper so he could teach his children. He dreamed of coming to the United States for the education his children could receive. He was so patriotic about the potential he perceived in a land of freedom that he named one of his sons George Bush. And in one of our interviews for *The Devil Came on Horseback*, I asked him what he wanted to say to the people of the United States. I expected a desperate and angry plea for help, but instead, all he had to say was thank you for the food aid and support he saw from the United States.

Adam lived in the Darfur refugee camps from 2004 to 2013. A true social entrepreneur, his big vision was to build a series of libraries for the camp. Most of the refugees in Kounoungo Camp are rural farmers, the majority of whom have never had access to education. With no independent gathering place of their own, the refugees lacked a center for their new community where they could draw together to learn from one another. So Adam began work on his idea by taking the library directly to the refugees. Using UN documents he obtained regarding refugee rights, Adam engaged his peers in the outdoor markets where they gathered daily to play cards. Enlisting the help of certain shopkeepers, the papers were read aloud while the men played.

He was pleasantly surprised to discover a level of interest among the men who had listened. They started to ask questions: "There's a legal definition of being a refugee?" "We have rights?" "What is the United Nations?" "What are they doing about Darfur?" A growing dialogue resulted, as displaced families discovered what it meant to be a refugee. Adam took this as proof that his people were eager to know more and all they needed was a structure that could serve as a place of learning.

Adam's vision involved constructing three library centers in Kounoungo camp. He dreamed of electric lights, satellite Internet, and television to bring members in to hear educational lectures on issues of refugee law, women's rights, children's rights, and UN resolutions on Darfur. He thought that having just one solar light bulb in a camp of ten thousand with no electricity would certainly draw attention after dark. Adam planned to address, as he called them, the "bad habits" of his culture, including the practice of female genital mutilation, child abuse, and domestic violence. Such a library would provide books, tools, and other informational resources to promote conflict resolution as well as psychological healing. Despite the fact that he barely had enough food to feed his family, his commitment to education was profound.

I was beyond inspired and wanted to fund his library as the first endeavor of Global Grassroots. I asked him for a plan, and he found someone who helped him create drawings of the structure. Adam wrote up a comprehensive budget and overview of what the program would entail. Should the day come when his idea could be spread to neighboring camps, he agreed to serve as an adviser. I returned to the United States energized, raised his construction budget of $12,000, and began to speak with international groups about assisting us on the ground. I couldn't exactly wire that money to Adam, who had no bank account, and even if he had a way of holding on to the money within his UN tarp, it would put him at great risk. So we tried to work within the umbrella of the United Nations. Unfortunately, even as a newly registered 501(c)(3) nonprofit in the United States, I was a one-woman, volunteer show with no legitimacy in these international environments.

To build a structure on foreign soil for a displaced population requires maneuvering through a whole host of restrictions and red tape. We needed to be a Chadian-registered NGO with local offices and a presence in the camp, which also required us to be an officially registered UN organization authorized by the United Nations to operate in the camps. Or we could identify a partner who met those requirements, and could facilitate the transfer of funds and building of the structure. Each organization I spoke with declined to partner in a venture that involved what seemed to be a political orientation and/or was for the benefit of one Darfuri refugee when they needed to apply their support equitably for all refugees. Those who were supportive and knew Adam would rotate out of their posts within six months due to burnout, and I would have to start again. Months went by.

I struggled to help. As I waded through international regulations, Adam began to build his library brick by brick with his own bare hands. In Konongo Camp, like many refugee camps, water is rationed daily, and women line up their water jugs next to a spigot and wait for hours until the water is turned on. A tiny jug, often no more than a gallon or two, is all they have access to for their entire family's cooking, cleaning, washing, and bathing needs. But Adam was able to inspire these same illiterate refugees to sacrifice some of their precious water in a desert—in 109-degree heat—so that he could dig a hole, make mud, and form mud bricks by hand for a library.

About a year passed, and a friend, Gabriel Stauring of iACT, who spearheaded the Darfur Fast for Life, visited Adam's camp. He sent back video of Adam with a library wall almost reaching beyond his own tall stature. I was overjoyed. And then word came that the rainy season—which tends to consist mostly of horrific dust storms—had disintegrated his wall. Nevertheless, Adam began again, working tirelessly to realize his vision.

Several years passed, and we lost track of Adam and placed our efforts with the project permanently on hold. He resurfaced in 2011 in Camp Djabal. He had moved camps to reconnect with family members who he had lost touch with when fleeing Sudan. There, iACT had also been working and happened to have brought in a mobile library to serve children in the camp. They were thrilled to find their old friend Adam, who was immediately recruited as librarian.

I have never met a more dedicated, humble, and wise soul. Adam exemplifies a conscious social change agent in many ways. Inner driven, he has selflessly dedicated himself to the needs of the common good, bringing mindfulness, compassion, and wisdom to each interaction. I do not know if he had a meditation practice, but from my own visit to the Islamic world of Chad and Sudan, I was deeply in awe of the discipline it takes to pray five times a day, no matter where you are. We would pass trucks and buses on the side of the road, in the middle of the desert, in extreme temperatures and dust, and yet people would be praying on their prayer rugs there in the sand.

Adam worked relentlessly, courageously, and resourcefully to address the roots of the issues his people faced, and enlighten them toward their potential rights and opportunities. He did not see opposition; instead, he sought to reconcile the tension of differing tribes and unify anyone struggling to survive as a refugee. He experienced great suffering, but found both an acceptance of reality and opportunity to advance change within that reality. He used not sticks and carrots but rather ways to motivate through inspiration and vision to find the resources and volunteers he needed to build his library. And he maintained a sense of gratitude and possibility wherever he looked.

Conscious Leadership

Mindfulness opens us to our unique calling and inspires innovation through an ever-deepening awareness. Nhât Hanh (1993) said, "Non-violent action, born of the awareness of suffering and nurtured by love, is the most effective way to confront adversity." Consciousness-based approaches to social change, learned through direct experience, enable change agents to advance social justice more effectively, creatively, and transformationally.

There are distinct qualities that conscious change leaders, like Adam, exhibit in their pursuit of justice. Inner driven, they make a commitment to their personal evolution through regular practice and the nonstop lessons for growth offered by the external environment. This requires discipline and prioritizing. It is not only reserved for moments when one can get away from the daily routine and go on retreat. It is an integral part of their lifestyle, and allows for both constant learning and intentional renewal. They are also guided by a mission and vision of what is possible, which takes priority over individual gain.

Conscious change leaders embody and regularly employ conscious awareness to understand as well as respond rather than react to an emotional charge. This is not to suggest that the ultimate goal is no emotion. The aim is to feel the entirety of one's experience—whether that is anger, grief, shame, or another such emotion, and use the experience as an opportunity for deeper clarity around what is needed in terms of one's self-care or in response to another.

Conscious change agents also attempt to bring their complete attention to their relationships. They work to balance their capacity for self-awareness and attunement to others. They know that the inner landscape affects the quality of their relationships, and their complete presence with the world around them is critical for contributing meaningfully to a better society. Cultivating this perspective of open acceptance, conscious change agents tend to consider circumstances that happen in relation to others as a chance to learn. When they are shown their blind spots, they inspire others with their self-compassion and humility as opposed to defensive reactivity.

Instead of sacrificing themselves beyond their capacities, conscious change leaders know when to attend to their own needs and also when to recognize they must let go of fixing others. They are committed to self-care so that their own needs do not detract from their ability to show up fully in their service. They model this commitment, not as an indulgence, but with acknowledgment that our true needs are intelligence that can guide us toward greater capacities. This in turn involves supporting the same in others, but with the recognition that if we intervene unconsciously and compulsively to fix, we may disempower another from learning a critical life lesson or having the opportunity to grow from their own experiences. In essence, the drive to act comes not from a rule of thumb or formula but rather from an attunement to the response needed in each moment, which is cultivated through mindfulness.

Knowing what change looks like from within, including the ways we suffer from wanting things to be different, a conscious change agent can look beyond reactivity to better understand human nature. Through compassion and attunement, conscious change leaders are capable of recognizing the essential goodness in people, can discern their underlying needs and intentions, and thus can act to support their highest potential. They will hold a vision for the highest benevolent outcome, even while recognizing it is not the end goal but instead the process that can be facilitated. Conscious change agents commit to live with integrity and attempt to do no harm. Though there will be times when it is necessary to act decisively with power, conscious change leaders are present enough to know when to take time to respond with wisdom and integrity, clear in their intentions, and aware of their impact on others.

Conscious change agents not only support others but also are unafraid to seek support when needed. And they do not simply shift from learning to leading once they hit some arbitrary level of authority. They continue to reach outward in both directions. They are grateful for the evolution and accomplishments they have been allowed to make, and give back to others through mentorship. They also recognize with gratitude that they have had many teachers they can credit with having supported their growth, yet continue to bring a quality of beginner's mind to each circumstance— a sense that there is always something new to learn. This openness fosters greater connection and collaboration with others as well as continual self-improvement.

Conscious leaders understand that completely transforming a system requires that we start with ourselves. They are willing to look at their own role in the inefficiencies or malfunctions of a system, seeking to live from a place of integrity in alignment with the change they seek to initiate. Just as Drocella redefined her approach to domestic violence after taking those critical three breaths before almost spanking her kids, change leaders operate from a place of direct experience with and deep personal understanding of change. From there, they are able to bring greater compassion to the stakeholders engaged in the targeted system. While still holding individuals accountable, they hold space not for blame but rather for personal growth.

As I have explored, our more mindful orientation fuels optimism, better relationships, and enhanced leadership capacity. It also sparks greater creativity and innovation, because we have more ideas, perspectives, and group assets to draw on so long as we remain free of judgment and unattached to a singular agenda.

Social Innovation

Conscious social change represents the intersection between mindful leadership and social entrepreneurship. In addition to the integration of mindfulness as a quality of their leadership approach, conscious change agents drive innovation.

Conscious change agents are inventors; they combine innovation, resourcefulness, opportunity, and business principles to maximize social value creation. They are not afraid of experimentation or risk taking. They rapidly prototype, test, and evaluate their interventions to see what works. Conscious social change is a mind-set as much as a process. As I mentioned previously, conscious change agents look at each circumstance as an opportunity to learn, but this extends beyond the personal domain to their work too, especially in circumstances others might consider failure. They are open and curious. They do not get stuck in one method or program but instead are continually driven to deepen their understanding and figure out what works best.

Conscious change agents find patterns in the way the world operates and determine their own theory of change—in other words, what dynamics and key components are necessary to create change, and what gaps in the system need to be filled and how for a better solution. Conscious change agents think about what we all assume to be true, and then turn those assumptions sideways and question if that is necessarily so. They dig deeply, identify patterns, and build an informed understanding of what is needed and helpful, so that they may set an inspiring vision for what is possible. They may start with a single intervention, but they will likely evolve their work over time. Taking into account the political, social, economic, and environmental dimensions of the system, their solutions ultimately strive to transform the entire system in order to alleviate the issue effectively. They are "systems entrepreneurs," not solo actors toward change (Walker, 2016).

Conscious change agents are also creative in the way they obtain the financial and human resources they need, and use strategic collaboration to maximize their impact. They are often not doing business using standard, traditional methods but instead are taking risks and experimenting with what works to refine their idea. They may be looking at long-term human transformation too, which is not always easy to measure in concrete, annual outputs. Most donors are looking for a track record and measurable outcomes that improve over time. Given this, conscious change agents frequently invent creative methods to obtain the resources they need from the community they are serving. Like Adam as well as the Rwandan literacy project that funded itself on rocks, sticks, and bricks, they are neither able to nor interested in waiting around for traditional channels to support them. But this in turn actually helps them design approaches that are more sustainable long term because they are supported by an interested base of stakeholders instead of outside funding sources. This is valuable because the growth in funding for social change is always surpassed by the growth in the seekers of that same funding. Ingenuity and resourcefulness become survival tactics in this work.

Finally, conscious change agents demonstrate the most remarkable compassion and commitment to the people and causes they serve; they often simply won't stop until they know they have made a difference, despite the odds they face. Social change, at its heart, is born of compassion. And compassion is fostered through mindfulness. With mindfulness, conscious change leaders listen better, learn better, intentionally seek compromise and collaboration, and thus inspire the most creative and effective ideas. They use mindfulness to understand themselves, and find their deepest calling and passion. They come to understand their own capabilities and gifts they can leverage in pursuit of their ideas, and understand what drives (or frustrates) change from a deep personal level. Mindfulness supports their capacity to deconstruct an issue, and integrate the needs, assets, and ideas of the collective. It helps them find insight and build partnerships. Conscious change leaders are therefore more capable of diffusing conflict, letting go of the unconscious material that obstructs clear thinking, and experimenting for change with curiosity, nonjudgment, and a willingness to learn. From this orientation, like Adam securing water donations from illiterate refugees in a desert, we too can inspire the impossible.

To cultivate the capacity to lead for transformation in this way as a conscious social change agent takes practice. The concept of contemplative practice reinforces one's commitment to self-reflection and supports the development of personal discipline through daily ritual. Furthermore, the process of personal transformation, like any change, takes time, and the actions that drive that evolution typically require a lifetime of continued practice. The final practice shared below can help catalyze the inner driven passion needed to step into a process of conscious social change.

Practice

Repeating Questions for Meaning and Purpose
Conscious social change invokes a paradigm that is inner driven and other focused. But how do we access a sense of purpose? How do we find meaning in our work or other endeavors? Following are three yogic question meditations that may support you in discovering some guidance from within.

Keeping a notebook and pen nearby, take a moment to sit and focus on your breath. Notice your three centers (mind, body, and emotional state), using the practices shared earlier in this book. Once you feel that you are as fully present as possible, ask yourself:

What do I most yearn to do in this life?

When an answer arises, write it down. Take a deep breath and ask yourself again. Repeat this process as often as it takes to run out of answers. Then try to ask the question ten more times. Be patient and just breathe, and wait until something arises beyond the ego's ready answers or any sense of what you "should" respond.

Then ask yourself, *What do I know to be true?*

Repeat the same process as the above.

Finally, ask yourself, *What do I need or need to do next?*

Continue to ask this final question with the process above.

When you are finished, look at what you have recorded in your journal. Compare your sense of what you are most passionate about and called to do with your own wisdom and truths. What is revealed to you about what you need or need to do next? See whether there is a way for you to pursue a path of meaningful work aligned with an inner sense of purpose.

For some, this process may bring them into awareness of something missing in their lives. For others, it may bring complete clarity about where they want to invest in passions that have gone unanswered. This may mean a change in career or the addition of volunteer work on the side. Finally, it may reveal deep wisdom or insight that can support a sense of confidence needed to dive into a new endeavor.

Conclusion

Having explored the neuroscientific and psychotherapeutic evidence for the benefits of mindfulness, considered the arguments contained herein as to the relevance of mindfulness to social change design, and experimented with the practices and frameworks that help you experience as well as apply mindfulness, I hope you feel poised to carry this approach into your organizations, communities, and social justice endeavors.

As mentioned previously, there are numerous applications for this approach and its capacities across all phases of social issue design, organizational development, and operations as well as a range of issues and fields of work. For example, what would a conscious social change approach look like in fund-raising, health care delivery, or a corporate form? In the appendix, I share a range of organizations, individuals, and initiatives that are employing a more mindful approach to their social change work and/or business model on a diverse set of issues. I invite you to explore their program models and methods, which might inspire new ideas for your own undertakings.

And if you are still uncertain where to start, let me offer you a suggestion: start within.

Take a breath. Cultivate the quality of presence—the ability to be here now without distraction. Like anything, especially in this overly stimulating world, this takes practice. You can begin with a simple ten minutes sitting upright on your bed or a chair before you start your day. Or you might choose a more intensive practice you do alone, or with a community or sangha. Look for meditation centers in your region. Find a teacher. Try a range of things until you find something that feels right for you. Take time in reflection each day, noticing your breath, thoughts, emotions, and body. Become your own observer. Notice the things that feel uncomfortable. The more you practice with discipline and dedication, the more you will become mindful in every moment and the more self-control you will have over your experience. As often as you can, ask, *What is happening?*

Let everything you notice become fodder for wholeness and personal growth. Every experience has intelligence for you—from a flash of rage to an aching neck muscle, to the gut sense gnawing at you that something isn't right. Take three breaths. Become your greatest expert. Find what fuels your potency from within and support that which nurtures the same in others. Take stock of privilege and your blind spots. Don't blame. Instead, as you work to let go of these conditioned ways of seeing and interacting with the world, invite compassion for the similar ways others are limited in how they experience change. Ask, *What is really true?*

Take care of yourself. Invest in your own well-being, so you can continue to be of service in your work without threat of burnout. Model personal sustainability and integrate self-care as a priority within your personal as well as professional life. Ask, *What is needed?* Check in regularly with your quality of peace, aliveness, and purpose, so that you can continue to heed your own wisdom as a guide toward finding what you most need.

Look first within, and then go deeper with the issues around you to understand *what is helpful* and *what is possible.* Only then can we begin to design for change. As we bring the capacities and key questions of conscious social change into each phase of our interaction with others along with the advancement of our work, we increasingly come to embody the qualities of a change agent who leads from within. We are guided by purpose for the sake of the common good. We use every opportunity as a chance to learn. We hold a vision for the highest benevolent outcome. We know how to inspire and leverage the best in others, aligning their contributions with their individual sense of purpose in service to a shared vision.

The great Sufi poet and mystic Rumi said, "Yesterday I was clever, so I wanted to change the world. Today I am wise, so I am changing myself." Conscious social change begins within.

May these stories of perseverance and innovation - from Adam Musa, building a human rights library with his bare hands, dirt, and water rations to Seraphine Hacimana, a woman with only a first-grade education combating sexual exploitation in exchange for water; from Zolecka Ntuli, an unemployed twenty-five-year-old in South Africa helping to end child rape to Aqeela Sherills, a man raised in the trenches of Los Angeles gang violence moving rival factions to forgiveness and peace - challenge us to find our own unique offerings to leverage for change. May they inspire us to use our relative privilege, freedom, and opportunity to fight for social justice wherever we see inequity. And may we all continue our own journeys of self-awareness so that we may serve as conscious agents of change fearlessly leading from within.

Appendix: Organizations Integrating Mindfulness into Social Change

Amani Institute (www.amaniinstitute.org) works to develop professionals who create social impact by creating new models of education and training that enable people to develop new practical skills and experiences for their professional toolkit, a personal understanding of their own leadership journey, and the global networks necessary for long-term career success.

Auburn Seminary (www.auburnseminary.org) equips leaders with the organizational skills and spiritual resilience required to create lasting, positive impacts on local communities and the national stage as well as around the world.

Awake in the Wild Experience (www.awakeinthewildexperience.org) is a mindfulness-in-nature art project that brings participants into intimate connection with the natural world through nature-inspired contemplations.

CARE for Teachers Project (www.care4teachers.com) is a unique professional development program that helps teachers handle the stresses as well as rediscover the joys of teaching to help students thrive socially, emotionally, and academically.

Center for Contemplative Mind in Society (www.contemplativemind.org) transforms higher education by supporting and encouraging the use of contemplative/introspective practices as well as perspectives to create active learning and research environments that look deeply into experience and meaning for all in service of a more just, compassionate society.

Center for Transformational Practice (www.transformationalpractice.org) is a meeting place and practice center for anyone wishing to advance sustainability through inner transformation.

Center for Transformative Change (www.transformativechange.org) is the first national center entirely dedicated to bridging the inner and outer lives of social change agents, activists, and allies to support a more effective, more sustainable social justice movement.

Compassionate Schools Project (www.compassionschools.org) is working to transform fifty schools involving twenty thousand children by teaching elementary school students to cultivate focus, resilience, and well-being for academic performance, physical education, character development, and child health policies.

Conscious Social Change (www.conscioussocialchange.org) is Gretchen Ki Steidle's hub for all things conscious social change, including the Toolkit for Conscious Social Change, mindfulness practice videos, classes, and a more comprehensive list of resources.

Contemplative Sciences Center (www.uvacontemplation.org) at the University of Virginia is committed to exploring contemplative practices, values, ideas, and institutions through analytic research and scholarship as well as helping to develop new applications and learning programs for integration into varied sectors of our society.

Courage of Care Coalition (www.courageofcare.org) works to empower both personal and social transformation by providing deep contemplative training coupled with powerful tools for systemic change.

CTZNWELL (www.ctznwell.org) is a political movement working toward a nation of well-being for all people using practice, community, and action to respond to issues with conscious as well as creative disruption for impact at a systemic and global level.

Cutting Edge Law (www.cuttingedgelaw.com) provides resources on Integrative Law, an emerging movement crafting values-based, creative, sustainable, and holistic solutions that build and strengthen relationships within the law built on dignity.

Dalai Lama Fellows Program (www.dalailamafellows.org) cultivates and supports a global movement of next-generation leaders applying universal values to solve global challenges.

EILEEN FISHER, Inc. (www.eileenfisher.com/behind-the-label-overview) is the largest women's fashion company to be certified a B Corporation, and is passionate about business acting as a movement toward sustainability, human rights, and personal well-being.

Empowerment Institute (www.empowermentinstitute.net) is a global consulting and training organization specializing in the practice of empowerment to achieve measurable as well as sustainable behavior change at the individual, organizational, and community levels.

Enneagram Prison Project (www.enneagramprisonproject.org) is dedicated to the self-awareness education of the incarcerated and the reduction of recidivism rates, using the Enneagram combined with mindfulness meditation and sensate-awareness practices.

Fetzer Institute (www.fetzer.org) is working to help catalyze and support a broad-scale, spiritually grounded transformation from an ego-centered way of being grounded in separation and fear, to an all-centered way of being grounded in oneness and love.

Garrison Institute (www.garrisoninstitute.org) convenes and supports those who are exploring the wisdom, values, and insight gained through contemplative practices to catalyze personal as well as social transformation.

Global Grassroots (www.globalgrassroots.org) is working to catalyze conscious social change among disadvantaged women in post-conflict Africa through a mindfulness-based leadership program and social venture incubator.

Global Gratitude Alliance (www.gratitudealliance.org) transforms intergenerational trauma into intergenerational healing, resiliency, and transformation.

Good Work Institute (www.goodworkinstitute.org) develops business education programs that aim to bring not just more knowledge to the professional world but also more wisdom to honor ourselves, the natural world, and all the people in our communities.

Hidden Leaf Foundation (www.hiddenleaf.org) is working to expand inner awareness within social change organizations in order to advance a more just, ecologically healthy, and compassionate society.

Holistic Life Foundation (www.hlfinc.org) is committed to nurturing the wellness of children and adults in underserved communities by helping children develop their inner lives through yoga, mindfulness, and self-care.

International Women's Partnership for Peace and Justice (www.womenforpeaceandjustice.org) leads workshops, retreats, and training courses in rural Thailand, which share in common the integration of feminism, social action, and spirituality for sustainability along with transformation at the personal, community, and society levels.

LIFE Camp (www.peaceisalifestyle.com) is working to develop teens and adults into peer leaders, to avoid becoming perpetrators or victims of violence, and effectively implement positive change within their own communities.

Mind & Life Institute (www.mindandlife.org) is working to alleviate suffering and promote flourishing by integrating science with contemplative practice and wisdom traditions.

Mindful Badge Initiative (www.mindfulbadge.com) offers mindfulness-based resilience training to law enforcement officers to improve compassion, awareness, and performance, so as to cultivate humanity, resiliency, and connection to community.

Movement Strategy Center (www.movementstrategy.org) provides training in transformative movement building through sharpening shared purpose and vision, deepening relationships, and embodying the qualities needed for transformation.

Omega Institute (www.eomega.org) offers diverse and innovative educational experiences that inspire an integrated approach to personal as well as social change.

Patagonia (www.patagonia.com) has a corporate mission to build the best product, cause no unnecessary harm, and use business to inspire and implement solutions to the environmental crisis.

Presencing Institute (www.presencing.com) is a growing community creating awareness-based social technologies for change makers around the world.

Prison Mindfulness Institute (www.prisonmindfulness.org) provides prisoners, prison staff, and prison volunteers with the most effective, evidence-based tools for rehabilitation, self-transformation, and personal and professional development to transform individual lives as well as the corrections system as a whole.

Reciprocity Foundation (www.reciprocityfoundation.org) is a contemplative nonprofit organization working to help homeless, runaway, and foster care youths from all five boroughs of New York City to realize their full potential.

Reverence Project (www.trproject.org) is an initiative working to shift the social and philosophical construct of present-day world culture rooted in violence, shame, guilt, and fear into a more balanced worldview rooted in reverence, forgiveness, compassion, and truth.

Rockwood Leadership Institute (www.rockwoodleadership.org) offers non-profit, philanthropic, and social change leaders from across the globe transformational leadership development trainings to change the way change is done as well as transform our world.

Roots of Empathy (www.rootsofempathy.org) is an evidence-based classroom program that has shown significant effect in reducing levels of aggression and bullying among schoolchildren while raising social/emotional competence as well as increasing empathy.

RSF Social Finance (www.rsfsocialfinance.org) is a nonprofit financial services organization envisioning a world in which money contributes to an economy based on generosity and interconnectedness, and where money liberates human capacity for compassionate action.

Social Health Concepts and Practice (www.mariselabgomez.com/socialhealthconceptsandpractice) is an independent consulting organization that facilitates alternative ways to transform existing oppressive, hierarchical models of individual and community change.

Spring Up (www.timetospringup.org) is a multimedia activist collective creating a space for analyzing interpersonal and structural violence through storytelling along with intentional myth making.

Thread (www.thread.org) engages underperforming high school students confronting significant barriers outside the classroom by providing each one with a family of committed volunteers and increased access to community resources.

Wellbeing Project (wellbeing-project.org) is focused on both modeling support to social change leaders and cultivating a shift in the culture of the field toward one that is healthier as well as supportive of inner well-being.

Zen Hospice Project (www.zenhospice.org) is working to help change the experience of dying and caregiving by creating a space for living that offers the opportunity for individuals, their loved ones, and caregivers to find comfort, connection, and healing in this shared human experience.

Notes

Preface

1. Among the business community, especially among corporate leadership, entrepreneurs, and the tech world in the United States, there has been a growth in the exploration of contemplative practices for greater productivity, creativity, well-being, and meaning. This is evidenced by several initiatives, including the proliferation of mindfulness conferences like Wisdom 2.0 (www.wisdom2summit.com), Google's Search Inside Yourself Leadership Institute (https://siyli.org), Otto Sharmer's Presencing Institute (https://www.presencing.com), the Good Work Institute (www.goodworkinstitute.org), and an increasing number of business management and leadership courses incorporating mindfulness at leading business schools.

2. For a powerful exploration of the divergence between the skyrocketing wellness industry and increasing inequality in the United States, take a look at the work of Kerri Kelly, founder of CTZNWELL, including her TEDx talk at TEDxWashington-Square in 2016 (www.youtube.com/watch?v=coJGRVU84ZM).

Chapter 1: The Science of Mindfulness

1. You can find guided mindfulness practices at www.conscioussocialchange.org.

Chapter 3: Cultivating Presence

1. As mentioned earlier, breathwork is a mind-body therapeutic practice that enables individuals to process deep pain on a mental, emotional, and physical level, certain methods of which have been clinically demonstrated to alleviate PTSD symptoms. I have been studying various breath practices since 2002, including Integrative Breathwork taught by Jessica Dibb of the Inspiration Community in Baltimore (www.inspirationcommunity.org) and Coherent Breathing taught by Dr. Richard P. Brown and Dr. Patricia L. Gerbarg (www.Breath-Body-Mind.com). I have run a small clinical practice since 2009, and have integrated breathwork for mind-

fulness-based leadership and trauma healing into Global Grassroots' work in Rwanda and Uganda.

2. You can read more about Darfur Fast for Life and iACT, including all the participant blogs, at www.fastdarfur.org/blog/ and www.iactivism.org, respectively.

3. Donald Rothberg's (2006) *The Engaged Spiritual Activist* inspired this meditation.

Chapter 4: Becoming Whole

1. The teachings surrounding suffering, aversion, and attachment are based on Buddhism's Four Noble Truths.

2. This framework was inspired by and adapted from teachings I received when I studied the intersection of Engaged Buddhism, feminism, and social change with Ouyporn Khuankaew of the International Women's Partnership for Peace and Justice in Chiang Mai, Thailand.

3. You can learn more about the Enneagram Prison Project at www .enneagramprisonproject.org.

4. These examples of unconscious compulsions or driving motivators are inspired by the Enneagram, a model for understanding our core wounds—patterns by which our ego compensates to protect us from vulnerability and prop ourselves up in the world. You can explore more about the Enneagram by reading Don Richard Riso and Russ Hudson's (1999) *The Wisdom of the Enneagram*.

Chapter 5: Ensuring Well-being

1. Brown and Gerbarg have created a program that is easy for everyone to learn, and takes only a little time to practice. If you are interested in learning the BBM technique, read their book, *The Healing Power of the Breath*, or for upcoming courses, visit www.Breath-Body-Mind.com.

2. You can learn more about Peng's work at www.robertpeng.com. You can find resources on Coherent Breathing as well as *Respire 1* by Elliot and the accompanying book at www.coherence.com. Fehmi has developed a relaxed form of nonexclusive, nonjudgmental attention to our diverse sensory experiences that supports relaxation while also addressing stress, pain, and anxiety. You can learn more in his book, coauthored with Jim Robbins, *The Open-Focus Brain: Harnessing the Power of Attention to Heal Mind and Body* as well as find workshops at www.openfocus.com.

3. You can learn more about Goerling's work and the Mindful Badge Initiative at www.mindfulbadge.com.

Chapter 6: Engaging Mindfully

1. To explore Mayoux's participatory learning tools, diagrams, and methods, see Gender Action Learning for Sustainability at Scale at www.galsatscale.net.

2. We had discovered there was no word for change agent or social entrepreneur in Kinyarwanda, the local language of Rwanda. So we asked our team members to make up a word they felt adequately represented who they were along with the work they were doing, and they chose *Abitangira Abandi,* which literally means "People who sacrifice themselves for others."

References

American Psychiatric Association. (2017). What is posttraumatic stress disorder. Retrieved February 4, 2017, from American Psychiatric Association: https://psychiatry.org/patients-families/ptsd/what-is-ptsd

American Water Works Association. (2010). Water use statistics. Retrieved February 26, 2011, from American Water Works Association: http://www.drinktap.org/water-info/water-conservation/water-use-statistics.aspx

Amnesty International. (2004, April 5). Rwanda: "Marked for death," rape survivors living with HIV/AIDS in Rwanda. Retrieved November 18, 2016, from Amnesty International: https://www.amnesty.org/en/documents/afr47/007/2004/en

Antares Foundation. (2012, March). *Managing stress in humanitarian workers: Guidelines for good practice.* Amsterdam, Neth.: Antares Foundation.

Bader, P., Boisclari, D., & Ferrence, R. (2011). Effects of tobacco taxation and pricing on smoking behavior in high risk populations: A knowledge synthesis. *International Journal of Environmental Research and Public Health, 8*(11), 4118–4139.

Baer, R., Smith, G., Hopkins, J., Krietemeyer, J., & Toney, L. (2006). Using self-report assessment methods to explore facets of mindfulness. *Assessment, 13,* 27–45.

Barks, C. with Moyne, J., Arberry, A. J., & Nicholson, R. (1997). *The Essential Rumi.* Edison, NJ: Castle Books.

Barnhofer, T., Duggan, D., & Griffith, J. (2011). Dispositional mindfulness moderates the relation between neuroticism and depressive symptoms. *Personality and Individual Differences, 51,* 958–962.

Begany, K., Cesaro, R., Bary, K., Ciccia, A., & Javk, A. (2009). Two domains of human higher cognition distinct brain networks underlie social and mechanical reasoning. Paper presented at the annual Neuroscience conference, Chicago, IL.

Bergman, A. L., Christopher, M. S., & Bowen, S. (2016). Changes in facets of mindfulnes predict stress and anger outcomes for police officers. *Mindfulness, 7*(4), 851–858.

Bhimani, N., Kulkarni, N., Kowale, A., & Salvi, S. (2011). Effect of pranayama on stress and cardiovascular autonomic function. *Indian Journal of Physiology and Pharmacology, 5*(4), 370–377.

Biss, E. (2015, December 2). White Debt: Reckoning with what is owed—and what can never be repaid—for racial privilege. Retrieved on April 16, 2017, from *New York Times*: https://www.nytimes.com/2015/12/06/magazine/white-debt.html

Bly, R. (1991). The Long Bag We Drag Behind Us. In C. Zweig & J. E. Abrams (Eds.), *Meeting the Shadow: The Hidden Power of the Dark Side of Human Nature* (pp. 6–9). New York: Penguin Putnam.

Brand, R. (2010). Biographical sketch: Otto Heinrich Warburg, PhD, MD. *Clinical Orthopaedics and Related Research, 468*(11), 2831–2832.

Brooks, A. C. (2014, December 14). Abundance without attachment. Retrieved on December 14, 2014, from *New York Times*: https://www.nytimes.com/2014/12/14/opinion/sunday/arthur-c-brooks-abundance-without-attachment.html?smprod =nytcore-iphone&smid=nytcore-iphone-share

Brown, R. P., & Gerbarg, P. L. (2012). *The Healing Power of the Breath: Simple Techniques to Reduce Stress and Anxiety, Enhance Concentration, and Balance Your Emotions.* Boulder, CO: Shambhala Publications.

Brown, R. P., & Gerbarg, P. L. (2017). Breathing Techniques in Psychiatric Treatment. In P. L. Gerbarg, R. P. Brown, & P. R. Muskin (Eds.), *Complementary and Integrative Treatments in Psychiatric Practice.* Washington, DC: American Psychiatric Association Publishing.

Calais-Germain, B. (2006). *Anatomy of Breathing.* Seattle, WA: Eastland Press, Inc.

Cameron, C., & Fredrickson, B. (2015). Mindfulness facets predict helping behavior and distinct helping-related emotions. *Mindfulness, 6*(5), 1211–1218.

Carmody, J., & Baer, R. (2008). Relationships between mindfulness practice and levels of mindfulness, medical psychological symptoms, and well-being in a mindfulness-based stress reduction program. *Journal of Behavioral Medicine, 31*, 23–33.

Chambers, R. (2009). *Whose Reality Counts: Putting the First Last.* Warwickshire, UK: Practical Action Publishing.

Chödrön, P. (2001). *The Wisdom of No Escape and the Path of Loving-Kindness.* Boulder, CO: Shambhala Publications.

Christopher, M. S., Goerling, R. J., Rogers, B. S., Hunsinger, M., Baron, G., Bergman, A. L., ... Zava, D. T. (2015). A pilot study evaluating the effectiveness of a mindfulness-based intervention on cortisol awakening response and health outcomes among law enforcement officers. *Journal of Police and Criminal Psychology, 31*(1), 15–28.

Corcoran, K., Farb, N., Anderson, A., & Segal, Z. (2010). Mindfulness and Emotion Regulation: Outcomes and Possible Mediating Mechanisms. In E.A.M. Kring & D. M. Sloan (Eds.), *Emotion Regulation and Psychopathology: A Transdiagnostic Approach to Etiology and Treatment* (pp. 339–355). New York, NY: Guilford Press.

Cox, S., Andrade, G., Lungelow, D., Schloetelburg, W., & Rode, H. (2007). The child rape epidemic: Assessing the incidence at Red Cross Hospital, Cape Town, and establishing the need for a new national protocol. *South African Medical Journal, 97*(10), 950–955.

Davidson, R., Kabat-Zinn, J., Schumacher, J., Rosenkranz, M., Muller, D., Santorelli, S., ... Sheridan, J. F. (2003). Alterations in brain and immune function produced by mindfulness meditation. *Psychosomatic Medicine, 66,* 149–152.

Davis, D., & Hayes, J. (2001). What are the benefits of mindfulness? A practice review of psychotherapy-related research. *Psychology, 48*(2), 198–208.

Dawson, J. R. (2014). *The CS Gender 3000: Women in Senior Management.* New York, NY: Credit Suisse Research Institute.

Early, J. (2008). Jay Early. In M. A. Edwards & S. G. Post (Eds.), *The Love That Does Justice: Spiritual Activism in Dialogue with Social Science* (pp. 57–60). Stony Brook, NY: Unlimited Love Press.

Elliott, S., & Edmonson, D. R. (2006). *The New Science of Breath: Coherent Breathing for Autonomic Nervous System Valance, Health, and Well-being.* Allen, TX: Coherence Press.

Enneagram Prison Project. (2017). Introducing the Enneagram Prison Project—a California non-profit. Retrieved February 3, 2017, from Enneagram Prison Project: http://www.enneagramprisonproject.org/home.html

Epel, E., Daubenmier, J., Moskowitz, J., Folkman, S., & Blackburn, E. (2009). Can meditation slow rate of cellular aging? Cognitive stress, mindfulness, and telomeres. *Annals of the New York Academy of Sciences, 1172,* 34–53.

Erisman, S., & Roemer, L. (2010). A preliminary investigation of the effects of experimentally induced mindfulness on emotional responding to film clips. *Emotion, 10,* 72–82.

Fast for Darfur. (2009). Retrieved March 18, 2017, from Fast for Darfur: http://fastdarfur.org

Fehmi, L., & Robbins, J. (2007). *The Open-Focus Brain: Harnessing the Power of Attention to Heal Mind and Body.* Boston, MA: Trumpeter.

Gallese, V. (2001). The "shared manifold" hypothesis: From mirror neurons to empathy. *Journal of Consciousness Studies, 8*(5–7), 33–50.

Gerbarg, P. L., & Brown, R. P. (2015). Yoga and Neuronal Pathways to Enhance Stress Response, Emotion Regulation, Bonding, and Spirituality. In E. G. Horovitz & S. Elgelid (Eds.), *Yoga Therapy: Theory and Practice* (pp. 49–64). New York, NY: Routledge.

Gerbarg, P. L., & Brown, R. P. (2016, November 30). Neurobiology and neurophysiology of breath practices in psychiatric care. *Psychiatric Times*, 22–25.

Gerbarg, P. L., Wallace, G., & Brown, R. P. (2011). Mass disasters and mind-body solutions: Evidence and field insights. *International Journal of Yoga Therapy, 21*, 23–34.

Gomez, M. B. (2013). *Race, Class, Power, and Organizing in East Baltimore: Rebuilding Abandoned Communities in America*. Lanham, MD: Lexington Books.

Gomez, M. B., & Muntaner, C. (2005). Urban redevelopment and neighborhood health in East Baltimore, Maryland: The role of communitarian and institutional social capital. *Critical Public Health, 5*(2), 83–102.

Gonzalez-Barrera, A. (2015, November 19). More Mexicans leaving than coming to the U.S. Retrieved February 14, 2017, from Pew Research Center, Hispanic Trends: http://www.pewhispanic.org/2015/11/19/more-mexicans-leaving-than-coming-to -the-u-s

Goyal, M., Singh, S., Sibinga, E. M., Gould, N. F., Rowland-Seymour, A., Sharma, R., … Haythornthwaite, J. A. (2014). Meditation programs for psychological stress and well-being: A systematic review and meta-analysis. *JAMA Internal Medicine, 174*(3), 357–368.

Gross, J. (1998). The emerging field of emotion regulation: An integrative review. *Review of General Psychology, 2*, 271–299.

Hartley, T. A., Burchfiel, C. M., & Violanti, J. M. (2008, June 30). Police and stress. NIOSH Science Blog. Retrieved February 9, 2017, from Centers for Disease Control and Prevention: https://blogs.cdc.gov/niosh-science-blog/2008/06/30/police

Healing Works. (2016). Healing Works: A Project of Common Justice. Retrieved February 3, 2017, from Common Justice: http://www.healingworks.org/peer/aqeela -sherrills

Hirondelle News Agency. (2008, April 28). Rwanda/genocide: Rwanda genocide orphans face loneliness and poverty. Retrieved November 18, 2016, from Hirondelle News Agency: http://www.hirondellenews.com/ictr-rwanda/412-rwanda-political -and-social-issues/21810-en-en-240408-rwandagenocide-rwanda-genocide-orphans -face-loneliness-and-poverty1086110861

Horwitz, C. (2008). Claudia Horwitz. In M. A. Edwards & S. G. Post (Eds.), *The Love That Does Justice: Spiritual Activism in Dialogue with Social Science* (pp. 53–56). Stony Brook, NY: Unlimited Love Press.

Hunter, J. (2013, April). Is mindfulness good for business? *Mindful*, pp. 52–59.

iACT. (2009a, May 19). "Congressional Black Caucaus joins Darfur Fast for Life: Announces a day of fasting in solidarity with Darfur." Press release. Retrieved February 9, 2017, from Darfur Fast for Life: http://fastdarfur.org/uploads/DFFL_Press_ Release_CBC1.pdf

iACT. (2009b). Congressman Donald Payne's blog. Retrieved February 9, 2017, from Darfur Fast for Life: http://fastdarfur.org/category/congressmanpayne

Jacobson, J. (2013, February 19). Book on Hopkins redevelopment by a leader of the opposition. Retrieved February 1, 2017, from Baltimore Brew: https://www .baltimorebrew.com/2013/02/19/book-on-hopkins-redevelopment-by-a-leader-of -the-opposition

Jerath, R., Edry, J., Barnes, V., & Jerath, V. (2006). Physiology of long pranayamic breathing: Neural respiratory elements may provide a mechanism that explains how slow deep breathing shifts the autonomic nervous system. *Medical Hypotheses, 67*(3), 566–571.

Kabat-Zinn, J. (1994). *Wherever You Go There You Are: Mindfulness Meditation in Everyday Life*. New York: Hyperion.

Kang, Y., Gray, J. R., & Dovidio, J. F. (2014). The nondiscriminating heart: Loving-kindness meditation training decreases implicit intergroup bias. *Journal of Experimental Psychology, 143*(3), 1306–1313.

Keefe, J. F. (2016). *Investing in Women in Smart Investing: The Value of Gender Diversity Is Proven in the Numbers*. Portsmouth, NH: Pax Ellevate Management LLC.

Khoury, B., Lecomte, T., Fortin, G., Masse, M., Therien, P., Bouchard, V., ... Hofmann, S. G. (2013). Mindfulness-based therapy: A comprehensive meta-analysis. *Clinical Psychology Review, 33*, 763–771.

Killingsworth, M. A., & Gilbert, D. (2010). A wandering mind is an unhappy mind. *Science, 12*, 932.

Kingsbury, E. (2009). The relationship between empathy and mindfulness: Understanding the role of self-compassion. *Dissertation Abstracts International*, Section B: Science and Engineering, *70*, 3175.

Kohn, A. (2006). Unconditional parenting: Moving from rewards and punishments to love and reason. Talk by Alfie Kohn.

Lanagan, P. A., & Levin, D. J. (2002). *Recidivism of Prisoners Released in 1994: Special Report*. Washington, DC: US Department of Justice, Office of Justice Programs.

Lazar, S., Kerr, C., Wasserman, R., Gray, J., Greve, D., Treadway, M., ... Fischl, B. (2005). Meditation experience is associated with increased cortical thickness. *Neuroreport, 16*(17), 1893–1897.

Leela, F. (2003). *Transforming Feminist Practice: Non-Violence, Social Justice, and the Possibilities of a Spiritualized Feminism.* San Francisco, CA: Anne Lute Books.

Lichtblau, E. (2016, November 14). U.S. hate crimes surge 6%, fueled by attacks on Muslims. Retrieved from *New York Times:* https://www.nytimes.com/2016/11/15/us/politics/fbi-hate-crimes-muslims.html?_r=0

Long, L. J. (2013, November 20). Criminal recidivism: The plight of African American male youth? Retrieved January 28, 2017, from psychosocialissues: https://psychsocialissues.com/2013/11/20/criminal-recidivism-the-plight-of-african-american-male-youth

Marcus Noland, T. M. (2016). *Is Gender Diversity Profitable? Evidence from a Global Survey.* Washington, DC: Peterson Institute for International Economics.

McKinsey and Company & LeanIn. (2016). Women in the workplace. Retrieved March 19, 2017, from Women in the Workplace 2016: https://womenintheworkplace.com

Meltzoff, A. N., & Moore, M. K. (1977). Imitation of facial and manual gestures by human neonates. *Science, 198*(4312), 75–78.

Mijares, S. G. (2009). Ancient and Modern Yoga: A Science of Breath, Healing, and Enlightenment. In S. G. Mijares (Ed.), *The Revelation of the Breath: A Tribute to Its Wisdom, Power, and Beauty* (pp. 3–23). Albany, NY: State University of New York Press.

Moore, A., & Malinowski, P. (2009). Meditation, mindfulness, and cognitive flexibility. *Consciousness and Cognition, 18,* 176–186.

Neff, K. (2016). What self-compassion is, the three elements of self-compassion, what self-compassion is not, tips for practice. Retrieved December 28, 2016, from Self-Compassion, Dr. Kristin Neff: http://self-compassion.org/the-three-elements-of-self-compassion-2

Nhât Hanh, T. (1993). *Love in Action.* Berkeley, CA: Parallax Press.

Nhât Hanh, T. (2008). *The Art of Power.* New York, NY: HarperCollins Publishers.

Ophira, E., Nass, C., & Wagner, A. (2009). Cognitive control in media multitaskers. *Proceedings of the National Academy of Sciences of the United States of America, 106*(37), 15583–15587.

Opportunity Collaboration. (2017). About Us. Retrieved January 30, 2017, from Opportunity Collaboration: http://opportunitycollaboration.net/about_us

Parker, A. S. (2016). *Putting Gender Diversity to Work: Better Fundamentals, Less Volatility.* New York, NY: Morgan Stanley Research.

Pattison, K. (2008, July 28). Worker, interrupted: The cost of task switching. Retrieved November 16, 2016, from Fast Company: https://www.fastcompany.com/944128/worker-interrupted-cost-task-switching

Powell, B. (2012, May 17). The law of unintended consequences: Georgia's immigration law backfires. Retrieved February 14, 2017, from Forbes Opinion: https://www.forbes.com/sites/realspin/2012/05/17/the-law-of-unintended-consequences-georgias-immigration-law-backfires/#18425a44492a

Quinn, R. E. (1996). *Deep Change: Discovering the Leader Within*. San Francisco, CA: Jossey-Bass.

Quinn, R. E. (2000). *Change the World: How Ordinary People Can Achieve Extraordinary Results*. San Francisco, CA: Jossey-Bass.

Reeves, E. (2016, April 28). Invisible, forgotten, and suffering: Darfuri refugees in eastern Chad. Retrieved April 24, 2017, from *Sudan Tribune:* http://www.sudantribune.com/spip.php?article58797

Riso, D. R., & Hudson, R. (1999). *The Wisdom of the Enneagram: The Complete Guide to Psychological and Spiritual Growth for the Nine Personality Types*. New York, NY: Bantam Books.

Rothberg, D. (2006). *The Engaged Spiritual Life: A Buddhist Approach to Transforming Ourselves and the World*. Boston, MA: Beacon Press.

Ryff, C. D., & Keyes, C. L. M. (1995). The structure of psychological well-being revisited. *Journal of Personality and Social Psychology, 69*(4), 719–727.

Salzberg, S. (2008). Sharon Salzberg. In M. A. Edwards & S. G. Post (Eds.,), *The Love That Does Justice: Spiritual Activism in Dialogue with Social Science* (pp. 71–75). Stony Brook, NY: Unlimited Love Press.

Segui, R. D. (1996, January 29). *Report on the Situation of Human Rights in Rwanda Submitted by Mr. Rene Degni Segui, Special Rapporteur of the Commission on Human Rights, under Paragraph 20 of the Resolution S-3/1 of 25 May 1994*. Retrieved November 18, 2016, from United Nations: http://hrlibrary.umn.edu/commission/country52/68-rwa.htm

Seppala, E. (2014, October 28). 18 science-based reasons to try loving-kindness meditation today! Retrieved November 2016, from Emma Seppala: http://www.emmaseppala.com/18-science-based-reasons-try-loving-kindness-meditation-today

Shapiro, S. (2013, February 27). Does mindfulness make you more compassionate? Retrieved November 2016, from Greater Good: The Science of a Meaningful Life: http://greatergood.berkeley.edu/article/item/does_mindfulness_make_you_compassionate

Shapiro, S., Brown, K., & Biegel, G. (2007). Teaching self-care to caregivers: Effects of mindfulness-based stress reduction on the mental health of therapists in training. *Training and Education in Professional Psychology, 1,* 105–115.

Sherrills, A. (2016, October 15). The reverence movement. TEDx Talks. Retrieved February 3, 2017, from TEDxWashingtonSquare: https://www.youtube.com/watch?v=kGJGYgoaPyI

Siegel, D. J. (2007). *The Mindful Brain: Reflection and Attunement in the Cultivation of Well-Being.* New York, NY: W. W. Norton and Company.

Specter, M. (2007, March 12). The denialists: The dangerous attacks on the consensus about H.I.V. and AIDS. Retrieved February 12, 2017, from *New Yorker*: http://www.newyorker.com/magazine/2007/03/12/the-denialists

Stoltze, F. (2012, April 28). Forget the LA riots—historic 1992 Watts gang truce was the big news. Retrieved February 3, 2017, from 89.3 KPCC Crime & Justice: http://www.scpr.org/news/2012/04/28/32221/forget-la-riots-1992-gang-truce-was-big-news

Strathearn, L., Li, J., Fonagy, P., & Montague, P. (2008). What's in a smile? Maternal brain responses to infant facial cues. *Pediatrics, 122*(1), 40–51.

Tang, Y.-Y., Hölzel, B. K., & Posner, M. I. (2015). The neuroscience of mindfulness meditation. *Nature Reviews: Neuroscience, 16*(4), 213–225.

Transform. (2010, February 11). Aqeela Sherrills | Beholding: An act of deep love. Retrieved February 3, 2017, from Transform: http://transform.transformativechange.org/2010/02/beholding-an-act-of-deep-love

UNAIDS. (2006, December). AIDS epidemic update. Retrieved November 17, 2016, from UNAIDS: http://data.unaids.org/pub/EpiReport/2006/2006_EpiUpdate_en.pdf

UNAIDS, UNICEF, & World Health Organization. (2004). Epidemiological fact sheets: On HIV/AIDS and sexually transmitted diseases, South Africa. Retrieved November 17, 2016, from UNAIDS: http://data.unaids.org/Publications/Fact-Sheets01/southafrica_EN.pdf

UNICEF. (2009, March 8). UN joint statement; statement on the humanitarian situation in Darfur. Retrieved December 28, 2016, from UNICEF Media: https://www.unicef.org/media/media_48507.html

UNICEF & World Health Organization. (2015). *Progress on Sanitation and Drinking Water: 2015 Update and MDG Assessment.* Geneva, Swit.: UNICEF and World Health Organization.

United Nations Human Rights, UN Habitat, & World Health Organization. (2010). The right to water. Fact sheet no. 35. Geneva, Swit.: Office of the United Nations High Commissioner for Human Rights.

van Dernoot Lipsky, L. (2009). *Trauma Stewardship: An Everyday Guide to Caring for Self while Caring for Others*. San Francisco, CA: Berrett-Koehler Publishers, Inc.

Velmans, M. (2009). How to define consciousness—and how not to define consciousness. *Journal of Consciousness Studies, 16*(5), 139–156.

Waelde, L., Uddo, M., Marquette, R., Ropelato, M., Freightman, S., Pardo, A., ... Salazar, J. (2008). A pilot study of meditation for mental health workers following Hurricane Katrina. *Journal of Traumatic Stress, 21*, 497–500.

Walker, J. C. (2016, October 15). Join the band: Meditations on social change. TEDx Talks. Retrieved January 18, 2017, from TEDxWashingtonSquare: https://www.youtube.com/watch?v=AOtRfk5oDxo

Wallace, B. A., & Shapiro, S. L. (2006, October). Mental balance and well-being: Building bridges between Buddhism and Western Psychology. *American Psychological Association, 61*(7), 690–701.

Way, B., Creswell, J., Eisenberger, N., & Lieberman, M. (2010). Dispositional mindfulness and depressive symptomatology. *Emotion, 10*, 12–24.

Weng, H., Fox, A., Schackman, A., Stodola, D., Caldwell, J., Olson, M., ... Davidson, R. J. (2012). Compassion training alters altruism and neural responses to suffering. *Psychological Science, 24*(7), 1171–1180.

williams, a. K. (2008). Rev. angel Kyodo williams. In M. A. Edwards & S. G. Post (Eds.), *The Love That Does Justice: Spiritual Activism in Dialogue with Social Science* (pp. 47–52). Stony Brook, NY: Unlimited Love Press.

Williams, W. W. (1991). The Equality Crisis: Some Reflections on Culture, Courts, and Feminism. In K. T. Kennedy (Ed.), *Feminist Legal Theory: Readings in Law and Gender* (pp. 15–34). Boulder, CO: Westview Press, Inc.

World Health Organization & UNICEF. (2010). *Progress on Drinking Water and Sanitation: Special Focus on Sanitation*. Retrieved February 28, 2011, from Joint Monitoring Program for Water Supply and Sanitation: http://www.who.int/water_sanitation_health/monitoring/jmp2008/en/index.html

Wresniewski, A., & Schwartz, B. (2014, July 6). The secret of effective motivation. Retrieved on July 6, 2014, from *New York Times*: https://www.nytimes.com/2014/07/06/opinion/sunday/the-secret-of-effective-motivation.html

Zimering, R., Gulliver, S., Knight, J., Munroe, J., & Keane, T. (2006). Postraumatic stress disorder in disaster relief workers following direct and indirect trauma exposure to Ground Zero. *Journal of Traumatic Stress, 19*(4), 553–557.

Zope, S., & Zope, R. (2013). Sudarshan kriya yoga: Breathing for health. *International Journal of Yoga, 6*(1), 4–10.

Zweig, C., & Abrams, J. E. (Eds.). (1991). *Meeting the Shadow: The Hidden Power of the Dark Side of Human Nature*. New York, NY: Penguin Putnam.

Index

Note: Page numbers followed by "f" or "t" refer to figures and tables, respectively.